MANAGEMENT: A POLITICAL ACTIVITY

MANAGEMENT: A POLITICAL ACTIVITY

Ted Stephenson

First published 1985

Published by
THE MACMILLAN PRESS LTD
Houndmills, Basingstoke, Hampshire RG21 2XS
and London
Companies and representatives
throughout the world

Printed in Hong Kong

British Library Cataloguing in Publication Data
Stephenson, Ted
Management: a political activity.
1. Management
I. Title
658   HD31
ISBN 0–333–38439–3 ✓

Contents

Preface

This book presents the view that management is substantially a political activity, based on power and characterised by conflict.

This viewpoint arises out of many years' experience of working with managers at all levels of a wide variety of organisations; including industrial and commercial concerns, the prison and hospital services and overseas large-scale private and public enterprises. The managers were not selected with research in mind; we were involved in examining and solving some real problems.

This particular approach to management has been considered in numerous seminars where discussion helped to clarify and develop the ideas born out of practice. I have also drawn on the literature of politics, international relations and military, political and industrial biographies.

My thanks must go to Donald Rutherford and to the numerous authors, managers, students and administrators who contributed to the shaping of this book, and to the colleagues who discussed with me the ideas expressed in these pages, in particular Bruce Partridge of the Department of Management Studies in the University of Leeds. I would also thank Ms Anne-Lucie Norton of the Macmillan Press, who gave me encouragement in the production of the final version. Without the support of my wife this book would never have been written and her patience in correcting many drafts has greatly contributed to the production of a readable script.

Notes, acknowledgements and references have been deliberately kept to a minimum.

T.E.S.

Introduction

My involvement with managers has confirmed for me the comments of Kenneth Morgan that:

> political truth possesses an intrinsically different quality from academic truth (which does not make it necessarily inferior), that political decisions are taken, often from instinct, in a confused turmoil of pressures and conflicts, with always the need to reconcile, to extract the basis of a working agreement, to relate the ideal to the practical realities, and to harmonize the desired end with the available, limiting means. Political judgements and decisions are not the product of relaxed, abstract speculation undertaken ... in a timeless continuum. They need to be understood in their own context and in their own terms.[1]

Management, like politics, is concerned with coping with differences. From the outset management is faced with the political and power differences that exist between and within organisations. The political system of every firm is characterised by a unique past, by differing degrees of sophistication and conflict, by varying distributions of political resources and skills and by different formal arrangements for sharing and exercising power. In consequence, managers use a variety of political strategies and tactics to cope with the situations they face.

It may seem that the results of this political process are often unedifying to the outsider, and for some the whole notion of managerial politics is sordid. But to discuss management without consideration of the political dimension is to fail to recognise organisational reality.

Undoubtedly there is a gulf between how organisations should be managed and how they are. This gulf is underlined by Pascale and Athos who point out that 'The inherent preferences of organisations are clarity, certainty and perfection. The inherent nature of human relationships involves ambiguity, uncertainty and imperfection. How one honours, balances and integrates the needs of both is the real trick of management.'[2] Political sensitivity, skill and practices are the essential elements of that trick.

Because managerial politics is complex, the argument developed in this book cannot always be simplified. As the central themes surface from time to time throughout the book, there may be some repetition. I have tried to keep this to a minimum but have not sought to eliminate it entirely, since these strands of the argument are what is really important.

1 Management Manifestations

The problems faced by managers are frequently shifting, complex and insoluble. Confronted with this daunting prospect many managers long to find the all-embracing solution, to shed the burden of responsibility for the problems that exist and the decisions that have to be taken. They are reluctant to accept the inescapable fact that there are no general solutions to individual and specific problems, only temporary expedients based upon the uniqueness of each managerial situation which is, in turn, constrained by personal relationships of the greatest subtlety and complexity.

To escape from their difficulties, these managers seek to simplify the world in which they work. Yet the very simplification that occurs is based upon some theory or other, on some model of man and the world he inhabits. Models dominate our thinking and from them we derive differing conclusions and attitudes to such matters as management, unions, government and politics. Models structure our thoughts; they lead us to see the world as mechanistic or organic, as the source of pessimism or optimism, of threat or opportunity, of man as perfectible or permanently flawed. The models we build, for they are not simply given to us, have important consequences for us as managers and human beings. They provide us with the first of many dichotomies; they are the source of the distinction between what we publicly say we believe and what we actually believe. This distinction is one of the threads running through this book and contributes to our understanding of the many facets and levels of management discourse and practice.

MODELS OF MANAGEMENT

The Greek poet Archilochus in his distinction between the characters of the fox and the hedgehog, provides us with

1

contrasting managerial models.[1] On the one hand there is the fox who knows many things and recognises that there are many objectives, often unrelated, even contradictory, and centrifugal rather than centripetal. On the other hand there is the hedgehog who knows only one big thing, has a single vision and operates in the belief that there is one coherent and best way of doing anything. These two models are applicable to human beings in general and to management in particular, where the desire to escape from the fox into the hedgehog manifests itself both in thought and action. There is the never-ending search for the one best way with its inevitable over-simplification. Now it is clear that we all select, simplify and look for certainty; the danger is that we often go too far so that the world we picture is far removed from the reality of the world we inhabit and the result is we create fresh difficulties for ourselves.

The concern with the one best way finds expression in a number of forms; for example, in managerial commitment to organisation structures, to human relations, to systems and techniques. Yet immediately we look closely at these 'solutions' to managerial problems we see their limitations and recognise the need for a further dimension – the political.

Organisation Structures

Formal organisation structures are frequently depicted through the organisation chart, which is an abstraction. It is not a picture of a firm in action. What we have in any firm is a series of different layers of reality: there is the manifest organisation as written in the charts and job descriptions; there is the assumed organisation as the various groups and individuals in it presume it to be; then there is the extant organisation – the firm as it actually operates.[2]

One of management's persistent concerns is with the development of the ideal structure and the belief that once such an artifact has been revealed, all other managerial problems will dissolve. This is most unlikely to happen, given the differences between formal structures and organisational reality. Structures are usually conceived in hierarchical terms which are generally at odds with the fine gradations of personal reality. When we examine the actuality we can see the limited impact of those in authority. The myth of hierarchy is exposed. Even in the hierarchical structures of the armed services, considered by many to be the most tightly organised of all organisations, there is abundant evidence that the orders of those at the top are not always carried out. Examples abound in military literature; there was the failure of the allied forces to carry out their directives to attack German communication targets before the allied landings in Normandy – they continued their own bombing policies;[3] there was General Mark Clark's refusal to accept General Alexander's strategy in the Italian campaign.[4] The same problem is underlined in accounts of the Cuban missile crisis when instructions from President Kennedy, regarding missile sites in Turkey, were evaded. Similar examples are to be found in managerial practice; for example, uncontrolled purchases of raw and semi-finished materials by divisional managers, unauthorised stock holding by production managers, the spreading of production and sales figures. The limited influence of those in authority is superbly highlighted in Tolstoy's analysis of the Battle of Borodino, and he makes the same point in many other sections of *War and Peace* – people at the top believe they are ordering affairs when it is the countless activities of those lower down which actually shape events.

Another misleading aspect of the managerial emphasis on formal structures is the belief that rules and regulations will be slavishly followed and that, in consequence, organisations can be managed as machines. Such a view has been criticised by others on the grounds that those who work in the web of formal orders will be stunted, their development retarded. This argument is based on the belief that members of bureaucracies develop 'trained incapacity'; having been trained to act in accordance with one set of rules they are unable to adjust to new circumstances, to situations that are not formally prescribed. In consequence there develops a fundamental imbalance in organisational behaviour so that, 'A way of seeing is also a way of not seeing; to focus on object A involves neglect of object B.' This tunnel vision may indeed develop in some highly formalised organisations but it is also in evidence elsewhere. What we need to recognise is that 'trained incapacity' can be a defensive strategy devised by the individual to help him cope with the world around. Adherence to rules, to established patterns of behaviour, to particular skills, ideas and ideologies is frequently the result of a fear of freedom. People want limited freedom and find too much freedom a burden. In a similar vein people do not always want their assumptions analysed in depth, they feel threatened and uncomfortable. To cope with freedom, whether a lack or surfeit of it, people develop informal strategies which do not usually find a place in models of management.

Both the optimistic assumption that formal organisation will produce effective programmed behaviour and the contrary pessimistic belief, that human development will be crushed within bureaucracies, contribute to an over-simplification of organisational assumptions about behaviour. Both miss out on a number of counts:

1. Many rules provide a defence for the weak against the strong, against the unbridled use of authority by those in the higher echelons of the organisation.
2. The rules, apparently so inflexible, are all-importantly subject to interpretation by those who apply them and by those who are affected by them, producing different interpretations as to 'what exactly a given regulation means.'
3. Rules are not simply applied, they do not arrive out of thin air; they have in the first instance to be made, and while there may be a presumption that they are made by those in authority it would be another over-simplification to believe that there is no contest over who frames the rules and what they contain. We must not take too facile a view of the prerogative of authority and lose sight of the ability of lower levels in the hierarchy to influence the shape and execution of rules. What is certain is that this influence cannot be deduced simply by looking at the organisation chart.

Much of the attack on bureaucracy arises out of the failure to recognise the multifarious factors that operate in the formulation and application of rules, regulations, policies and plans, and that there is an immense degree of subtlety in the way formal structures and their attendant rules operate.

Structure – the Managerial Lifeline

Why do managers overlook the intricate behaviour that builds up in organisations and why do they hold, at least publicly, to the need to develop ideal structures and adhere to them?[5] There are a number of reasons:

1. Formal structures emphasise authority and generally place it in the hands of managers, which is naturally where they want it to be.

2. Formal structures have the appearance of certainty, and as such seem to provide a court of appeal, a fixed point, to which the manager can turn when things go wrong. Additionally, concentration on structure diverts attention from the short-comings of a firm's management, so that when it faces a critical problem it will seek to restructure rather than look at the question of managerial competence. In consequence, the same managers, competent or not, continue to operate in the new structure.

3. The emphasis on structure arises in part out of the nature of managerial activity; managers are essentially clinicians, in their jobs they continually confront difficulties which demand resolution. They have to decide what is to be done and who is to do it. These decisions are frequently taken under pressure with time as an important element. Analysis which is or appears to be time-consuming is likely to be rejected in favour of intuition.

For many managers it is not analysis but intuition that is satisfying. It is satisfactory because it seems to be trustworthy, having been developed and tested over a considerable period of experiment and experience; it is habitual, the manager frequently has little else to rely on; it is unique in the sense that everyone's intuition is in some measure individual and singular to its possessor: it is well adapted to the context of affairs, it makes quick decisions possible in the face of limited information and meets the constraints of time, cost and knowledge imposed by the manager's environment.

Formal organisation with its theoretical simplicity fits well with the clinical approach; it can be taken as given, as an inevitable feature of the manager's landscape. The principles of organisation which underpin it are few in number, apparently straightforward and relatively free of jargon. These principles have a directness which appeals to the manager and they have the additional bonus of being pre-scriptive, of telling him what to do and so cut down the time that has to be taken on problem solving. The principles pave the way for speedy action, or so it appears to many managers.

4. Formal organisation and its underlying theory is also attractive for some managers because it appears to avoid the personal. It is devoid of emotion which is seen as a barrier to getting the job done; the emphasis is firmly on managerial rationality.

5. Formal organisation is acceptable to the manager because it provides him with an article of faith. It offers him reassurance and provides him with a 'myth' which supports him and simultaneously trains him to use this 'myth' to legitimise his position in the eyes of the managed. He is psychologically armed in much the same way as the nineteenth century entrepreneur was by the Protestant ethic.

Over the years it has been pointed out that the principles of formal organisation are unsophisticated and contain numerous contradictions, but this line of attack does not prevent their acceptance, for the principles have a significance far beyond their intellectual content. Managerial beliefs are not truths or untruths in any absolute sense. There is usually enough truth in them to keep them intact and ensure their persistence. This largely explains why the belief that structure is an all-powerful problem solvent continues to be held by many managers.

Behaviour in Organisations

Turning from the structural to the behavioural model the focus of attention shifts to the human being in the management situation. One recent example of this behavioural approach is that of Organisation Development[6] which, in the language of Argyris – one of its outstanding proponents – is concerned with the vitalising, energising, actualising, activating and renewing of organisations through technical and human resources. In spite of the mention of technical, the emphasis is almost wholly upon people in organisations. Such a position might be valid if the behaviouralist worked with a complex model of man, one which recognised the peaceful and not so peaceful coexistence in man of incompatible attitudes, values and goals. A more valid understanding of the human being would emerge if it was appreciated that the differing facets of the individual surface in different

situations, at different times and at different stages in the
individual's life. Then those managerial theories and practices,
which are based on over-simplified versions of man, would be
seen for what they are, barriers to the process of comprehending
problems, of reaching effective solutions and of successfully
implementing them. But, all too often, in place of a complex,
shifting model of man, managers are advised to base their
practice on idealised end-states of human behaviour. Too frequently managers are expected to accept the values of the
behavioural scientist and organisation development practitioner
as his own. According to Argyris, managers rarely express
feelings, experiment with ideas, evince trust and display openness to others.[7] Instead of accepting the probability that managerial beliefs and behaviours reflect the legitimate perceptions
of managers and are based upon their experience of both
organisations and the wider society, he takes the view that
people ought to be different, they ought to be open, trusting,
sharing and more committed to experimenting with new ideas
and feelings so that others can respond in a similar way, and so
contribute to organisational effectiveness. In practical terms
much of this is allied to the call for more participative and
consultative management styles. What the advocates of this
approach are reluctant to face is the question of why managers
persist in their traditional behaviour if it produces ineffective,
uncreative and unproductive organisations. The answer the
behaviouralist gives is that managerial behaviour is largely the
result of the emphasis society puts on bureaucracy. Here is the
source of managerial ills; bureaucracy is considered in black and
white terms and rarely is attention given to the richness of
behaviour that is to be found in organisations in action. It is
argued that innovation and creativity is thwarted in bureacra-
cies, yet their members display considerable ingenuity and
creativity in dealing with the organisations they inhabit. Behaviouralists stress the need to develop adaptive, coping and
learning skills when they are already widely practised. The rub
for the behaviouralist is that these attributes are developed by
organisational members in order to protect themselves, to
control their immediate environment and generally survive.
These 'desirable' skills are not necessarily used in the service of
the organisation, indeed they may be used to thwart its operations. It is here that the ambiguity of the organisational role of

the behaviouralist comes to the fore. While he advocates development, creativity and the like, it is evident that these
qualities are to be used for the benefit of the organisation and are
not to be exercised to question the basic purpose of the firm.
Constrained creativity is the order of the day.

Managers who embrace behavioural ideas subvert their own
positions; they are blurring and confusing issues of power and
authority. Why then do some managers accept these ideas?

First, because they feel under pressure and are prepared to
look for any lifeline.

Second, because much of the behaviouralist approach is
couched in 'hurrah' words which fit in with some element of
current social values. Democracy, participation, consensus,
reflect current values; to go against them, to query their
operational validity is to be swimming against the tide. Yet
underlying the acceptance of these general ideas are other levels
of human experience which emerge in new forms to cope with
new conditions. For example, when overt authoritarianism lost
its social acceptability it was largely replaced by covert manipulation. In this process, wittingly or not, the behaviouralists
have provided management with tools which increase the repertoire of manipulative strategies.

A third reason for managerial acceptance of a behaviouralist
approach is that it emphasises the idea of progress, of development and growth, all of which fit in with managerial ideology
and provide a justification for managerial prerogatives. There is
an underlying assumption, shared by managers and behaviouralists, of the inevitability of progress; further evidence of
the reluctance to look at the reality of human behaviour and
history.[8] On some criteria, say housing, education and general
standards of living, it may be claimed that there has been some
progress for some people, but not for others such as the
unemployed and the inhabitants of many of the 'developing'
countries. However, away from this quantifiable and material
progress there remain patterns of human behaviour which
appear to have changed little. The characters in Shakespeare's
plays display in pointed form many of the feelings, emotions and
behaviours of modern man. Basically in much management
literature there is a lack of a sense of history; a concern with the
future overrides the need to think about the past; new ideas must
be better than old ones because they are new. This rejection of

the past appears strange when it is so evident that the past helps shape the present and the future, and that these periods have one factor in common, the complex human being. It is difficult to see how we can understand any organisation in action if we do not take account of its past.

Allied to this concern with progress is an everpresent sense of optimism and a rejection of pessimism. At the core of this attitude is the belief in the perfectibility of man, and, according to Gouldner,[9] to reject this hope leads to a state of bleak pessimism. To accept the bureaucratic form of organisation with its alienation of its members is, in his view, to retreat into the past and accept defeat. He exhorts us to advocate ways of mitigating bureaucracy, of fortifying and extending democracy and of moving towards perfectibility. What is omitted from this viewpoint is the recognition that we need to be both pessimistic and optimistic, and that history and human behaviour give us grounds for both states of mind.

The emphasis on progress and perfectibility meshes well with a managerial ideology based upon a simple model of man, for around them cluster ideas of efficiency, of rationality and of linear progress. A measure of hope is undoubtedly necessary but an oversteadfast belief in the inevitability of progress and of the universality of optimism is to move too far away from the actual world of management.

Strangely enough the belief in progress and perfectibility has its other side. The members of bureaucratic organisations are seen as victims, incapable of modifying their organisational situation. This impotence suggests a plastic image of man, shaped by the forces around him but not able to influence them. In behavioural literature there is no view of man possessing some enduring integrity and seeking to shape his environment as well as being shaped by it. What surely happens is that people respond to situations and in varying degrees seek to alter them in ways that are significant for them. To the outsider, especially if he is seeking dramatic changes in human values and behaviour, the adaptations and shifts of the individual may seem small and insignificant, but all-importantly they are significant for the individual. This failure to perceive the significance of acts for those who perform them arises in part, at least, from a commitment to a view of the ideal organisation and the ideal man. In consequence the idealistic element in the behaviouralist approach becomes a block to sensitivity and to understanding the importance of minute incidents and adjustments for the individual concerned.

Behavioural solutions

Given the critical stance of the behaviouralists towards bureaucracy, what alternative do they offer? Their answer appears to lie in more organic structures which will provide people with the opportunity to become more humane and democratic.

This alternative is supported by the belief that man is essentially good. Man is not seen as inherently evil, lazy, destructive, hurtful and narrowly self-centred; he develops these characteristics, it is argued, through his life experiences. But the evidence for the case that man is inherently good is highly selective, and the human propensity to be both good and bad at different times and within the same person needs to be taken into account in any model of management that we adopt.

The human qualities which Argyris and the behaviouralists seek to develop are admirable in the abstract but they have to be placed in the context of the competitive, stratified society in which managers live and work. The emphasis on trust and confidence, so much a part of the behaviouralist case, can be queried on two points.

1. Trust has to be related to specific situations and relationships: there are some people whom we would trust in one set of circumstances, for example, in technical matters, but would not trust in another, for example, in human relationships.
2. People live in a society where trust and confidence are uncertain factors.

There is frequent discussion of the question of openness, encouraging the individual to tell all, but this is a denial of the view that a person has a right to privacy, to withholding information about himself and those around him if he so desires. Openness, if wholeheartedly carried through, is liable to destroy confidence rather than build it. Against the argument for openness it can be held that the individual's goal should be effective behaviour; should we not foster in ourselves the behaviour which works to accomplish what we want? 'Openness should be seen as a means to an end (effective behaviour) rather than an end in itself. Being 'open' becomes one more item in our repertoire of behaviour, to be used to get us what we want.'[10] Hence it can be considered a form of manipulation. Stanford, in the article just quoted, noticed that other people tended to like him when he was 'open' about his weaknesses, fears and shortcomings and that he tended to like other people when they were 'open' about these matters. In consequence to achieve rapport, he frequently behaved in an 'open' manner, revealing weaknesses that most people were not comfortable talking frankly about. In return they were more expansive. His openness was a way of getting what he wanted, it was a manipulative device, one of the games people play.

Real trust and openness require selfless interest and concern for others, based upon an appreciation of them as persons in their own right and not simply as means to an organisational end. Disinterestedness appears to be missing from much of the behavioural literature – trust and openness are to be developed not because other people are human but because as instruments they can be used to increase organisational effectiveness.

The possibility that openness, trust and creativity may have adverse consequences for the organisation is rarely, if ever, considered, yet why should we presume that these attributes will always work for the good of the organisation? It is widely believed that individual and organisational goals should be in harmony; if they are not, the individual's goals must be brought in line with those of the organisation. Here the behaviouralist's managerial stance emerges, ultimately there is an identity of interests.

Frequently the behaviouralist appears to suggest that personal relationships can be made effective through exposure and the employment of a series of techniques. In pursuing this view there is a failure to recognise that personal relationships may be spoilt if they are too self-consciously pursued or promoted, and that behavioural techniques become dehumanised when they are packaged for use in organisations.

In the behavioural approach to management there is a stress on the need for 'authentic' behaviour in the attributes already discussed. Now one of the features of 'authentic' behaviour is the feedback of information from one party to another concerning how he perceives, feels and reacts to the other. Yet how valid is such feedback? There must always be the possibility that, for a variety of reasons some of which are entirely worthy, it will be faulty; that for protective purposes people will distort information or hold it back in order to retain some power in the situation. This behaviour is decried as 'maskmanship', 'game-playing' and 'non-authentic', but to hold this view is to fail to recognise the individual as a private person. It also fails to see that organisational members operate in reward/punishment systems in which information can be used for and against the individual. To claim that this situation is unhealthy is to disregard the fact that organisations are plural political systems in which information is a significant element of power.

This leads in to the notion of organisational health: much use is made of medical terminology in discussion of organisational functioning and this is significant as it suggests,

1. A set of criteria against which organisations can be judged to be either healthy or not. These criteria are usually centred on the human factor and in the values already discussed. Clearly there is a basic assumption that these values are right and that not to hold them is in some sense to be unhealthy.
2. That the unhealthy organisation needs to be cured and this requires intervention from an organisational 'medical' man. The use of the medical analogy is pointed as it transfers some of the mystique of medicine to the interventionist and provides him with additional support – it gives him added authority. However, acceptance of this analogy is dangerous as the knowledge of the behaviouralist is much less certain than that of the medical doctor.

A final point arising out of so-called 'authentic' behaviour is the basic question of likes and dislikes. A manager reacts to different people in different ways, liking some colleagues and disliking others; this is not something laid down in any job description, there can be no requirement that he likes everyone. Liking is particularised and cannot be commanded or legislated for.

Successful managers are very diverse in their styles. Many sound managers remain remote, showing a respect for and understanding of their colleagues without evincing any great personal interest in them. The distance a person wishes to keep between himself and other people will vary; a manager may work with colleagues with or without being involved in any friendly relationship; he may on some occasions seek companionship then at other times wish to be on his own. The pressure to behave as though everyone is friendly is a manifestation of the phoniness that can pass for good human relations. Too often the back-slapping, the immediate first name approach is a facade behind which conflicts and antagonisms are powerfully played out. What we have in these situations is the ultimate in self-deception; the 'authentic' is in fact 'non-authentic' and the attributes which characterise the truly personal are hidden beneath a morass of dubious sentimentality. The result is that organisations are less, not more effective; the illusion distorts the reality and management is acted out at a number of confused levels.

Quantitative and Information Models

This chapter has taken issue with two powerful basic organisational and managerial models and criticised the faulty assumptions upon which they are based. Other models exist which build on these two and provide management with other perspectives.

The technical model suggests the solution of managerial problems lies in the application of techniques, using that term in its broadest sense to include administrative systems as well as the hardware. This model is grounded in quantification, mechanisation, automation and applied rationalisation, and in doing so it allies itself with the somewhat dehumanising implications of strands of contemporary ideas of progress. It is essentially rational and scientific. It places a heavy emphasis on the accumulation of factual information and consequently fails to take account of the probability that managers can be so overladen with data that imagination is submerged. There is the other possibility that a strong emphasis on quantification will lead to a false sense of security, to a belief that we know because we have the facts, to a failure to recognise that the data puts us at least one further remove from reality. The assembling of data into differing packages and categories inevitably obscures the unique quality of the material and distorts the fact that behind the information there are large numbers of human situations. Of course categorisation is necessary, but we need to be aware of its limitations and the pitfalls into which it can lead us. We oscillate between feelings of futility and mastery; to help us cope we rely increasingly upon the processors and the interpreters of information who become yet another barrier between ourselves and the reality behind the data.

One practical example of the technical model is that of forecasting and planning, which has to come to terms with the great complexity of many contemporary problems. The solutions proposed for these problems often have short lives, because by the time they are formulated the problems have changed, or may no longer exist. This is not an argument for the abandonment of forecasting, planning and the techniques associated with them, but for an appreciation of the nature of the world that has to be managed and of the issues raised by the techniques at management's disposal. Recognising the limitations of the available systems is better than accepting the claim that order exists when there is only a desire that it does.

Another recent approach to the management of organisations has been based upon contingency theory. This theory seeks to relate different features of an organisation to the environment in which it operates, and in attempting to establish effective structures and relationships between the two, it utilises structural, human and technological components. In drawing attention to the outside world the systems and contingency approaches have usefully broken down much of the insularity of the other models, although it has to be said that they retain their appeal because they match the felt needs of many managers.

CONCLUSION

This chapter has been concerned with models of management which stress what 'ought' to be; they are prescriptive, indicating how managerial goals can be achieved. They demonstrate that there is a choice of models; managers can accept one model and reject the others, or they can accept their existence and utilise whatever model seems appropriate in a given situation. Basically however the operative models and practice of management are to a large extent determined by how managers perceive the process of management; in other words the form management takes depends in no small measure upon the way people think, talk and write about management.

This book takes the view that the models so far developed and presented to management have omitted any substantial consideration of conflict, power and managerial politics; all fundamental aspects of organisational behaviour. The approach proposed is concerned with what 'is' and how to cope with it; it recognises the significance of other models and makes use of some of their attributes. It does not claim that all management is conflict, power and politics, but it suggests that these are important aspects of management which cannot be overlooked in any realistic appraisal of the subject. This chapter has cleared the ground for the study of management as a political activity.

2 Management in Action

CONTRASTING VIEWS OF ORGANISATIONS

In addition to the models discussed in the last chapter, there are two other views of organisations we must take into account. The first is the unitary view with its emphasis on integration and the second, the pluralist with its stress on conflict. Both are oversimplifications, for the reality is that organisations embody the two elements of co-operation and competition.

Allied to the structural model, outlined earlier, is the unitary view of the firm.[1] This regards the firm as a harmonious whole, characterised by the following beliefs – there is a single source of authority in the organisation; a team jointly striving to achieve common aims; no rival leaders and no conflicting loyalties; a close link between morale and success and a leader whose acts maintain loyalty.

The unitary view serves three functions for management; first, it provides reassurance: for many managers a belief in a basic harmony of purpose helps to sustain their self-confidence. Second, it is an instrument of persuasion: it represents the firm as a unity, disrupted only by the actions of fools, knaves and faulty communicators. Third, it helps to secure legitimacy: the notion that the interests of everyone in the firm are identical goes some way to conferring an aura of legitimacy on managerial action.

Linked to this view of the firm is a complementary set of ideas relating to management. These ideas, comprising the rhetoric of management, involve a collection of beliefs which together can be seen as the ideal; management as it 'ought' to be. According to this image the manager is faced with clear goals; he has time to plan for the achievement of these goals. He has adequate resources, including information, upon which to base his plans, and he makes decisions in a thoughtful, rational manner after the evaluation of all the factors involved. In the translation of these plans into operations he organises rationally and devises systems and procedures which will be acceptable to his staff and will lead to speedy implementation of his instructions. He has the authority appropriate to the responsibilities he carries and his position is in no way threatened by those in advisory positions. The overriding impression is one of unhurried pace, orderliness, control and rationality. From these ideal characteristics emerges the professional image of management, and an accompanying stereotype.

In considering this view it is clear that many managers not only believe that a firm and its management ought to be like this, but that it closely resembles this. Why do managers hold this image? The answer has much to do with the nature of beliefs; 'once a belief has been established the people concerned live with it, with the result that they can no longer be analytical about it and become reluctant to accept that it can be analysed'.[2]

Practically, the acceptance of the unitary perspective can lead to widely oscillating views of what is said and what is done: there is confusion between what ought to be and what is; the validity of conflict is at one and the same time denied and recognised to exist.

In contrast to this idealised version of the firm and its management there is another perspective which is rather more in accord with reality. This is the pluralist approach, where the firm is regarded as a plural society containing many related but separate interests, each with different objectives and rival leaders. In the pluralist view there is a recognition of the inevitability of conflict and an acceptance of the need to keep conflict between the differing interests within bounds, so that the firm is not totally disrupted and destroyed. It is recognised that the degree of common purpose in a firm is limited. The unity that exists arises mainly from the interdependence of the different groups who recognise their survival is linked with that of the whole. The main concern of the individual groups is with the prospects for short-run survival and, in consequence, long-term considerations are generally relegated to the background. Finally, for a variety of reasons, managers act to protect their own departments against the interests of others, making decisions which are likely to constrain the performance of others. Every organisation and set of linked organisations tends to display this divisive quality. It might be thought that the armed forces would be united by a common purpose in time of war, yet there is abundant evidence in the different accounts of the 1939–45 War of examples of inter-service rivalry of a most serious nature.[3] Memoirs and diaries of Cabinet Ministers repeatedly stress the competition between the Ministers; a situation summed up by the late Lord Boyle, former Conservative Minister for Education, in these terms, 'One had to fight not only against the Treasury, but compete with other Ministers for resources.'[4] Social movements such as trade unions and co-operatives exhibit similar tendencies to fragmentation; each trade union and co-operative society has its own interests to protect and these take precedence over the wider demands of their respective movements. In both cases the word 'movement' is part of the rhetoric with little bearing on what actually occurs. Within the individual organisation the same divisiveness appears, as different departments seek to protect their own interests; examples of this will be considered at length in later chapters. What is evident from this wide range of examples is that, in spite of the appearance of overwhelming common purpose, whether military, political or social, far reaching differences exist and shape the actual behaviour of the organisations involved.

The existence of a variety of leaders is regarded as inevitable by the pluralists, who also accept that much of leaders' behaviour which appears restrictive and resistant to change is logical and rational from their point of view if not from that of the outsider. Given this situation there is an acceptance of negotiation and bargaining as essential and inevitable elements of management, with compromise as a necessary outcome of managerial behaviour. Behind these activities is the fact of power and its unequal distribution within organisations.

Linked to this pluralistic approach is a view of management very different from that characterised in the unitary view. This pluralist view is concerned with the day-to-day behaviour and piecemeal give-and-take of management. It emphasises the need to negotiate and cope with the unanticipated, the ambiguous and the contradictory. Management is seen as open-ended; much of it as hectic, fragmented, paltry, unfinished, contradictory and characterised by busyness. What emerges is that managers prefer brevity and interruptions, they gravitate towards the most active parts of their jobs. They are more interested in current information and gossip than in formal reports.[5] In most cases the pressure of the manager's job does not encourage planning but rather the development of short-run information as a basis for short-term action. Managers develop the ability to continuously adapt. To the onlooker they may appear to exert little control over what they do, being set in a network of contacts involving superiors, subordinates, colleagues and outsiders. Yet they exert control in two important ways; first, as the initiators of numerous activities, and second, by extracting information from those around them. Mintzberg[6] remarks that the distinction between the successful and the unsuccessful manager is that the former decides who pulls the strings, how they will be pulled and then takes advantage of each move they are forced to make; the latter is unable to exploit this high-tension environment and is swallowed up. The manager emerges as a conductor or puppet depending upon how he manages his own affairs; in this context the conductor is the one who knows how to manage his boss, the puppet is the managed.

The pluralist sees the manager working through a whole series of relationships which are largely verbal and involve personal contacts characterised by interdependent chains of exploration and bargaining. The world in which the manager operates is volatile, ever-changing and fraught with competing claims and conflicts.

Originally the unitary and pluralistic approaches, as developed by Alan Fox, were applied to the relations between management and the work-force. One of the arguments of this book is that the pluralistic approach has a wider validity, being applicable between and within management and the work-force. The idea of a unified management facing a unified set of employees is part of organisational mythology. It may provide comfort to management, but is largely illusory and liable, if adhered to, to make the task of managing more difficult. To be realistic we need to recognise that a firm's management is fragmented, with different leaders, different goals and different resources, each in conflict with one another. The production manager, the sales manager, the financial and personnel controller each have their different goals; one concerned with how many 'widgets' his department has produced, the other with how many have been sold, the next with how much profit is being made and the last with how many people are employed, and so on. The attainment of these and a myriad of associated goals depends upon successful acquisition of resources, and given that these are scarce, conflict is the outcome. In a similar way the work-force is split and often in conflict; one has only to consider the many forms of inter-union dispute to appreciate this. Where unions have merged the inter-union disputes have become intra-union.

THE MANAGERIAL NETWORK

The relationships between managers embody both co-operation and conflict. If we look at these relationships we see that they can be broken down into a number of different styles, each with its associated problems.

1. There is the workflow relationship where a manager is faced with departments which precede his and which feed goods and/or services into his unit and, with succeeding departments to which he feeds his output. In this relationship the manager is dependent upon the efficiency and effectiveness of other managers whom he does not control and who may be judged against different criteria from those applied to him. They may have different time-scales for their operations and may be concerned with different aspects of the work process.
2. There is the service relationship in which the manager is the recipient or the producer of services for other departments; for example, the personnel controller provides initial screening interviews for positions in the production department.
3. There are those relationships which are essentially advisory where the manager is giving or receiving advice. Closely linked with this is the innovative relationship where the manager is required to change his methods of operating or to recommend others to change theirs. An O.M. department could be active in both relationships; giving advice on clerical systems and suggesting new ways of administering a system.
4. There is the monitoring relationship where the manager is monitoring others or being monitored. Any manager operating internal systems or, at the receiving end, being subject to forms of budgetary control, is a party in this relationship.
5. There is the stabilising or hierarchical relationship, the aim of which is to ensure stable relationships through the giving and taking of instructions. The traditional management hierarchy typifies this relationship.[7]

All of these relationships, except the hierarchical, involve managers who are subject to differing controls, criteria, goals and values. With no exception, there is inherent in them a trading relationship based on bargaining and negotiating, both of which call for implicit and explicit trade-offs. Examples of this include the tacit agreement between an advisory or innovating unit and a production department, whereby the latter accepts the advice or proposed change as long as it is not pushed too hard or is faced with changes which imply criticism of its previous activities. Behind this trade-off is the recognition by production that, if there is too obvious or precipitate a rejection of advice or change, the initiating unit will have a case for going to senior management and complaining along the lines, 'You employed us to utilise our expertise and it is being rejected, what are you going to do about it?' There is also the appreciation, by the initiating unit, of the ability of the production department to covertly produce results which appear to show the ineptitude of those proposing change or advocating particular advice. Another example occurs where a unit with a monitoring or control function requires information upon which to base its assessment: this information comes from the department under review and the monitoring unit is aware of the ability of that department to make life difficult for it, say, by producing information just within the stipulated time limit but so close to it as to make it hard for the monitors to process. Clearly there is a reply to such a tactic and what may develop is a battle of dates. To avoid such a situation some form of compromise may be reached which goes something like this, 'We will not produce too critical a report if you co-operate,' to which the reply is 'We will co-operate if you give us some indication of the lines of your criticism so that we can take action to deal with it before senior management come down on us.'

In this network of relationships managers occupy many different and shifting positions, and any one manager may operate in a number of relationships. For example, a personnel manager may operate on some occasions in a service capacity, in others as an advisor and still others as an innovator. In all these activities he is involved in negotiating and trading and his ability to handle these differing activities will be a partial measure of his success.

Behind these relationships there are certain objectives which the manager has in mind and there are appropriate strategies and tactics he will employ to achieve them. The first aim of a manager is to achieve a position where the balance of initiations favours him, that is to say, he makes more important demands on those in his network than they do on him. To achieve such a favourable balance a manager could attempt to move from being in a service position where others initiate demands upon him, to an advisory position where he is able to give advice without waiting to be asked, then to a monitoring position where he requests, even demands, information from others and ultimately to a hierarchical position where he gives instructions. This pattern of progression is one that can be widely observed in organisations as departments seek to increase their power and control over others. This shift is not blatant and obtrusive but gradual and barely perceptible. For example, there are the information providers who begin with the provision of data, who move on to interpreting the data and then advise on matters relating to the data, and then as their advice becomes regularly accepted it achieves the character of instruction. Another tactic is for a department to take on additional functions; for example, there is the personnel department which started as a welfare function and acquired a recruitment role, an industrial relations function and a management development involvement, each of which were presented in a way that moved the department into a more favourable balance of initiations in relation to other departments in the organisation.

A second aim is that of moving to positions of greater control and influence in the work sequence and in the decision-making process. Coming into either of these chains of activity at a late stage is to be involved when the work is well advanced; the decision is already firm. In both instances the possibility of influencing the process is limited; people have already made commitments, the work sequences and the decisions have taken firm shape. The only way to influence the situation is to become involved while operations are still fluid and the decision-making process has not reached the firm stage. A pattern emerges of managerial behaviour aimed at achieving positions in the firm, not necessarily formal, from which it is possible to influence the work pattern and the decision process. An example of this tactic would be the new financial controller who wished to lift his department up the organisational pecking order. In the first place he widened the scope of his department by stressing that it was much more than a mere provider of financial information, it had a function as a financial analyst and reporter. The second stage was one of developing a financial strategy for the company and on the strength of it a right to an early place in all corporate decisions. He was the initiator of each of the moves which placed his department at the centre of affairs, a position it had never previously occupied.

What is evident from any study of managerial networks is that managers operate in an arena of negotiated order in which the problem of power is central and conflict is not far below the surface.

The Special Relationship

One relationship of particular significance in the examination of management as a political activity is that of the superior–subordinate.

Any manager has a wide variety of relationships with his subordinates. One of these relationships involves direction aimed at achieving results which are satisfactory in the eyes of the superior. In the achievement of this end it is a fallacy to assume that subordinate satisfaction can be the prime concern of management. It is misleading to think that satisfied subordinates necessarily admire their superiors or that they perform more efficiently and effectively if they are handled according to some satisfaction formulae. The relationship between the manager and his subordinates is complex; general prescriptions do not necessarily fit individual cases.

The manager–subordinate relationship is influenced by differing factors on both sides. The position of the superior is more likely to be accepted if he displays technical or organisational ability; his credibility will be enhanced if he shows understanding of the rules of the game and of the expectations of his subordinates. His behaviour as the representative of his staff, his ability to act as a buffer between them and other parts of the firm and, where appropriate, from the environment external to the firm, are key factors influencing the relationship. His subordinates evaluate him on his ability,

1. to bring back to the department extra resources, for where there is growth there is the probability of more security and greater prospects;

2. to obtain at least a fair share of promotions and better still a more than fair share of what is going;
3. to obtain recognition for his staff and with that an acceptable share of current benefits; and
4. he is judged on his skill in protecting his staff from unpleasant and threatening changes, from redundancies, from the loss of the departmental position in the firm's pecking order and from undue pressure which might disturb the accepted operation of the department.

Wherever there is discretion the manager is expected by his subordinates to interpret the situation in a manner most favourable to his own department. He must exercise his skill to obtain resources and information from lateral groups.

In all these many aspects he is an advocate using the repertoire of strategies and tactics available to him to trade and negotiate successfully with those who have authority and power. However, these skills are not reserved for activities outside his department, he is also involved in bargaining and negotiating with his subordinates. These activities are rooted in two facets of his ability to manage his staff.

The first relates to the fact that much of his external activity is the result of initiations upon him from his own staff. These take a number of forms: there is the request for organisational aid where a subordinate has a problem elsewhere in the firm and needs the power and authority of his senior manager to help resolve it; there is the situation where a subordinate asks for technical aid knowing that his manager has entrée to sources of experience and expertise located in different parts of the firm; there is the subordinate's request for information as to how well he is doing, or for assistance in a personal matter or for support in an application for promotion or transfer, all of which may require contact with other departments.

The second relates to the manager's role as monitor, which involves assessment of how the work is progressing; effective appraisal of the operational system; the establishment of criteria against which to detect deviations and to judge performances and the initiation of corrective action when faced with deviations.

A key element in the superior–subordinate relationship is the ability of the superior to manage his boss on behalf of his own unit and staff. He has to act as a buffer absorbing pressure from above and below.

In all these activities the behaviour of a manager is a reflection of how work is progressing in his department, not of abstract and static conceptions of democratic or autocratic ways of dealing with people. The development of subordinate satisfaction is secondary to his ability (a) to represent and protect his department in such a way that his subordinates recognise that he has acquired a fair share of the available benefits and resources for them, and (b) to respond to their initiations. This is not one-way traffic, the subordinates have their part to play in the trade-offs; in return for effective management of their interests, they make their contribution by recognising that part of the power base of their superior rests on their readiness to co-operate. The manager who knows he carries his staff, feels that his back is protected when he negotiates with other departments. The greater his successful track record in operating on behalf of his department, the more readily will his staff support him. The ability to succeed, to obtain resources, to secure the benefits, produces commitment to local rather than to overall organisational goals. Success contributes to support and to the acceptance of the superior's position and to some appreciation, not necessarily firmly given, of the fact that some of the manager's decisions will limit the freedom of his subordinates. The effective manager will be in a stronger position to perform his monitoring function and get the necessary responses from his staff if he is aware of the ongoing trading nature of the process in which he is involved.

The relationship will remain fundamentally a trading one with everyone giving and taking, and while the superior carries the formal authority he will, if he is wise, recognise the power of his subordinates. Through their ability to control, distort and delay information they can make life difficult for him. Similarly they can create problems by going slow, by working to rule and by resisting change. Faced with this type of behaviour a lower level manager may collude with employees to ensure continuation of the work-flow for which he is responsible. Brown[8] gives an example of how supervisors in a piecework situation used their discretion to bend management rules: when a worker was paid less while waiting for a machine to be repaired than when he was assisting the fitter to repair it, the supervisor would give the worker a spanner to hold. This type of action is not so much a question of fiddling the company so much as a means of getting work done through collusion with lower levels in the firm. Lower and middle managers protect their seniors from involvement in work-flow problems if, and this is the important caveat, they are of the opinion that these higher levels are able and willing to protect them on other matters. These behaviours are not necessarily recognised by higher management, who often have only limited understanding of what their lower levels do, or of their subordinates' practices for coping with what is expected of them. Where they are aware of them, they are often deliberately forgotten so that the myths of hierarchy and formal control can be maintained.

When subordinates feel they are not well protected by their seniors they can always use the tactic of delegating upwards, of referring every problem to their superior, who ends up making decisions which should be taken by his subordinates, who can then disclaim responsibility. Delegation upwards is a powerful tactic for subordinates. For any manager who feels overloaded it is worth trying to pinpoint where all the extra work comes from. To do this he can analyse his time and separate it into three categories, the work that is delegated from above, the work he himself generates and the work his employees' 'delegate' to him. He will quickly learn how much control he has over his own problems, how much is exercised from above and how much control his employees have.

Managerial Choice

The pattern of relationships based upon trading and negotiation has to be seen against a background of managerial choice. In the first place the norms and values of organisations, indeed of the wider society, do not constitute a coherent whole, but are discrepant and vague. It is this that allows for the exercise of choice and for the manipulation of norms by organisation members, in the furtherance of their own interests and those of their own department. In the second place, the individual manager, in reality, does not have a clearly defined job with neatly prescribed authority, responsibilities and accountabilities; he is faced with demands, constraints and choices set in the middle of a network of relationships which he must fashion into a pattern that will accomplish his objectives. He is engaged in a set of strategic behaviours in which, faced with the moves of other parties, he has to make compensating moves which, in turn, impact on the others and the process goes round again. These activities involve new agreements, commitments and assurances from those with whom he has been and is negotiating.

Managers exercise choice in both what they do and how they do it;[9] this takes place within the context of their environment, their level and function in the organisation, their personality and style, and the situation as they perceive it. Much of this choice is embodied in their coping strategies within the framework of relationships outlined earlier. Child and Partridge[10] put forward three strategies aimed at dealing with conflict and pressures in the supervisory role. The first strategy reflects a concern for unit output, quality, cost-effectiveness and dicipline and is linked with strong dependence on higher management through the reference of issues upwards rather than taking the initiative. The supervisors in this group are task-oriented and tend to delegate upwards.

The second strategy emphasises the maintenance of high morale and effectiveness among subordinates, coupled with the managers' desire to settle problems on their own initiative; they keep conflict latent and collude with their subordinates. They are employee-oriented with an emphasis on training, recruitment, supply of appropriate tools and the progressing of work.

The third of these strategies stresses withdrawal from conflict and pressure. These supervisors spend much time on paperwork, looking after equipment and frequently doing the work of their subordinates.

In the actual situation there are shifts between these alternative strategies. The discretion existing in the supervisory and managerial positions allows for this shifting of patterns, although it is evident that various factors in the manager's development, such as training, experience and inclination, will lead him towards one alternative more than to others.

Underlying the various activities and strategies available to the manager is the relationship between himself and his staff which is, in part, a series of reactions to the expectations and behaviour of the other party. Each takes cues from the other; for example, when a manager schedules his time, he is indicating his perception of the interests of his department and is setting priorities for action; he is announcing, however obliquely, what is important and what is not. His subordinates then react to these implied priorities and their associated values and behaviours, learning which matters interest him and should be taken to him and which should be kept away from him. The agenda for their actions is determined by their perception of the manager.

Managers and Specialists

A similar pattern of choice, negotiation and strategy emerges in the relationship between a line manager and specialist staff. This relationship is based on certain formal assumptions: the contribution of the specialist staff will be welcomed; applied by line management, if feasible, and recognised as based upon unique knowledge. In practice this relationship operates within the context of a confused set of values which are unlikely to provide much guidance to either specialists or users; in consequence many of the assumptions are unlikely to be met. Moreover it is complicated by the specialist's definition of his role, which affects both his attitudes and behaviour and also the line manager's perception of the specialist's task. Important in the manager's assessment of the specialist is his judgement of the likely effects of any suggested innovation upon his power and that of his unit. Additionally, the work background and career prospects of both parties differ and the criteria and control systems applied to them are dissimilar. Studies of the way the relationship of computer specialists and users operates show that joint decision making is often characterised by bargaining rather than problem-solving, by the rationing of information; by rigid formalised relations and by suspicion, hostility, manipulation and defensiveness.[11] If this appears to be too harsh a view of this relationship, it is necessary to remember that both parties are concerned with their present positions and the power associated with them. As a result of this there is a continuous process of bargaining, whether implicit or overt, between the parties involved, with the negotiations being influenced by the power and expectations of the specialists and users. The track record of the parties can be crucial: the success or failure of previous proposals from the specialists will influence the stance of the users, and the previous ability of the users to apply proposals will shape the attitudes and expectations of the specialists. At the same time the parties are aware of external pressures, such as senior management or the external market, and this awareness will influence the style of the relationship. Where pressure is brought to bear by specialists who have enlisted the support of top management, there is always the possibility of the self-fulfilling prophecy becoming operative – starting from a position of declaring that 'This proposal will not work' the behaviour of the reluctant managers can produce the result they had prophesied.

An added dimension arises when the specialism is new, for then its practitioners seek to gain status and impress those around them. This is not always easy because new specialisms are often experimental and their benefits less obvious than the tried and trusted methods. As a result their promoters may make excessive claims which are out of line with their capability; in such a case they put themselves at risk, especially as early failure may make it difficult for them to establish themselves. Clearly there are dangers inherent in the situation for both parties; a line management which believes that the specialist has the full backing of top management may react overenthusiastically, uncritically accept the specialist's recommendations and end up with his unit disrupted. The behaviour of both parties will be influenced by the degree of commitment of senior management: if there is a high level of commitment for the specialism the specialist can move with more confidence and exert more pressure on line management; if the commitment is low the specialist may be placed in a weak position and have to tread carefully in his relations with others. Thus the relationship of the specialist to line management is affected by their relative power which is in turn affected by the commitment of top management. This commitment is fluid, for example, in American industry in the early 1980s there was a sharp move away from top management support for specialist activity, to a renewed awareness of the importance of line management; in a great number of large industrial concerns specialist staffs were severely cut back and the responsibility for decision making which had drifted to the specialists was thrust back to line managers.

Where there is severe conflict between specialists and line management there is the danger that the value of the advice offered will not be recognised; fewer alternatives will be generated and examined; short-term gain at the expense of long-term development will be the main concern of the interested parties and additional rigidity and polarisation of positions will be the order of the day. From the point of view of the specialist the task is not simply one of possessing scarce expertise and information but of controlling and using them skilfully in the pursuit of his own goals. For the line manager his prime concern is with the defence of his department, which entails the careful acceptance or rejection of advice in the light of its impact upon the power of his unit.

Lateral Relationships

The lateral relationship is the final one we consider in this chapter. In any firm there will be lateral interdependence, based upon the flow of men, materials, money and information. The problems of managing lateral relations usually arise because no one in the chain has the formal authority to manage the others. Additionally these relationships are often characterised by irregular operational patterns. This leads to attempts to programme them, or, if that is not possible, to isolate the stages in the lateral chain from each other. The irregularity of lateral relationships can interfere with routine and precipitate events which lead from small local difficulties to major upsets. They can also be the source of ambiguity, presenting a steady stream of unsettling issues for the manager to face; for example, a production manager may be faced with an erratic supply of semi-finished products from an earlier stage in the production line; a management services manager may irregularly receive information which should arrive at a steady rate from operating managers. In both instances the stability of their own department's operations is put in jeopardy. Coping with these problems involves selling, persuasion and influence and their management has been defined as 'a process of working interfaces', raising such questions as 'who is expected and/or required to do what, with whom, when and where?'

An example of lateral relationships can be found in the purchasing department[12] which has two primary functions, one to negotiate and place orders on the best possible terms, but only in accordance with the specifications laid down by others and second, to expedite orders and ensure that deliveries are made on time. The department is at the receiving end of the work-flow process and is subject to a wide variety of pressures generated both inside and outside the firm. The purchasing manager may have power when dealing with external pressures but have limited power internally, except in periods of acute shortages of crucial supplies. In the general situation the purchasing manager seeks to extend his function to that of providing market information about new materials, sources of supply and price. To perform in this way he needs to be consulted before internal departments submit purchasing requisitions. If he achieves this consultative role he is in a better position to suggest alternative materials and parts, recommend more economical lot sizes and changes in specifications or design of components which will, in his view, lead to a saving of money or result in higher quality products or to quicker delivery. He will also be able to influence 'make or buy' decisions. Here we have another example of the tactic of shifting the direction of initiations; normally orders flow in one direction which the purchasing manager seeks to reverse so that he can take the initiative in matters relating to his unit. This attempt to reverse the flow of initiations and increase the power of the purchasing manager in the decision-making process, is likely to be viewed with some hostility by those who presently determine the specifications and frequently deal directly with suppliers' salesmen, undermining the purchasing manager in doing so.

The purchasing manager may have little or no choice with suppliers because of the tight specifications laid down in the design office. He may be faced with deadlines which necessitate his seeking delivery on short notice and at premium prices; asking favours of suppliers and placing himself under an obligation to them. The root of the matter is that he only becomes involved when other departments have made the decisions. Faced with this position, the purchasing manager has a range of tactics open to him.

1. He can act in a rule-oriented manner and in doing so appeal to higher level management for support. He can request the requisitioning department to justify in writing the timing and order size of the requisition. He can comply with the strict letter of the law, knowing full well that a late order coming

from a requisitioning department cannot be delivered on time, and use the defence, 'I did as requested'.

2. He can use more personal and political tactics to gain admission to the decision-making process, relying on friendship, or on favours exchanged, or on trade-offs with the implied threat that a failure to involve him will lead to reprisals, such as delaying the processing of the requisitions of the offending department by returning them for clarification. He may use allies in other departments to bring pressure to bear on the recalcitrant unit.

3. Using an organisational approach he may seek to change existing systems and procedures, so that other departments must check with his unit on matters of timing, quality and quantity. He may seek to restructure the purchasing function so that specialist buyers are attached to internal departments rather than being centralised, the rationale being that he spreads his influence throughout the operating units. He may seek to convince those with power of the need to regroup a number of activities so that a powerful unit emerges, at the head of which is purchasing. He will couch his arguments for organisational change in terms of efficiency, cost saving and the like, but in the background there is the aim of improving his power base. To achieve these changes the purchasing manager must 'prove' that the present procedures and structures are inefficient by ensuring that they are not.

It is clear that there are a number of options open to the purchasing manager. Individual purchasing managers will react differently: some will seek more formal authority, or more influence and power through greater involvement; some will withdraw behind formal arrangements; some will think in terms of developing a long-term organisational position and some will seek to cope with each conflict as it comes along. The success of any of these tactics will depend upon the purchasing manager's political skill in using formal and informal approaches, by the technology of the major operations and hence their supply requirements and by the management philosophy of the firm. The position of the purchasing manager illustrates the highly political nature of lateral relationships, and underlines the variety of tactics that is open to him and the need to be ready to shift from one tactic to another as other managers respond with their own tactics.

When we examine the performance of managers in similar jobs it becomes clear that they respond in differing ways because of their varying perceptions, expectations, abilities, information and experience. The choice of what the manager does will be influenced by the factors already mentioned and their relationship to the network of power in which he is involved.

A manager determines what work he shall do and how he will do it; this latter includes choosing the tactics he will use to improve his power base. Admittedly his choice will be constrained by the cultures of the organisation and the habits and preferences of his superior, but always the question of power can never be far away. Discretion is a key element in managerial politics, both in extending present power and in developing political skills for promotion to higher levels of management. To fill a series of management positions where the element of political thinking is very small is poor preparation for more senior posts. To avoid such a deadend position a manager needs to be on the alert to move to positions where the managerial job has been restructured to increase the discretionary element in it, or to newly created positions where the first occupant does not inherit constraints from the past, or to posts where he is the expert and his superior is not.

The manager exercises this choice with respect to a limited, approximate picture of the world which he has developed. His definition of the situation is itself the outcome of selection, of what the manager considers important to himself and his department, and of his ability, willingness and opportunity to search for alternative strategies, tactics and solutions. The critical factor is that the choices do not come to him neatly packaged; he has to find them and shape them. Looking for alternatives is time-consuming and competes with other time-demanding activities. Where the manager lives in an ongoing atmosphere of crisis, his opportunity to think in terms of choice is limited. It is clear that some managers do not think in these terms, or develop a strategic conception of management behaviour, based on choice and ultimately directed to the maintenance and development of their power.

CONCLUSION

What emerges from this consideration of management in action
is its contradictory nature and its internal tensions. For example,
it is often argued that subordinates need to be given a clear
understanding of their jobs, yet inevitably jobs overlap and
boundaries become blurred and as a result there is room for
manoeuvre and negotiation. Winston Churchill recognised the
value of ambiguity when it suited, for, of his appointment as
Minister of Defence in 1940 he said, 'we must be very careful not
to define our powers too precisely'.[13] Then there is the desire to
establish routine and regularity, much of which comes under
pressure and has to be abandoned in the face of change,
ambiguity and uncertainty. Managers are portrayed as decisive
yet it is sometimes difficult to know when and where a decision
was made; indeed decisions are often in a state of flux and are
often 'made' in retrospect. Firms are pictured as hierarchical yet
much managerial time is spent coping with lateral relationships.
These and many other contrasts expose the shifting nature of
management, the almost universal doing rather than managing,
the everpresent factor of power and the complication of choice.

This chapter has presented management in terms of contradictions and choice, set in the midst of a network of relationships
which involve trading, negotiating and bargaining. The actuality
is evershifting, confused and far removed from the rhetoric of
management. In the words of Lord Armstrong, it is evident that
'people who are doing the job ... are not actually doing what the
book says ... they have adapted it to themselves, how they like to
work, how they like to behave and how it looks to them'.[14] The
manager is enmeshed in a clash between the rigorously rational
and the social and political aspects of human behaviour. To cope
with that clash it is essential to view management as politics, as
the art of the possible.

3 The Politics of Management

Having asserted that management embodies a political element, it may well be asked, 'What is political in this context?' For our purpose politics is a many-sided activity; it arises from fundamental differences of interests, structures, opinions, power and resources. These differences lead to disagreement and conflict which have to be managed. Politics aims to bring about change or to resist it. It includes both a struggle for power and resistance to it. Politics is one of the mechanisms by which people seek, through the exploitation of both human and physical resources, to achieve control over others. Political behaviour is central to competition for scarce resources. Political activity involves the deployment of strategies and tactics through bargaining and negotiating, aimed at the protection of personal and departmental interests.

The political view of management has its basis in the plural model of organisations and is unlikely to be welcomed by those who adhere to the unitary view. This rejection stems largely from the failure to see managerial politics as an outcome of the way organisations function. For those who reject the pluralist view, political behaviour may be regarded as a bore – slow, repetitive and equivocal, ending in compromise and concession; far removed from the black and white of victory and defeat of a 'cleanly fought' contest. Frequently managerial politics is seen as the cause of managerial and organisational failure; for example, the American magazine, *Businessweek*, frequently highlights 'executive infighting' as a cause of a firm's poor performance. This may on occasion be the case, but it is the argument of this book that organisational politics, more often than not, facilitates change and adaptation and the resolution of problems: it may not always be fast moving but in the end may be no slower than the more 'rational' approaches that are advocated.

An example of the political process in action is to be found in the debate in the United States over the development of the

Polaris missile. The Polaris has frequently been cited as one of the most successful and effective of the military weapons development programmes undertaken in the USA. It was regarded as a model of good managerial practice. When the programme was studied in depth it was concluded that it was 'the skill in bureaucratic politics of the backers and managers of the Polaris project that largely accounted for its success. Interservice rivalry was successfully managed; congressional and administration political support was obtained; scientific expertise was garnered as needed; and the network of interagency and interorganisational contracting relationships were successfully negotiated and managed.'[1] An example of the political tactics employed was the use of sympathetic scientists who were coopted on to the programme to give the appearance that current scientific opinion supported the feasibility of the programme. Even well-established management techniques, such as PERT and critical path analysis, were used more for window-dressing than for substantive reasons. As the proponents of Polaris eliminated competitors, outmanoeuvred reviewing agencies and coopted congressmen, admirals, newspapermen and academics, it became clear that politics was an organisational requirement and that what distinguished advocates and opponents was not that some played politics and others did not, but rather, that some were better at it than others.

Acting politically requires taking a strategic view based, not on some idealised model of human behaviour, but on how people actually behave. Thus a strategic view rests on a sense of what is effective, a recognition that the ideal cannot be achieved, that management acts within the realm of the possible. This underlines the importance of managerial philosophy, of how managers view such notions as opportunism, utopianism and realism.

THE MANAGERIAL NETWORK

The last chapter described the various relationships in which managers are involved, with the one enduring objective of management being to initiate, hold and master a predictable and reciprocal network of relationships. To build such a network a manager requires an awareness and knowledge of the people with whom he deals. He has to identify those from whom he can readily ask favours and information and those whom it would be useful to have involved in his schemes but whom he does not know well. The manager seeks to make these contacts effective for furthering his personal and unit goals. To achieve this effectiveness is a matter of tactics, of how relationships can be strengthened or where necessary initiated. On a specific issue the manager needs to know who in his network will support him, who will be lukewarm and who will oppose him actively or passively. A key part of the political equipment of the manager in these circumstances is sensitivity, based on his assessment of the distribution of power within his network and his perception of how any changes might upset the power balance. He must also recognise that support is achieved at a price; his relations with others are based upon interdependence; each and every party is dependent on the other in varying degrees. He has to assess the price and consider whether he has overdrawn the balance of goodwill with those whose support he seeks. Another considera-tion must be his estimate of what trade he has to offer a particular contact, and whether he has the necessary resources for the trade. Information is one important dimension of these relationships and the question a manager has to face is, who controls the important information which is currently available?

Within this network the manager acts in an accommodative and manipulative manner, seeking to restructure the conditions in which the manipulated operates, so that the course of action he desires is accepted. The manipulated should not be aware of the manager's intentions to influence him, whether through changing the environment or through altering his perception of it. The latter is achieved through communication, often involv-ing the use of symbolic images and language. Changing the titles of managerial posts, the location of offices; providing company cars; identifying real and imagined external threats are but a few of the tactics which contribute to shaping people's attitudes.

The task of political language and symbolic activity is to rationalise and justify proposals, plans and decisions in order to make them acceptable and legitimate to other members of the network. Management can be regarded as a manipulator of myths, symbols and images aimed at building support for whatever is proposed. Around managerial activities there are generated attitudes, beliefs and values, all of which can be manipulated. It is possible to influence feelings about choices

and decisions independently of the activities involved because of
the socially constructed nature of reality. Through language we
shape the world we inhabit, and sharing a common language
with other people in a network provides the subtlest and most
powerful of all tools for controlling the behaviour of network
members, to the advantage of the manager concerned. Language
is another of the critical elements in political activity, it can
cloud the analytical process, dull the critical faculty and provide
symbols rather than substance for those with little political
power. Brzezinski, President Carter's National Security Adviser,
illustrates the subtle use of language and the need to be able to
interpret it in the following example, 'When he (Carter) said, "I
understand" he was saying "I don't want to argue the subject
with you any more, and I don't want you to go away feeling that
I have disagreed with you, but I am not going to say anything
which you can later use to the effect that I agreed with you." In
effect, "I understand" was a pacifier – and it often produced
misunderstandings with those who concluded that "I understand" meant "I agree."'[2]

The propensity for managerial decisions to be taken before
any adequate explanation of them has been made, offers the
opportunity for manipulation of those who carry out the decisions. The reasons for a· decision can be rationalised after the
event, to justify the success or failure of the decision and to gain
acceptance of the results.

The activities of rational analysis and planning, contribute to
the development and use of political language to justify decisions
and orders, while at the same time making the politics less
obvious. Analysis and planning give decisions the appearance of
rationality, yet they basically justify actions that are based upon
political predilections.

Ideologies held with conviction and not empirically tested can
help to hide the use of power and legitimise non-rational
behaviour. They simplify a complex reality and provide a feeling
of orderliness and rationality that is much valued. In this
connection 'rational' decisions and planning provide a sense of
order and control; in consequence actions are 'good' because
they are planned and are less likely to be critically examined.
Whether they are as planned as the outsider assumes them to be
is another matter: for example, the German drive through the
Ardennes and the Japanese attack on Pearl Harbour suggested
they were the implementation of long-prepared plans, solidly

supported by the military hierarchy; in neither case was this wholly true.[3]

Within his network the manager seeks to manipulate other members through the use of political language and symbols, trade-offs and the like, and in turn they seek to manipulate him.

The notion of the manager as a manipulator may be distasteful to some, but it is one necessary aspect of the manager's role. In his competitive situation he can pose a threat to those above him, appear disciplinary to his staff and even negative when he refuses requests which appear reasonable and legitimate to those who make them. He may seem restrictive when he makes a decision which favours one individual or group at the expense of others. Further, if he is realistic, recognising that power is needed to achieve his goals, he will also know that the acquisition and retention of power through the use of political skills will be at the expense of others.

The manager is concerned to influence and control the environment in which he operates, and manipulation is one of the means of achieving that control. Within many of the standard ideas of management there is the element of manipulation; for example, if the subordinate is to be given wider discretion and if organisational homogeneity is necessary, these apparently conflicting aims can be achieved through selection, special training, appropriate reward and punishment systems and indoctrination. Significantly, senior management manipulate the situation when they provide the basic premises upon which subordinates make decisions. In the extreme it can be summed up in the words of the chief executive who said, 'My managers can make any decision they like as long as it is the decision I would make.' He made sure it was, by using the tactics of manipulation listed above. The reality of freedom is much less than the rhetoric of management would have the onlooker and indeed the practitioner believe.

POLITICAL STRATEGY AND TACTICS

Political strategy is concerned with the acquisition of power. It can take a number of forms.

1. The manager can seek to exercise countervailing power, so as to set limits to the extensiveness of the power of other

managers – he can seek to constrain the number of people affected by their decisions; he can attempt to limit the comprehensiveness of their power by limiting the scope of topics covered by their discretion; he can attempt to minimise the extent to which they can push him, that is, he seeks to limit the intensity of their power.

2. He can seek to destroy their integral power altogether, leaving the basis of their power open for grabs by anyone and everyone.

3. He can seek to supplant his competitors by acquiring and exercising their power.

His success will depend upon his own power. This is most effective when used unobtrusively and with an aura of legitimacy, hence the widespread attempt to make the use of power covert and to legitimise and rationalise actions and decisions that are the result of power.

Within a network the manager of a unit will seek to establish some measure of autonomy, by protecting the boundaries around it and resisting absorption by other units. When a unit manager sees another department embarking on activities already included in his own unit's operation or sees new tasks going to a competing unit when he believes they should come to him, he will take some form of political action. When faced with powerful demands for integration into another unit the manager can make visible those 'special' qualities which, he claims, can only be exercised if he has a measure of independence. Many managerial actions which appear threatening to other members of his network are defensive measures on his part, and in reverse many activities of other network members which seem aggressive to the particular manager are part of their defence.

The reciprocity between different units within a network is not necessarily symmetrical, some units are more dependent than others; some suppliers are more dependent on some customers than on others, some customers are more dependent upon their suppliers than others. These different dependencies produce different balances of power within the supplier–customer relationship. It is clear that interdependence is problematic, unbalanced and shifting. It is not fixed and permanent. There is, for example, a conflict between network membership and privacy; managers seek to defend the privacy of their own units while proclaiming the virtues of openness. The tactics of defence include avoidance rituals, such as setting up meetings to share information but which in reality are designed to obscure a position and avoid the declaration of significant information.

We can now examine some of the tactics which are used to manipulate managerial networks.

The Criteria Tactic

There is the selective use of objective criteria. In any firm there are multiple interests with multiple goals; for example, it can be argued that business policies group round three dominant concerns: growth, efficiency and social action.[4] In consequence of this multiplicity the assessment of managerial activities and decisions is both difficult and uncertain. The individual manager faced with this situation can employ a number of tactics:

1. he may advocate the use of criteria favourable to his own position;
2. he can hold constant on some criteria and show improvement on those of interest to the elements in his environment upon which he is most dependent;
3. he may employ those criteria most visible to important elements in his network; and
4. if it is difficult to score effectively on internal criteria he can turn outwards and make comparisons with selected external criteria.

Underlying these tactics is the recognition that efficiency criteria are only one aspect of organisational effectiveness. Basic to all these tactics is selective perception; information is selectively collected and used in decision making to provide support for the decisions that have already been taken or favoured. For example, there was the company which was undertaking a major development and its senior management had two viability studies undertaken. Both of these were kept under wraps; the study which was closest to the results of the development were later brought out in its justification, the other was quietly forgotten. This type of behaviour is often made possible by the multi-faceted and ambiguous nature of the data that is used in the establishment and operation of criteria.

In examining the relations between operations and maintenance departments, Dalton[5] demonstrated how the use of rational procedures can produce subtle and unobtrusive political behaviour. Recognising the pressure of costs on operations management, he highlighted the link between a manager's cost record and his future promotion prospects. This led managers to search for loopholes in the cost system. In his sample of firms, levels of costs were affected by the efficiency of the services provided by the maintenance department. This led operations departments to put pressure on maintenance for the speedy completion of repair work. To achieve this managers used bullying, implicit threats and friendship. Among the tactics they used were,

1. threatening to block informal favours to maintenance – favours which took the form of covering up the mistakes of maintenance men, and, if discovered, of sharing responsibility for them; and
2. supporting maintenance department requests for more personnel and resources and generally helping to fight off threats to maintenance from other departments.

The aim of these tactics was to obtain speedy and regular maintenance service, which would enable the operations departments to keep part of their costs at a low level and thus ensure that they were seen in a good light by senior management.

When maintenance was required to make a surprise inspection of operations departments, it would confer with those to be inspected and agree to telephone the starting point, the time and route to be followed by the inspectors. This allowed operations departments to move materials and equipment, which they did not want examined, out of sight by shifting them from the route. To appear to be working along the guidelines provided by senior management the maintenance department varied its starting points, times and routes but always tipped the wink to operations. What we have here is the tactic of 'nominal surprise'; a common device in inspection and auditing relationships. Basically maintenance avoided seeing things that would call for corrective action and disturb friendly relations with operations managers. Encapsulated in this example are some of the key political activities of trading support and favours, and of entering into bilateral agreements and coalitions.

The Consultant Tactic

A second tactic is the use of the outside expert or consultant. By bringing in the outside expert, decisions can be influenced covertly. Attention is distracted away from one's own proposals to the recommendations of the expert. The consultant's views can also be used to support a view already held by those who have the power to invite him in. It may be asked whether it is necessary to call in a consultant when the knowledge often exists within the firm. One answer is that it enables the firm to check its own knowledge against that of an impartial outsider; another is that the consultant can legitimise decisions that have already been taken and at the same time provide an aura of rationality. The consultant is assumed to be objective, expert and expensive, the first two legitimise his proposals and the third fosters commitment to his recommendations.

Thus the consultant can be used as part of the firm's power structure. He is likely to be used when power is widely dispersed and those in authority feel the need for support. He may also be involved when the issues at stake may lead to a substantial shift in power; for example, when a firm is being restructured and when new information systems are being installed. The consultant is involved in a series of advisory and monitoring relationships in which he operates in a political situation, subsumed in a rational framework. However, if he is to be effective he has to define problems in his own terms in order to be seen to be objective; if he fails to do this he will be too obviously a part of the organisational contest for power and control and his credibility will suffer. Clearly the key question in these activities is, who has the power to bring in the consultant? Certainly the sponsoring manager will try to keep control of access to the outside expert, and determine who can talk to him, when, in what conditions and on what issues. To preserve his own identity the consultant has to resist these constraints, recognising that there is the ever-present tendency for every outsider to become an insider.

The consultant has to assess the power structure of the firm in which he is working. He has to determine the key leverage points within that structure and operate them to the benefit of the host firm, in a manner which is not detrimental to his future in and out of the firm.

The Agenda Tactic

A third major tactic relates to the formal and informal agenda of discussion. Here the concern is with such questions as, what topics are generally discussed in the firm, what topics are on the formal agenda of various meetings and what decisions are made? Just as important are such queries as, what issues are not discussed generally, what decisions do not appear in any formal sense and what decisions are not taken?

It is the power to prevent issues surfacing and decisions being made that can be crucial to the functioning of organisations and their management. In any meeting, formal or otherwise, there is the need to be aware of the hidden agenda; why some issues are not being discussed and who keeps them suppressed. Thus the basic question is, who has control of the agenda, both formal and informal? Clearly, those in power, who, when threatened by the possible emergence of new ideas, proposals for change or evidence of their own shortcomings, exercise their power to determine the agenda. Here it has to be recognised that it is power and not authority that is important in determining the agenda.

For any manager to break into agenda making, he must have an issue that is so widely recognised as significant that it becomes difficult, if not impossible, to keep it off the agenda of discussion. In addition he must build up an adequate groundswell of support by demonstrating to sufficient people, who together have power, that it is in their own interests to get the matter discussed. He has to build a coalition. The astute political manager always thinks in terms of the ripeness of the issue. Issues that never surface may suffer because their sponsors have sought to introduce them too soon or indeed too late. There is a crucially right time and the manager has to develop his sensitivity to the timing of issues.

The order of consideration of an issue is important: where does it come on the agenda? This is most clearly demonstrated on the agenda of formal meetings, for the specific order of discussion and, where relevant, of voting can be crucial. A decision on an early item on an agenda can well affect the way in which a later item is dealt with and whether a decision on it will be taken at all. The agenda represents a series of decisions, and the tactics of agenda building can help determine the success or failure of discussion of its items. For example, if there are two items dealing with similar issues it is advisable for the supporters of these items to seek to have the weaker proposal placed first, as this maximises the possibility that both or at least one of the proposals will be approved. Similarly the use of dummy and bogus proposals which are put up to direct attention to later items is a tactic of consequence. The use of ceremonies and rituals, for example, the manner in which the minutes of the previous meeting are handled, and the use of reports, have their part to play and are often aimed at pushing critical issues to the end of the agenda when time is short and members are wanting to get back to some other work, committee, social occasion or are simply tired by the meeting. Frequently members will spend a great deal of time discussing an issue which involves the expenditure of a relatively small sum of money yet will deal very quickly with another matter involving a very large sum, simply because of its position on the agenda.

Few managers regard the agenda either as an item of public discussion or as an element of political strategy, yet it is a key factor in shaping not only the way issues are discussed but also whether they are acted upon or left dormant. It is part of the control system exercised by those with power and it provides a focus of conflict as those with less power seek to gain it through the agenda.

The Committee Tactic

Fourth, the committee itself emerges as a political tactic. To coopt various internal interests onto a committee helps to build legitimacy and support. This is particularly important when acceptance of a decision is problematic because of strong differing interests, the lack of any clear-cut answer or when the issue is not susceptible to a technical answer. The move must be to build the conflicting interests into the committee, because when decisions are taken in a public forum and with clear choice, those involved are then committed to the decision.

Cooption is largely an attempt to change the position of powerful people who, if left outside, could threaten the committee's decisions. The coopted person is exposed to informational and social influences which produce a pressure towards conformity to the decisions taken and to a justification of its acceptance. Coopted members are frequently recipients of information that is not widely available and they are in the company of people with interests and viewpoints that may be different from their own. They are under pressure because they are to some extent isolated from the interests they represent, and they become associated and identified with their new affiliation. In consequence the expectations of those they 'represent' may be unfulfilled and they are regarded as turncoats. Indeed, in some instances they may well have changed their attitudes and from the point of view of the organiser of their co-option, the move can be regarded as effective if they align themselves with him. Cooption can bind the coopted individual to decisions, by providing new roles, new expectations and a label that produces an appearance of consistency with the newly-acquired affiliation.

Cooption of people external to the organisation may be aimed at obtaining financial support, information, additional status, building into a new external network and so on. In cooption there are costs; the coopted individual acquires knowledge of the organisation's workings which he can take back to the interests he represents, and there is also the possibility of some loss of control to the coopted party.

Those who coopt members, whether from other parts of the organisation or from external bodies, have to trade off the gains of constraining difficult interests against losing some measure of control. This is a specific case of the general problem of balancing the costs and benefits, in the light of what is the best and the worst that can happen in any particular trade-off.

Given such factors, as the size of committees and the degree of heterogeneity present, it is evident that committees can be slow. However the slowness of a committee can be a useful attribute to those who wish to remove an issue from the active agenda of discussion.

If some issue arises which cannot be kept off the agenda but is disturbing to those in power, a number of possible tactics exist. One is to set up a sub-group or committee to discuss the issue and allow it a long time before it has to produce any conclusions which have to be reported back to the decision-makers.

1. Involve in the group a number of people who have widely differing interests and views and ensure that among them is a high proportion of analytically skilled people.

2. Isolate the group from responsibility for making other decisions, particularly of the short-term nature.

In contrast if there is an issue upon which some quick action
has to be taken, the opposite tactics can be employed,

a. enforce a short deadline; and
b. keep the number in the group very small and ensure that
they have similar interests and are not analytically skilled.

This is but one of many tactics which someone in power may
employ in order to get the type of answer and report he wants at
the time he requires it.

In a committee the individual members bring to bear their
own tactics, each hoping to achieve his particular goal. Underlying some of these tactics are such precepts as, 'do not act in a
manner which raises expectations that future actions will follow
the same pattern', and 'do not set dangerous precedents'.[6]
Cornford also makes the point that 'There is only one argument
for doing something; the rest are arguments for doing nothing.
The argument for doing something is that it is the right thing to
do. But then, of course, comes the difficulty of making sure that it
is right.' This somewhat tongue-in-cheek attitude is at the basis
of many tactics to prevent change that might disturb the status
quo.

Other tactics for delay embody some of the following:

1. There is the 'fair trial' stance which maintains that anything
new should go through existing systems and not through any
new system that might be proposed – 'let us keep to the
systems we know and give them a fair trial'.
2. There is the perennial argument that the time is not ripe; the
right time has not yet arrived.
3. Another obstructive view is that the matter under discussion
should not be activated because, if it were, it would prevent
the later introduction of sweeping changes; of course it always
transpires that the time for such reforms is never right.
4. There is the claim that the machinery for achieving the
present proposals already exists – no new machinery is
needed; this is an argument that can be used when the
opposer knows that the existing machinery has never worked
and there is no chance that it will.
5. Faced with the proposal that outside specialists should be
brought in, it is persuasive to argue that all reform should

come from within; on the grounds that if there is to be any washing of linen it is necessary to be sure beforehand that everyone knows that it is clean.

6. If delay is required, the submission of a number of seemingly balanced alternatives can ensure that time is consumed and majorities brought against them all at different times. If speed is important and the proposer knows that the submission of a single offering will lead some committee members to argue, often with justification, that there must be 'other ways of going about this', he can produce three possibilities, two of which are patently absurd whilst in the middle is the proposal he supports. In the words of Kissinger, 'the strong inclination of all departments is to narrow the scope for Presidential decision, not to expand it. They are organised to develop a preferred policy, not a range of choices. If forced to present options, the typical department will present two absurd alternatives as straw men bracketing its preferred option – which usually appears in the middle position.'[7]

7. A general blocking device is the request for more information on the pretext that the committee can make a more informed decision. A reverse ploy is for the proposer to provide a group with so much information that its members are overwhelmed by the piles of documents supplied to it. Many of the members will be unable to read them because of pressures of time, but they cannot afford to admit that they have not done so. This gives the person making the heavily documented proposals, or indeed counterproposals, the opportunity to achieve his goals. He can make the running knowing full well that his colleagues are unlikely to have read the documentation and will be in no position to argue against him.

Further lines of defence in a committee include the following:

1. If a member is opposed to a proposal, the submission by him of a few bad reasons for not doing something will help to neutralise all the good reasons for doing it – he will raise doubts, cast aspersions and generally delay matters.

2. A member can claim that he will fight to the last ditch for or against the proposal under discussion. If he has already acquired a reputation for obstinacy his fellow members may well be reluctant to become embroiled in a long drawn-out struggle.

3. A long established committee man can recall that exactly the same proposal was put forward twenty or thirty years ago and got nowhere.
4. There is the tactic of bear bait or bull fight, that is, knowing the topics which will be a red rag to a bull, a committee man can start them going in the discussion. This will either lead to a long delay while the bull chases the rag around the committee or, if the proposer is angling for it, achieve a sharpish victory because the bull upsets the others by his raging and they coalesce against him.
5. There is the comma hunting, pointing out that this or that is badly written and that the proposal should go back for rewriting so that it will be more clear.
6. Finally there is the tactic of the 'great yawn', when the argument is kept going by bringing in the irrelevant, by generally wasting time and boring the rest of the meeting to tears. In a formal meeting, the raising of 'points of order' can contribute to yawns.

In all these delaying tactics the practitioner is aware of the value of manipulating time, he recognises that time is a scarce resource and, properly managed, can provide him with a power base in the group. His aim is to demonstrate that even if there is an argument for doing something there will be great difficulty in discovering if it is right; that all important questions are complicated and in consequence difficult to determine, hence the doubt as to whether anything can be achieved. In this circumstance, the argument goes, the only justifiable, rational approach is suspension of judgement, of delay. At the highest level the political manager makes the issue one of principle and that can be the end of any proposal. In these circumstances the principle is not really a principle at all but an interpretation of someone's vested interests.

Some of the delaying tactics outlined above can be used, not to prevent action so much as to drive people who are opposed to a proposal to leave the meeting before the conclusion of the discussion. Once the sponsor feels the opposition has departed or is in a weak minority, he can seek approval from those whom he knows will support him and who have stayed on – stamina in politics can be all-important.

These are a few examples of the countless moves in the political games of managerial life and they reflect the enormous diversity that exists within that life. In practice these tactics are always couched in appropriate managerial language and make use of the rhetoric of management.

The Coalition Tactic

Coalitions are an integral part of organisational and committee life, providing power and support for contestants in the managerial arena. They are the result of multifarious groupings of individuals, groups, units and external contacts.

Coalitions are sought by both the powerful, seeking to maintain or increase their power, and the less powerful, seeking to reduce the power gap. More specifically coalitions revolve around the issue of control; some are designed to strengthen the coalition members' control over others, while others aim to weaken the control exercised by the powerful. Coalitions are also used to protect their members from unwanted change and the aggressive intent of others. They are used to advance policies, programmes, systems and personal interests. Hence to form successful coalitions, would-be members need to know other people's interests and how they stand on particular issues. This requires an awareness of the informal communication channels in which occur exchanges of information about individual interests. When an organisation attempts to limit the development of informal communications, by having everything go through the 'proper channels', it is indirectly influencing the opportunity for developing effective coalitions.

The development of coalitions will also be influenced by the degree of conflict in the firm and the divergence of interests between the members of the organisation. Where the gulf between members is great, it may be impossible to form coalitions; there must be some common denominator between would-be members, if a coalition is to come into being. For this reason, sensitivity to people's interests is one of the key skills required by the coalition builder.

The formation and continuation of coalitions depends upon the priority given to specific issues and upon the importance of those issues as perceived by members and would-be members. The political strategist can ensure that some issues are more visible than others and, in consequence, is able to exercise control over the order in which issues are discussed. Thus the ability to present and time issues provides important means of controlling coalition formation, but this ability is exercised within the structure of the firm which itself can facilitate or constrain coalition behaviour. The division of labour within the firm, the grouping of activities, the means of coordination, the geographical distribution of units in a company, all shape coalition formation and activity. For example, it may be that the greater the centralisation of authority in an organisation, the less scope there is for coalition and counter-coalition building, and the more limited the scope of the issues raised and fought for by coalitions. Where coalitions do establish themselves in these circumstances, the greater is the likelihood of them achieving stability through adversity.

The establishment of coalitions between the internal members of a firm and people on the outside, represents a special case. These coalitions usually arise out of the relationship of boundary spanning departments, such as sales, supplies and personnel, to relevant segments of the environment. One important factor in the operation of these coalitions, is the knowledge of the inside members that the external elements are unlikely to be competitors for internal resources, and cannot easily enter the internal decision process. At the same time the internal members of this type of coalition are able to use the information generated within it to further their own internal position. They can advocate proposals based on the selective information provided by their external colleagues, knowing full well that others in the firm are in no position to check up on that information. The cost to the internal members who embark upon such coalitions is the charge of disloyalty to the firm and their exclusion from some phases of internal decision making. To avoid this they may feel it expedient to be flexible as to the extent they parade their external links and only use them when their power is clearly recognised by those within the firm.

Ultimately a coalition must be a winning one. With the winning coalition, its maintenance becomes a primary goal of the members. It makes individual members susceptible to compromise in order to keep it alive and ensure its continuing success. To maintain the coalition, members will develop ways and means of reducing internal conflict and of increasing stability. These include the partial exclusion of those issues which might threaten the unity of the coalition, the right of members to exercise a veto over important decisions and the emergence within the coalition of a central broker, whose task is to smooth out local difficulties between members.

While coalition members have some interests in common, they may have substantially different individual goals and priorities, hence the potential for internal conflict is always there. The goal or goals of a coalition are often the subject of bargaining between its members. Where there is a wide divergence of interests the life of the coalition will be tenuous and the goals are likely to be ambiguous and even inconsistent.

A successful coalition does not have any fixed booty to divide among its members; rather the spoils depend upon its composition. The question of power is at the root of coalition formation and activity; the more powerful the coalition is in relation to others, the greater the prize will be; the weaker it is, the less will be its winnings. Within the coalition there is likely to be an unequal distribution of power, with bargaining to determine each member's share.

The resources of a coalition and the individual contributions of the members tend to be both ambiguous and negotiable.

How do people become involved in a particular coalition, what is the basis of their choice? They look for the coalition which offers maximum gains with limited cost and limited commitment.

1. They will prefer the coalition which controls a maximum number of relevant individuals and groups.
2. They will also be influenced by their perception of their own power and ability to shape the behaviour of any coalition they join.

There will be a balancing of costs and benefits; this calculation will be a blend of the intuitive and the rational but it is the ability to size up options that is the mark of sound organisational politicians. However, given the imperfection of knowledge and the subjective nature of their perceptions, people may find they have joined the wrong coalition and have to extract themselves; either acting as individuals or seeking to join another coalition which is more appropriate to their interests and has every appearance of being successful. To gain acceptance in a new coalition they may be required to give substantial evidence of having something worthwhile to offer – the entrance fee is higher if they are fugitive from another coalition.

The world of coalitions is dynamic, comprising new, emerging and established groups. Within and between these coalitions bargaining takes place, however it is not confined to them. Bargaining goes on between coalitions and individuals. Those organisational members who are excluded from any coalition can act in a variety of ways; they can attempt to break up a coalition by weakening their pay-off demands so that the pressure on the coalition is reduced to a point where there is no need for it to exist. They can make positive advances; their offerings may be such that individual coalition members begin to defect because there is more to be gained from leaving the coalition. Behind this decision to leave a coalition, as indeed in joining one, is a calculation of the link between resources and power; the coalition must demonstrate through its aggregate resources that it is able to do more for its members than they can do individually. In the two cases mentioned above the individual has power which he brings into operation to produce a recalculation of the costs and benefits of coalition membership.

Coalitions are linked with conflict and retaliation, and the greater the retaliatory capacity of a counter-coalition, the greater will be the task of mobilising a coalition. Faced with the threat of retaliation the members of a coalition may seek to strengthen the bonds that link them together. They may seek to expand the coalition to include individuals who have no strong immediate commitment, but whose presence will be symbolically useful or whose power can be called upon at a later date. In this way the coalition seeks to improve its defensive and offensive capacity. This is the benefit, but as always there are costs to be considered; the larger the coalition becomes the greater the possibility of internal conflict and the more ways the booty has to be split.

The ability of a coalition to achieve its goals may be very specific; for example, a group which is crucial to production may well be able, with its resources, to change the hours of work without being able to modify the nature of the product. A coalition having achieved a specific goal may dissolve and its members go their separate ways, either joining other coalitions with specific goals or reforming the winning coalition when the need arises. In contrast, some coalitions will persist with their members making every effort to keep them going. What we see emerging is a picture of an organisation as a collection of coalitions; some parts will be subject to frequent change, others will remain unaffected. It would be taking too simplistic a view to believe that firms are in a state of either perpetual change or permanent stability. The extent to which the pattern of coalitions shifts or not depends on the issues raised, the power that is threatened or mobilised, and external pressures.

Among this multiplicity of coalitions there is likely to be one that is dominant; it is not necessarily identified with the formally designated holders of authority. It is only dominant while it retains power; its position may be undermined by any of the factors already discussed, notably the power of other coalitions to effectively influence its activities, to change the agenda and modify the significance of the different bases of power. Critically the dominant coalition is dependent upon other coalitions for information and for the implementation of its suggestions, recommendations and advice. To achieve cooperation from the other coalitions requires the operation of the political process which can be time-consuming, and if those outside the dominant coalition wish to make themselves felt they may use time as a bargaining counter. There may be activities and areas where the power of the dominant coalition appears to be unassailable, indeed some might argue that this is the permanent condition in all organisations. However, this is to fail to recognise the fine organisational, managerial and staff differences which work together to produce changes in the distribution of power, which in turn alters the position of the dominant coalition.

External events contribute to this shifting, unobtrusive pattern of coalitions so that the power of different internal coalitions will be modified by changes in the external world. Additionally, political and social beliefs are brought into the organisation by its members and, as these change, so there are shifts within the organisation. As a result the organisation emerges as an arena in which the social and political differences of society are manifested. Much of this change is slow, piecemeal, wayward and in no sense dramatic; indeed to those who are short of political sensitivity it may not seem to be there at all.

Membership of the dominant coalition is affected by such a factor as the spread of managerial discretion. The manager who is in a highly discretionary position and who is able to handle crucial ambiguities is likely to obtain a place in a dominant coalition – hence the more numerous the areas in which the organisation must rely on judgemental decisions, the larger the dominant coalition is likely to be. Also, the more heterogeneous the environment with which the firm has to negotiate, the larger will be the number of boundary spanning personnel who may be candidates for membership of the dominant coalition.

Promotion and Coalition Building

Coalitions develop for a variety of reasons, one of which is to bolster the position of a particular manager. Important processes in coalition building are the identification of common interests and the working out of terms of exchange between the potential members. This process of exchange is highlighted in the use of promotion as a coalition builder; in return for promotion support is obtained – there is an exchange of favours. The judicious use of promotion opportunities can give a manager important allies, both in his own department and, where he has the authority, in others. This can be particularly effective when a manager promotes an 'unobvious choice'; that is, someone who is not an obvious candidate for the post – not only does the manager place someone of his own choice in the position but he powerfully earns the loyalty of the person who has unexpectedly been promoted. A particular example of the use of promotion to build a coalition is the exercise of 'nepotism' – the promotion of members of the family – the relatives may not be worthy of promotion on the grounds of merit but their support is strengthened by the promotion. Such behaviour carries with it the danger that the members of the family will be ineffective and endanger the life of the firm; there is also the possibility that family disputes will spill over into the firm and destroy the coalition. Nepotism and promotion of the 'unobvious choice' need to be seen for what they are, political moves to build support and ensure control by those with power.

The much condemned 'old boy' network performs a similar coalition-building function; the manager who selects and places someone from a similar background to his own, whether it be school, university, regiment, union or political party, is taking steps to build support. Though this behaviour may appear to be dysfunctional for the organisation, it is functional for the manager; it provides him with support, it helps him build coalitions and strengthens loyalty.

In this particular process stress is laid upon the idea that everyone is a winner, and to underline this, positions may be created so that it appears that everyone has been given something, even if it is only a new title. Thus support may be generated through the proliferation of positions.

Coalition Bargaining

The main characteristic of coalition behaviour is bargaining over policies, people, procedures and practices. But this bargaining process, like so much in management, leaves many issues unresolved. These problems are submerged by:

1. The inability of the parties, whether as coalition members or as individuals, to appreciate all the issues – there is limited rationality.
2. There is the infrequent need to deal with more than one or two issues at a time – in consequence there is sequential rather than parallel attention paid to issues. One or, at most, two matters, rather than a cluster will be dealt with at any one time. As a result some concerns never come up for consideration.
3. Problems are avoided by ambiguous assessment and measurement – no operational objectives are used.
4. As long as the organisation is not fully stretched to meet its commitments, it has the capability of simultaneously satisfying potentially conflicting demands. This raises the importance of organisational slack in managerial politics. If a firm has spare, under-utilised resources there is more left to go round and there can be greater give and take. However, if there is little slack, win-lose situations come into the open more clearly and bargaining positions between and within coalitions become more tight and tense.

Summary

The existence of coalitions, with their political and bargaining activities, transforms the picture of management as a clear-cut activity, moving towards clearly defined goals within a clearly defined structure. The manager emerges as a member of one or more coalitions, some stable, some shifting. Power, control and change are hallmarks of these coalitions.

This examination of the functioning of coalitions in organisational politics has been based largely upon utilitarian considerations and has taken little account of ideological factors. Over a period of time people may become committed to each other because of their interaction and, in consequence, the coalition is held together beyond the period of its usefulness. Human likes and dislikes play their part in the development, maintenance and functioning of organisational coalitions, the main purpose of which remains utilitarian.

The Routine Avoidance Tactic

To decrease the control exercised by top management over his department, a manager needs to avoid the routinisation of his unit's work. Where that work is substantially automatic, lacking discretion, it is relatively easy to control. The individuals performing such work are easy to substitute, so that the manager is not able to protect his staff on the grounds of their unique contribution to his department. He will have to seek other ways of defending them.[8]

To avoid routinisation the manager can seek to professionalise the work by structuring it so that only he and his staff understand it. He surrounds the work with a mystique, often through the use of language and a technological overkill – making the simple, complex. In developing this uniqueness it has not to become so specialised that it cannot be adapted, otherwise the unit will become inflexible and unable to cope with a new innovation which makes the present unique skill obsolete. A fringe of flexibility has to be maintained around the core of uniqueness.

The ability to restructure work and professionalise it demonstrates the opportunity that exists within managerial activities to shape work through emphasising particular aspects of it.[9] While this freedom to restructure is constrained by technological factors, it would be inaccurate to believe that managerial work is wholly determined by technology – choice does exist. The manager's aim at this stage is to establish the critical nature of his department for the firm's well-being. If he succeeds he has created the opportunity to acquire more than his 'fair' share of the firm's resources.

In addition to making sure that his unit's work does not become routinised, a manager can use the further tactic of acquiring activities which maintain the internal regularity of his unit's work and by doing so reducing the need to negotiate with others for their services. He can also attempt to add an appraisal function to his operations as the right to monitor others gives him a measure of independence.

To achieve success with these modifications of his unit's work a manager has to become involved in the necessary organisational restructuring and, through this change, the division of labour in his favour. This means that he has to have sufficient power to get to first base – the restructuring, and this he will seek to do through some of the strategies available to him.

Another tactic allied to the avoidance of dependence arising from routine operations, is that of attempting to move from a late to an early stage in the decision-making chain, so that the manager and his department are not the recipients of firm decisions which cannot be changed. To achieve involvement early in the decision process he has to demonstrate that he has something to offer the current decision-makers.

The Position–Personality–Bargaining Tactic

When a manager seeks the advancement of new ideas, new technologies, new structures, he has to be heard by the decision-makers. This may require forceful presentation, as top management generally responds rather than initiates. If a manager cannot make himself heard he has to choose someone in the hierarchy who is at a level to be noticed. That person must have the character to persist with the advocacy of an idea or plan which is not his own. He may be encouraged to be advocate if there is some pay-off for him – this may take the form of being given property rights in the idea or plan. Position and personality have to be allied to bargaining power; the advocate has to have something to give if whatever he is proposing is to be accepted – not only has there to be bargaining skill but there must be resources to go with it.

The championing of change, whether directly or through someone else, needs to be done opportunely and with political sensitivity but not over-persistently, as it inevitably involves risk and may be counter-productive. An over-persistent advocate of change is liable to meet with the response, 'he never leaves anything alone', or, with a groan, 'not another bright idea.' In contrast, the advocate of judicious change acquires power as people with ideas come to him for support. For his part he gains the support of an innovative network and acquires property rights in new schemes and ideas.

The Visibility Tactic

Another tactic is to gain visibility through building new programmes, sponsoring innovative ideas and displaying critical skills. This involves self-projection and the seizing of opportunities to put oneself on view at the right time and in the right circumstances, and in the presence of the people who can influence your future. The style of self-projection has to fit in with the dominant culture of the firm; it is not very useful to project oneself as brash, abrasive and pushing if the generally accepted culture is one that avoids such characteristics. Having said this, it is possible to face a situation where an organisation is ripe for a cultural shock, and to project a sharply contrasting style to the currently dominant one may be successful. In such a case the comment may be, 'He was like a breath of fresh air.' Political sensitivity, awareness of possibilities and of timing, are crucial attributes of the successful managerial politician.

Visibility carries risks, the manager who makes himself conspicuous may do so at the wrong time, with the wrong ideas and to the wrong people. He may make a mistake – what is certain is that he has to choose whether to take the risk or not.

At the root of many political tactics is the development of monopolistic practices, such as the control of information; of the entry of others into the firm; of the development of new ideas and technology. The managerial politician acts as a gatekeeper to protect his position through control over training and recruitment, and he strives to gain acceptance of the idea that outsiders do not have the necessary competence. He develops protective myths; for instance – his department cannot work effectively under tight time constraints, or that his staff is specially qualified. He builds up the notion that some information must be kept secret, as wide distribution would be disadvantageous to the firm. He withholds information to keep other people uncertain. All these ploys are aimed at maintaining a monopolistic position in order to maintain power.

For reasons connected with the search for certainty, there is a tendency for managers to concentrate on technical issues to the extent that they become ends in themselves; efficiency rather than effectiveness becomes the main concern. Those who do not take this position, who look beyond technicalities and raise questions of ends, are likely to be branded as 'unprofessional'; a significant accusation when so much managerial energy goes into building the notion that all managerial activities are professional. The use of the term 'unprofessional' is an example of the tactic of 'credibility destroyer', an exercise frequently undertaken to counter those who are putting forward arguments which are in opposition to a manager's proposals and threaten his position. To give support to the view that someone's credibility is weak, the manager can manipulate a situation so that his opponent makes mistakes which he then uses to justify his view of their 'unprofessional' incompetence. This links with the notion of the pre-emptive strike, where a manager takes action before the opposition can fight back.

Tactics and Key Values

All of these tactics take place within the framework of a firm's key values, which largely but not wholly determine what is and is not acceptable. Now the power and practices which contribute to the shaping of these key values are of critical importance, with the central questions revolving around who makes and maintains those decisions which create the key values. Here the role of the dominant coalition and key management is crucial, not only in the choice of key values but in creating the social structure which supports them. Their task involves creating a myth or series of myths which embody habits; conformity to a myth helps management deal with external threats and provides an internal integrating factor. Of course senior management are themselves constrained by the power and political activities of others; they do not act in isolation. In any case when a culture develops, a counter-culture is likely to arise; beneath the myth of organisational unity there operate conflicting sets of interests. The stronger the myth, the more subtle and submerged are the activities and counter-beliefs that oppose it.

Decisions which create and support key values include:

1. those around the recruitment of management. Such decisions become part of the critical experience of the firm, in so far as management selection takes account of personal commitment to the organisation's key values;
2. decisions relating to management and staff training, for it is in this area that people are indoctrinated with the ethos of the firm. Here it needs to be stressed that managers themselves are involuntary educators, for it is from their behaviour that subordinates pick up cues as to what can and cannot be done;
3. those decisions which relate to the structuring of the firm, for it is in this process that a system is established for the representation of internal sectional interests. The way different activities are grouped reflects what is considered to be important. Further, in designing structures and determining procedures connected with them, the deliberate making and continuance of ambiguous rules allows for differing interpretations to develop, which may ultimately lead to the modification of existing key values; and
4. decisions relating to the degree of cooperation with other firms, for this has undoubted power implications within the firm and reflects the key values that exist.

Managerial Politics

There emerges from this examination of political tactics the essentially competitive nature of much managerial activity. Power is being sought at the expense of others. Intergroup struggles are emphasised and, in this connection, who wins depends on who has the appropriate resources and the political skills to manage them.

Clearly the profession of management is politics. Political processes embody the clash of interests, their definition and embodiment in key aspects of the organisation. Politics has little concern with technology or efficiency, though much of its language is couched in such terms. Technology is a tool in the political activities of managers.

Political skills are based on the recognition that 'coercion and conscience, enmity and goodwill, self-assertion and self-subordination, are present in every political society'[10] and a firm is just such a community. The various political skills call for a high level of sensitivity to the changing facets of any situation, with the recognition that success often depends upon an inconsistent style. Improvisation and spontaneity are essential, combined with the calculative element inherent in the political process.

Political sensitivity arises from understanding that the work of a particular manager, at a given time, is determined by the potentially dynamic environment in which he operates; his job – its level and functions; his personality and the overall situation with its power and time dimensions. Much is heard of the need for managers to manage their time efficiently, but there is more to it than present time. The manager also needs an historical awareness, a sense of the past as well as the present and future. Without accepting that the past wholly determines the present, the manager needs to be conscious of the many ways in which it has affect, influencing the distribution of resources and the ways of thinking and operating. To reject the significance of the past is as misguided as to be bound by it. Yet much management thinking is non-historical, with the result that some managers and their advisers go through the process of rediscovering the wheel.

Political sensitivity at senior management level is concerned with the subtle skills of control at a distance. The top manager has to find ways of penetrating internal units and external organisations in order to assess what is happening and to influence them so as to gain acceptable responses.

In all his roles the manager acts in a political manner. As disturbance handler, resource allocator, authoriser, negotiator, monitor and evaluator, he is concerned with the politics of power. His skills in these roles help to shape the organisation's working, influence the distribution of power and evoke responses.

Around the activities and skills described in this chapter there are generated attitudes, beliefs and values which provide a measure of predictability and enable people to act and endow their acts with enough legitimacy to make them acceptable. If they succeed in this, power becomes less visible and less likely to be challenged. Much of this legitimacy is achieved through the use of political language, ritual and ceremony. For this to be effective, some organisation members must not see too clearly what is happening. As long as they fail to discriminate between reality and symbol, the symbolic action has been effective. If people are convinced by political language, for example, 'promotion is based on efficiency not service' when this is not true, they have been successfully manipulated. How is this achieved?

1. When people are unsure of their priorities and preferences they cannot be sure they are getting what they want.
2. When they are uncertain of how to act they become susceptible to organisational influences and information, they look round for guidance. This is exemplified in the position of new entrants to a firm; given their initial insecurity they are highly sensitive to organisational influences. It is at this early stage that future perceptions will be shaped, giving a remarkable opportunity to those with power to provide the cues and symbols to indoctrinate the newcomers.
3. The vast majority of people are not deeply involved in their work situation and symbolic gestures are sufficient to convey the impression desired by the powerful.
4. People respond to the symbolic to avoid evaluation by reality.

Manipulation through political language, rituals and symbolic action is not restricted to internal members of organisations; many firms use these tools to protect themselves from critical evaluation. There is selective release of information, emphasising the effort expended in the firm and concentrating on the inputs into the organisation while deflecting attention away from the outputs. In consequence, organisations are judged by the effort they make rather than on actual results – attention is directed to the efficient production of a given product and away from the problem of its selling potential. Symbolic action occurs when a firm is faced with demands and complaints from customers and responds by creating a customer complaints unit to convince people that action is being taken to put things right – self-regulation is a form of organisational defence. More obvious forms of symbols are to be seen in advertising, in the language of the company annual report, and 'image' building generally.

CONCLUSION

The political manager should never underestimate the significance of language, symbols and ceremonies.

1. Language shapes the perceptions and actions of organisation members; it influences the way people view reality.
2. Ceremonies play an important part in organisational politics. Meetings have a ceremonial character, they can provide an important assurance that a significant interest is being given appropriate consideration by inviting its representatives to join the committee. An outstanding example of a symbolic meeting is the annual shareholders' meeting which creates an illusion of control. On occasion the illusion becomes a reality, as when very large institutional shareholders decide to use their power on a given issue, but this is the exception.
3. There are symbols provided by the organisational structure in terms of charts and schedules of responsibilities, authority and accountabilities. These can be used to indicate the formal situation without disclosing the actual way in which the organisation operates.
4. There is the physical setting, such as physical separation from head office; the size of office, its location, whether or not a manager has a private secretary or not. There are the significant seating arrangements at functions and meetings.

All of these are capable of manipulation, of being used to increase or maintain power. They distance people from the actual use of power; they make people more malleable and make more legitimate the underlying actions of those with power.

4 Power

Underlying organisational politics is power. This power finds expression in relationships of the kind where one manager has the means, and is willing to use them, to get another manager to act in a manner which is contrary to that manager's interests. In consequence it is characterised by resistance and conflict.

The impact of power can be judged along three dimensions:

1. The weight, that is to say, the amount of effect the exercise of power has on others.
2. The domain, which is the range of persons and groups that are affected.
3. The scope, the range of issues covered by the use of power in a given situation.

These dimensions are unlikely to lead to a useful, quantified assessment of power in a particular instance, but they provide us with some sensitising guidelines as to the nature of power. They take us away from an oversimplistic view of power and remind us that power is complex and its use frequently covert and subtle.

Power involves relationships and dependence. This means that individuals take each other and their respective power into account when making and acting on decisions. This interaction is an essential ingredient of organisational politics. For example, a manager often blames his subordinate for the poor perform-ance of his unit and in doing so fails to see that he himself is a contributor to that situation – his assessment of his staff is an assessment of himself; what happens in his unit is in part an outcome of the power relationship between himself, his sub-ordinates and others. The manager operates in a network of dependencies which vary in their degree of difficulty, frequency and nature.

Dependence is based upon, first, the availability of relevant alternatives and second, the importance attached to the particu-lar resources involved. For example, a firm requires a particular raw material, semi-finished product or other resource from a supplier. The extent of the firm's dependence on that supplier will be affected by the existence of other suitable suppliers, the importance of the commodity to the firm's operations and the availability of substitutes for it. One significant ingredient in this situation is the subjective element in power and dependence – the use of power is based not only on the objective conditions of dependence but also the judgement people make about those conditions. This subjectivity contributes to the fact that power and dependence are not constants; they vary over time and across relationships and settings. While remaining the essence of organisation, power is linked with changing issues and conditions. Power involves the possession of relevant resources and the political skill to use them to affect the behaviour of others.

SOURCES OF POWER

What then are the sources of power in a firm?

Strategic Scarce Resources

There is the possession, in a given situation, of strategic scarce resources held individually or collectively in the firm.

Organisational change and the degree of convertibility of a resource help determine the strategic nature and power of that resource; for instance, money clearly represents a resource which can be readily converted and can be transferred across boundaries. Posts, promotions, equipment, expertise and information exhibit varying degrees of convertibility and sources of power.

Power linked with control over rewards implies some right to create, maintain and fill posts. This power enables the manager to build on his existing strengths, for in exercising the right to appoint people he makes it clear that they are there because of him and to some extent owe him allegiance. This becomes very evident in the case of promotion; for the manager who exercises his right to promote has to be recognised not simply as having power based on the authority of his position but also on his discretion, his choice and interpretation of the criteria for promotion. This goes some way to explain why some managers are often reluctant to see their right of appointment and promotion being diluted by the emergence of personnel and similar departments. It also goes some way to explaining their reluctance to see formal evaluation systems becoming too significant; anything which takes away from their discretionary power is likely to be resisted. This is why some managers will seek to prove that they and they alone know the qualities and skills that are required for specific promotions and appointments. In support of this contention they may well use evaluation schemes in such a way that everyone is assessed as average. In doing so they attempt to demonstrate the weakness of such schemes through their use of the self-fulfilling prophecy. This may not be the only reason why formal evaluation schemes have had a chequered career, but it is a political dimension that cannot be discounted.

Managers are also concerned to maintain their control over rewards in general; they resent any organisational move which threatens to constrain that power. Faced with the possible loss of power in the areas of appointments, promotions and rewards through the introduction of more formal systems, managers are likely to seek to regain their power through more covert political behaviour. Formal systems and procedures do not eliminate managers' political activity, they simply divert it into different forms.

Those who control capital development in an organisation are in positions of considerable power. The decision to expand or not is fraught with consequences for the existing distribution of power. Expansion means more resources are to be allocated, new posts created, promotions made; some managers will have more patronage at their disposal, others will lose out. It is for these and other reasons that decisions on capital development are surrounded by a high level of political activity. While the devotees of rational behaviour would like to believe that capital decisions are made on the basis of rational procedures, in the final analysis these procedures produce evidence that will be diagnosed, interpreted and presented in the light of the existing power structure – decisions will be made to a large extent on the basis of political criteria.

Scarce resources are critical to the distribution of power in a firm, but a resource only has strategic value if it is critical to the functioning of the firm or specific departments. And what is critical is not static; as environments change, as organisational goals shift, as new ways of operating emerge and as the organisational structure is altered, so will the critical nature of given scarce resources alter. For example, a scarce labour skill may be critical to a key operation in the firm; in consequence the possessor of that skill will have power in the operating system. With the introduction of an automated process which replaces the old skill, the power based on that skill is liable to shift to some other group.

In any organisation there will be some slack resources; these are resources which, at a given time, are in excess of what has already been committed or promised to different members of the firm. These slack resources can quickly become part of the firm's regular operations through the machinery of allocation. It is while they are slack that competition for them is intense, because it is recognised that a manager can increase his power through the acquisition of relatively small amounts of slack resources so long as they are the only discretionary parts of the firm's budget. Most resource allocations are made using the principle of incrementalism: budgets are regularly based on the preceding year's allocations, plus increments reflecting growth, inflation or the incorporation of new activities by different departments in the firm. Budgets also reflect a desire to keep the peace. Each year's budgets become the basis for the formulation of the requests and demands for a share of the available slack resources. It is the incremental gains from this source that contribute to shifts in power. The absorption of slack into the ongoing operations of a firm is one reason for the strong managerial preference for organisational growth, not simply because it enables new activities to be entered into without cutting back on existing ones, but also because it creates slack resources. The presence or absence of organisational slack helps shape the political behaviour and power distribution in a firm.

Having acquired a share of the scarce resources, managers work to make others dependent upon them. It is not enough to provide monetary or other resources, there is the need to control them, to be able to increase or decrease the flow of funds or resources to others. This discretionary control over limited resources gives power to those who possess it. Resources that are once allocated can become essential to a department's working and where power exists to withdraw them, the threat to do so will tend to bring the recipient into line.

Power in a dependence relationship derives from having something that someone else wants or needs and which is difficult to obtain from another source. The balance of dependence is not static, it can be altered:

1. If manager B reduces his operating need for the resources provided by manager A.
2. If B cultivates alternative sources for the acquisition of those resources.
3. If manager A is denied alternative dependencies with whom he can trade.
4. If B can so structure his operation that the withdrawal of A's resources does not have a wide impact upon his organisation or unit.

Politically dependence needs to be built up before the firm or individual with the greater power in the relationship attempts to exercise control. To show one's hand too quickly may send out warning signals so that other managers and/or firms will make every effort to avoid dependence and keep their options open.

Linked with the scarcity of resources is the control of alternatives; if substitutes become available the manager or firm who possesses the previously scarce resource will need to make every endeavour to obtain control of the substitutes. If he fails to do so he is liklely to lose control of the relationship, which was based upon others' dependence upon him. The politically aware manager will keep alert for the development of threats to his power through the emergence of substitutes for his resources.

Scarcity, power and conflict go together. Where resources are scarce they must be in demand if power is to be generated; resources must be critical. But what is critical? What is scarce? Resources that are defined as scarce are perceived as important, so managers claim that what they have is scarce and behave as if it were. This strategy is augmented by developing elaborate allocation mechanisms and establishing formalised, ritualistic procedures, so that people come to believe that whatever is subject to such mechanisms and procedures, must be important and scarce.

Scarce resources can be created by defining a resource in such a way that scarcity is ensured; this is one way that prestige and status are managed.

However, the defining of a resource as scarce or critical sets up a dynamic situation and reaction may result. Those who feel their positions threatened are liable to redefine the scarce resources upon which they are dependent, so that it appears of less significance than was previously thought; or they may redefine their own resources as more important. This entails the redefinition of the problems and opportunities faced by the firm – a shift in products manufactured, or services rendered, or a realignment of the market.

Formal Authority

Another source of power lies in formal authority, that is, who legitimately decides, who instructs, who reports to whom and who evaluates? At the core of formal authority is hierarchy and the division of labour, both of which affect the distribution of power within a firm, through their definition of which tasks are formally regarded as important and crucial. Who defines what is critical in these circumstances? This question can be the subject of dispute, creating conflict and political behaviour. Hierarchy ensures some degree of coordination; it is the management of interdependence through structure and is an attempt to control individual and group behaviour. However, it is only an attempt and not always a very successful one.

Legitimate power – authority – based on formal position and buttressed by rules and regulations, conditionally establishes the context in which power is initiated and resisted. In the formal structure, the confrontation between power initiators and those who resist is mediated by the legitimacy built into the role of the superior, who acts as coordinator, controller and conciliator. Authority represents 'coercion by consent'.

The degree of centralisation in a structure can influence political activity within the firm. In a highly centralised organisation the views of the dominant coalition are likely to be reflected in the imposition of preferences relating to structure and technology. Through the use of concentrated authority, decision making appears to be more orderly and rational because

technological uncertainty and goal disagreements are submerged
in the way choice is exercised. Politicising continues, but it is
buried and conflict is suppressed or takes on different and more
subtle forms. This acceptance of centralised authority is based
upon power differentials, upon legitimacy and upon the desire to
escape from freedom – there is a preference for the appearance of
rationality if not its substance.

Where authority, power and control are dispersed, politics is
likely to be more overt and conflict more evident. It would be a
mistake to think that centralisation will remove all political
behaviour, but it does drive it into different forms from those of
the decentralised structure. What can happen is that top management in the centralised organisation believes there is no
political behaviour in the rest of the firm. Such a view may be
comforting to those who hold it but it divorces them from what is
actually happening in their organisations.

In considering authority within the formal structure there is a
tendency to conclude that, because the organisation chart is
infrequently changed, the power structure is also stable. This is
to accept the appearance for the reality, for behind the formal
structure lie changing issues, changing coalitions and shifts of
power.

In placing authority in its structural context it is worth
remembering that he who has the money makes the rules, but it
takes less money if you know the rules.

Formal authority not only contributes to power through its
coordinating function, but also because it bestows a degree of
legitimacy. Hence it is to the benefit of those in authority to
develop this sense of legitimacy and to manipulate it to ensure
acceptance of that authority and its associated power. This will
be achieved partly through the management of language, symbols and rituals. However, the legitimacy of a position of
authority is limited by its place in the structure, which formally
indicates both its domain – the numbers subordinate to that
authority – and the range and depth of issues on which that
authority can be exercised. Authority as a source of power is
constrained.

In considering the structure of the organisation as a source of
power it may be thought that technology determines structure,
but the all-important fact is that technology is chosen. The
routinisation of a task through the application of technology is

not decided by the task, but by the manager's decision as to how he defines the task and how he divides the total work. The choice of different tasks and technology can be used by those in authority to maintain control, or by contestants in conflicts over control.

The structural consequences of technological choice are not neutral. The development of routinisation through technology serves the interests of higher management, by facilitating further centralisation of power. The choice of routinisation and other technological developments is a political choice, which is liable to be resisted by those who see a potential loss of control over their work situation.

Information

A key source of power lies in the possession of information and access to it. One contributory factor is the position of the manager in the organisational structure; his centrality in the communication network affects the amount and quality of the information he possesses. A manager's possession of exclusive information which is crucial to others' performance or decision making, will make them dependent upon him. As the holder distributes the information his power declines, unless he is able to obtain other critical information to ensure continuation of his power. He may also seek to jargonise his information so that he is not simply its disseminator but also its interpreter. Access to key information is important, particularly if a manager can act as a gatekeeper controlling access to it. In his book 'Under New Management', Professor Tony Eccles describes how the directors of the Kirkby Manufacturing and Engineering worker co-operative, effectively the two union convenors, preferred to keep information to themselves and not inform the members of the Advisory Council. They took the view that it would be quite a time before the shop-floor could absorb and understand fully the problems of running a business and that in the meantime there would be information which should not, in the interests of the enterprise, be disclosed to the work people. If knowledge was power, it was also a way of centralising power.[1] This access gives power to many staff positions – and to those in boundary posts – linking the firm and its environment. The presence of alternative sources of information and the willingness of a firm to search for data beyond its regular informants not only provides the possibility of new information, but weakens the power of the present source. Any restructuring of an organisation which leads to the redistribution of control over access to information is likely to be the setting for a great deal of political activity.

The ability of the manager to buffer, filter and selectively provide information enables him to control it and, what is crucial, to set up the premises upon which decisions are made.

In view of this, one of the important decisions in any firm is determining who controls the search for information and the information processing departments in the firm.

In the final analysis, information has to be organised and structured. In these processes information is filtered and shaped and the form of its presentation determined; who undertakes this task helps to shape the discussion of key issues. The structuring of reports and recommendations all contribute to moulding discussion and decision. The problems associated with the presentation of information are mapped out in Sandy McLachlan's 'The National Freight Buy-Out'; the production of the Consortium Prospectus was a long and difficult process with tempers running high among those involved. All those involved wanted to achieve a common end, but different groups had different positions to defend and in many cases compromise was not easy to reach. The discussions were far removed from any picture of a group of men sitting round a table coolly dissecting problems and producing neat solutions.[2]

Position within the organisation structure is not the sole determinant of power derived from information. It is not only the people at the top who acquire power; those at lower levels in a firm can manipulate the flow of information up the organisation. They are able to time information flows and in consequence acquire power and defend positions. In 1982 Olympia, the 51 per cent AEG–Telefunken owned office equipment manufacturer, admitted that its turnovers for the five years from 1975 to 1979 were falsely inflated through fictitious sales transactions. A small group of employees had been booking these sales shortly before the year end, in order to inflate the sales and present a more flattering picture to the parent company. In many cases goods were transferred out of Olympia factories before the year end as if they had been delivered to customers. They had merely been placed in 'interim storage' and were returned later when the 'order' was cancelled. This example sharply highlights how information can be shaped in the interests of lower levels in the organisation.[3]

Power is also exercised by those who know where information is stored and how to get at it. The information memory bank not only rests in files, or in computer tapes and the like, but also in the minds of long-serving members of staff; people to whom others go to ask, what happened years earlier, how a particular problem was dealt with in the past, who certain people were and are. These memory people have power, in that they can provide past solutions for current problems. At the same time they can be irritants to those who do not wish to be reminded of the past. This is but one instance of the fact that subordinates exercise power; they are not the passive recipients of a downward trickle of power but are active participants mobilising power for their own ends.

Power is dispersed and those who seek to mobilise it must be able to diagnose and understand the distribution of information holding, along with other sources of power. In this connection organisation members have to be assessed on a number of measures, for example, on committee membership, who sits on the important committees and what type of information they are likely to acquire. Here we have an instance of the effect and cause of power – people are put on committees because they are powerful, and as they sit on committees they become more powerful. Another dimension is that of resource allocation: which departments receive the most favourable budget allocations and who has the rules, policies and procedures most favourably interpreted and implemented for them? In all these dimensions information plays a key part.

Uncertainty

Power arises out of the ability to cope with uncertainty for other people. This ability rests on the manager's position in the firm, access to information, position in the communication network and possession of valued resources and skills. This power is a critical resource for those who possess it. It helps to create others' dependency; the greater the ability to cope with uncertainty for others, the greater is the dependence of others.

Other factors influencing this dependence will be the critical nature of the uncertainty, the extent to which those with coping ability can be substituted and their position in the organisation's work flow. A manager's power is increased if he cannot be substituted and if his department is critical in the sense that (a) if it fails the output of the whole organisation would be rapidly affected, and (b) the work flow connects it pervasively to all or most other departments. These variables of immediacy and pervasiveness contribute to the existence of differing amounts of power, because they give units differing degrees of control over contingencies that affect the work of other departments. If the uncertainty coped with by the department is neither central nor critical, immediate or pervasive, the power arising from it is limited. Coping with uncertainty is insufficient in itself, there must be work-flow pervasiveness, centrality and non-substitution.

Uncertainty may be reduced by subdividing a task so that it is easy to substitute employees, by routinisation and the reduction of discretion. It can also be diminished through the development of standard operating procedures; forecasting; buffering that permits the rationalisation of organisational activity. The position remains dynamic, for what may happen is that the reduction of uncertainty in one area may lead to its creation elsewhere, with the result that there is a shift in power. The substitution of machinery for skilled labour may reduce the power of the latter while increasing that of the maintenance workers.

As with all power holders, those who rely on their ability to cope with uncertainty seek to become irreplaceable. All have a series of strategies available to them.

1. The first strategy is that of monopolising the knowledge which provides the basis for the reduction of uncertainty, through non-disclosure and secrecy. While much is made of the need to keep certain information secret for the 'good' of the organisation, the real question is for whom is it 'good'. Any answer to that must take account of the fact that whoever keeps the information secret is in a position of power, hence the tenacity with which information is held and safeguarded.

2. There is the use of jargon, of making communications appear more substantial and difficult than they really are.
3. The firm can be discouraged from bringing in outsiders who have similar knowledge to the insider. If an outsider does come in, the insider is liable to find that his 'cover' has been blown; his information will no longer be scarce and his ability to reduce uncertainty for others will have been diluted. Not only will there be an increase in the number of people who possess the scarce knowledge, but those who do not have it and need it are no longer faced with a monopoly situation. Hence the debate as to whether to bring in an outsider to cope with an uncertainty is liable to be complicated. What does emerge is that substitutability is a dynamic property varying over time.

The significance of the ability to cope with uncertainty emerged in a company which decided to enter into a new area of activity and did not have the necessary skills. Senior management experienced considerable uncertainty as to how to develop the new activity; an outside manager was brought in and the price for his reduction of their uncertainty was their acceptance of his decisions and their dependence upon him. Although new and of a lower level in the hierarchy, his power in relation to the senior management was very substantial and his control over the new activity almost total – even his seniors felt unable to challenge him.

Where a particular skill is necessary for coping with uncertainty, the possessors of that skill will seek to retain it, prevent its dilution and attempt to keep out any outsiders who have the skill. Where uncertainty is reduced through the utilisation of external networks and contacts, those who operate in the networks and through the contacts will seek to keep others in their organisation from acquiring entrée to them. This may be achieved by stressing the 'professional' nature of the network, and the special nature of the social relations involved. The myth of 'professionalism' plays an important part in protecting the power of those organisational members who can cope with uncertainty, and distinguishes them from those who are unable to do so. A sidelight on coping was the rash of courses, developed in the early 1980s, aimed at improving coping skills; they were frequently related to the problems of coping with interpersonal relations. They were aimed at widening the numbers who could cope and in doing so, consciously or not, reduced dependencies and diluted power.

Prestige

Prestige can contribute to a power base. Individuals, groups or firms are often willing to work with and for others who have prestige. The 'halo' effect which involves the spread of approval from one feature of an individual or organisation, works to build up dependence. In consequence we have the strategy of prestige or image building: this is not a paper exercise, people only wish to associate with prestigious people and organisations if there is evidence that the prestige is well-founded. An example of the significance of prestige is to be found in the relations of Marks and Spencer with its suppliers; the latter being ready to accept a high degree of dependence because of the reputation of the retailer.

In any dependency there is an exchange of commitment and both parties must accept their responsibilities. So it is with prestige where the significance of past behaviour becomes apparent; people must have honoured their commitments over a period of time.

A person with prestige and charisma has unique personal qualities which attract others. These qualities provide a source of power, but it is a shifting source; unique qualities used in one situation may not be effective in another. For example, the charismatic military leader is not necessarily successful when in charge of an industrial or commercial organisation.

Stakeholding

In an organisation power arises out of the importance of the different interests represented by the members. Any firm can be regarded as a collection of stakeholders, each with particular interests or involvements in the firm, each directly or indirectly represented in the organisation. They include the general public, the customers, managers, employees, suppliers, loan services, owners, trade unions, trade associations and so on. Each group has different degrees of involvement and commitment and their importance in the organisation will depend upon the significance of whatever they represent to the firm. If finance is scarce, then those in the firm who represent the sources of finance are likely to be powerful; if labour is short, the personnel department will become significant. In other words the internal representatives of these stakeholders will be important depending upon the critical nature of the stakeholders they represent. Here we have a dynamic situation:

1. because events in the market or wider environment may change and disturb the relative signficance of the different stakeholder groups and so change the power profile of their representatives in the firm;
2. each of the stakeholder groups evaluates the firm against different criteria – suppliers are concerned with speedy payment of accounts; employees with the levels of earnings, conditions of work and tenure; shareholders with the dividend and capital appreciation of their holdings; customers with the quality of the product and where appropriate, the service back-up. They compare the present firm with available alternatives and move away if these offer a better return against the criteria. The performance of the firm is pivotal and allied to the degree of dependence that has developed between it and the stakeholders; and
3. the importance of a stakeholder may be reduced because the firm obtains substitutes; for instance, if there is a severe shortage of skilled labour the firm may substitute machinery and so reduce the significance of labour and with it the personnel department. In turn the personnel department will attempt to find or create a function that will maintain its importance in the eyes of the firm.

(The representatives of the stakeholders have to manage the relationship between the firm and their particular stakeholding group, ensuring that the group remains important to the firm and retains its power.) Where this is not possible the representatives will take action to protect themselves, witness the personnel department cited above. Now it may be argued that customers are all-important and this is clearly true, but their degree of importance will shift if there are critical developments in relation with other stakeholders. No representative can assume that present power is guaranteed forever; then have to work to retain that power.

Another aspect of these relations is their impact upon political decisions internal to the firm. As the importance of a particular stakeholder group rises and falls, so the power of its representatives to shape and influence internal decisions is modified.

This implies a situation where there is speedy adjustment between environmental change and the internal power structure. However, the speed of adjustment is unlikely to be as quick as this; (a) because of inertia – once a framework of power has been established in a firm, people are liable to go on adhering to it, partly because the threatened powerholders will endeavour to obscure the fact that change has occurred and partly because the others may not be fully aware that any change has taken place, (b) those threatened may not only deny that any change has taken place, they may seek to obtain new knowledge, new capabilities and new issues with which they alone can cope, (c) the skills and personalities of those involved will influence the shift of power. In this situation, as in many others, the political manager recognises that there is no single direct cause-effect relationship; the impact of change is mediated through a number of variables.

Any group representing a stakeholding faction will seek to make its external relationships unpredictable, in order to increase its power and avoid being taken for granted. But here is an example of the many dichotomies that exist in situations of power. If a group dwells on the unpredictability of its external relations it may be seen as lacking control over them and increasing the vulnerability of the firm. If this is believed, others will attempt to reduce the significance of that particular stakeholding group or to increase the control of the internal representatives by changing the structure or personnel.

What emerges is the variability of what is critical, what is scarce and what is substitutable. The ability to manage this variability is important, yet it would be incorrect to overstress the extent of change. In an organisation much happens with little apparent change, though even marginal changes can lead to major shifts in the distribution of power. What is important is the management of marginal differences.

For a manager to gain power he has to identify the key power holders and their positions and understand what would happen without the intrusion of different power holders. Power can be assessed by studying its source and its consequences; for example, by considering who benefits from its exercise. This is easier said than done; it is not easy to identify power because it is imprecise, diffused and often hidden. The culture of many firms stresses the illegitimacy of power and politics, leading to the suppression of overt manifestations of power and to the concealment of political behaviour. Organisational members in the pursuit of their own interests may so scrupulously and skilfully camouflage their political behaviour that their activities appear to be in harmony with organisational goals and ideology. By stressing the language of managerial ideology, such as efficiency, techniques and teamwork, they further obscure their own goals.

For the effective use of power there must be the following: interdependence; heterogeneous or inconsistent goals and heterogeneous beliefs about technology, that is, about the ways of achieving these goals. Finally there must be scarcity which creates choice. The greater the scarcity relative to the demand, the greater is the potential for power. Disagreements about meansends relations and performance levels lead to conflict and to the use of power and politics to resolve the differences. Even where there is agreement about general goals, this will not necessarily prevent power conflicts over their implementation. Managers can readily agree on the need for greater profitability, for cost-cutting, for improved efficiency; but strongly disagree on how these can be achieved. It may be argued that business organisations are less overtly political than other types of organisation, not because they are more rational, or more analytical, but because there is reasonable agreement about the goal of profit. This belief should not be too readily accepted, for while the general goal of profit may receive approval, this does not obviate disagreement or defensive behaviour on the part of those who are protecting their own interests. Profitability can mean very different things to production managers, financial controllers, personnel managers and sales personnel.

THE SIGNIFICANCE OF LANGUAGE

We have considered the different sources of power but suffusing the whole edifice is language, for the meanings attached to language are themselves evidence of power. The language of an organisation is an indication of its power structure, indeed 'power' is itself an example of the subtle manner in which language influence thinking in particular directions.

Actions arise out of the meanings which are used to define the situation – the firm defines the manager who defines the firm. The manager defines the firm from the position he occupies in it and from the functions he performs. Clearly these different views, arising from the complex of managerial positions and behaviour, and the language that encapsulates them, can be a source of conflict, complexity and procrastination. It goes some way to explaining the lengthy nature of much negotiation, bargaining and decision processes. However it would be a mistake to think that faulty communication and the ensuing misunderstandings are always conducive to conflict; they can equally well act as dampers of conflict, preventing organisation members from fully recognising their own interests or forming interest groups for their advancement.

The point has been made that language helps define the managerial situation and becomes the basis for action. Nowhere is this more evident than in considering the word 'organisation', for behind the word lies the fact that it is both a cooperative system and a place where people compete for advancement.[4] At one and the same time managers compete for organisational rewards and resources and cooperate in a common enterprise. The organisation chart is itself a control system and a career ladder. What is more, this dichotomy reflects the order prevailing in the wider community where there is both cooperation and competition, where the few succeed and the many are confronted with the possibility of non-advancement. Given this situation there will inevitably be disputes about the criteria which determine success, about the justice with which they are applied, their relevance to career development and the capacity of the firm to survive. Clearly the rules of the game which determine success are themselves the subject matter of organisational politics and the result of the exercise of power. He who shapes the rules must initially have power based on one or many of the sources outlined.

As we have seen language can be a means of obscuring reality; managers use language as a defence against the fact of conflict and discord among themselves.

RESISTANCE

Power generates resistance, and leadership as the exercise of power cannot avoid resistance. Attempts to avoid it can lead to the corruption of the powerless as well as the powerful. Resistance is often diffuse, unstructured and an emotionally saturated activity while opposition is a powerful and specific activity. However, resistance is not simply a response, it has its own positive quality, its own origins, functions and effects. The effectiveness of opposition and resistance can be measured by the extent to which change is resisted or modified.

The effort to overcome resistance is an essential and necessary aspect of management, and the problem for the manager is how to use power to reduce resistance and opposition without generating greater difficulty. While the elimination of resistance and opposition may be desired by those who aim to impose their will, the chances of achieving this are unlikely. At most resistance may be weakened, or made dormant by compromise and manipulation. Opposition to specific issues can be reduced, but a probable consequence is that the defusing of opposition leads to resistance – the specific gives way to the general. It may be that resistance and opposition can only be avoided by forestalling devices, so that before an issue surfaces or takes a firm shape some compromise is achieved: 'The processes of organisational control will shift from authority and away from standards set by analytic experts, and toward negotiation, arbitration and brokerage.'[5] This suggests that managers should take resistance into account when formulating a change and devise appropriate tactics for coping with it. One such tactic is to localise resistance by means of segmentation, by making the issue a matter of local and limited concern; another is to present the issue in impersonal terms as though no one will be affected by the proposal.

The avoidance of overt resistance is widely practised in order to avoid a public awareness of the existence of confrontation. In such circumstances indirect and more subtle forms of resistance are likely to occur and these may well be more effective than more obvious forms – a 'go-slow' may be more effective than a strike. Where managers mobilise power to crush resistance or where too obviously they seek to manipulate resistance, they are liable to create counter responses which may be difficult to control. Skilful management directs its attention to encouraging the transformation of resistance into opposition so that the unfocused and non-articulated responses become more sharp, more capable of being grasped and on occasion more readily coped with through bargaining and compromise. Part of this approach recognises that among those who resist there will be the 'satellites' who always follow the lead of anyone who is powerful in the organisation and the 'chameleons' who are shrewd judges of how an issue is going to turn out and know when to shift their position. Identifying and dealing with the 'satellites' and 'chameleons' is an essential part of managerial strategy, for the rest it is 'rule by anticipated reaction', in other words the manager formulates issues in the light of what he expects others to want.

POLITICAL ACTION

If an organisation is regarded as the mobilisation of bias, then a critical resource, or an important contingency, or uncertainty can be seen as a matter of social definition based on power. What is emphasised can then be open to manoeuvring and negotiation. Indeed 'it is because of the potential for redefining situations and using language and other forms of symbolic politics in acquiring power that strategic action as well as personal skills, can be important in the process of acquiring power'.[6]

Political skills can ultimately be seen as determinants of power. The underlying scarce resource is political skill, for without it the possession of the other sources of power are of much less value. The capability and willingness of managers to engage in political action enhances those resources derived from organisational structure and from positions in the formal and informal communication networks. Personal characteristics can strengthen the power exercised by the occupant of a given structural position:

1. articulateness in arguing one's case;
2. sensitivity to and knowledge of the power distribution;
3. understanding the decision process and the rules of the game;
4. belief in one's own position and argument plus the knowledge of when to stick and when to modify one's stance; and
5. when to manipulate and use power and influence.

For an example of political skills it is worth recalling an appraisal of Harry Hopkins, a confidant of F. D. Roosevelt, 'He knows instinctively when to ask, when to keep still, when to press, when to hold back, when to approach Roosevelt direct, when to go at him roundabout ...'.[7]

No political manager is effective unless he knows the rules of attack and defence in the political arena, recognising that politics is a competitive game. Beyond that it becomes a fight in which the object is not to defeat the opposition according to the rules but to destroy the 'game' and establish another – here is the political ultimate. The politician has to learn the appropriate language and rules of the game before he can play it effectively. These rules include, first, the criteria to determine who wins the prizes, second, the specification of who is eligible to play, third, the delineation of the competing groups, fourth, the guidelines for the operation of the competition and finally, the rules to be followed when a rule is broken.

The real nature of politics is often a complex mixture of duty, fear, love, status-seeking and self-interest and the power holder makes use of them all to extend and diversify the forms of power he exercises. He seeks the attainment of stable long-term control which is moderately comprehensive and strong. He operates in the knowledge that tougher forms of power may weaken milder forms. There is ladder of escalation and each form of power tends to change into a different form over time; for example, when power is regularly expressed through persuasion it tends to become authoritative.

Conflict is the guarantor of both freedom and social progress[8] and along with this dichotomy there is another form of ambivalence in that the will to power and the will to submission can coexist in the same person – the latter being the price that is paid to feel secure. The effective manager recognises that both consensus and conflict are present and interact in different mixes in virtually all power relations.

The importance of the power structure – the pattern of power relations – must not detract from the significance of the processes by which that structure is maintained, threatened and changed. Time reveals instability in power relations, and here again there is tension between change and resistance.

Power mobilisation is one factor in the shifting pattern of power distribution. The effective political manager generates support through an accurate perception of where and with whom power rests on a given issue. When an issue arises within the political process the critical determinants of the way in which it is received and acted upon are,

1. the importance of the source of articulation – who puts it forward;
2 the audience who hears it; and
3. how widely it is diffused in the power network.

From the subsequent mobilisation of power, decisions emerge.

CONCLUSION

This chapter has concentrated on power rather than influence. The two can be differentiated: power can be thought of as a means of changing a situation, while influence can be regarded as a way of restructuring someone's perception of the situation. Influence may also be seen as unspecific, more characterised in personal qualities and expertise than in structure. It rests on rapport based on prestige, credibility and reliability rather than on threats. It is exercised through occupying important positions in the communication process; it builds up alternatives in such a way that people feel they are exercising choice and by this means commitment develops. In many ways influence overlaps with power while being different from it; they are both aspects of political behaviour.

5 Bargaining and Conflict

In previous chapters there has been frequent reference to the process of bargaining and its attendant skills. Given the view of the firm as a political arena there is virtually no organisational relationship which does not involve negotiation – decision-making is a prime activity involving bargaining and conflict. Individual negotiations are related to particular structural arrangements, which influence such questions as who negotiates with whom, when and about what – in other words negotiations are not random, they are patterned.

The products of negotiations are contracts, agreements and rules, all having a temporal dimension: they have to be reviewed, re-evaluated, revised and on occasion revoked. Negotiated order has to be worked at on a continuous basis; it is the sum total of organisational rules, policies, understandings and contracts, achieved at different levels of the firm, at different times and to meet diverse situations. In the main they are informal; they are covert rather than overt. In addition to the daily bargaining process through which the work of the firm is carried on there is also the periodic reappraisal in which existing arrangements are reviewed, again often informally, and again requiring active bargaining. The emergent pattern in the firm is one of complex, shifting relationships between the ongoing, everyday process and its review counterpart.

These negotiating processes have to be seen against a background of change, for the introduction of new staff, new technology, and new structures can disrupt the continuity of bargaining, leading to the jettisoning of established relationships and arrangements and to calls for the renegotiation of existing agreements. Thus change can usher in a hectic period of negotiation, bargaining and conflict.

This negotiating, bargaining system is at the same time influenced by external forces which limit the freedom of choice of those involved, though the extent of that curtailment will partly depend upon the bargainers' perception of the power of those external forces. One factor at work in this situation is environmental time, that is to say, the differing time perspectives of the various external stakeholders. Depending upon these time perspectives, negotiations will vary between the leisurely and the hectic.

Managers have obligations to many groups and individuals both internal and external to the firm, all wanting action which, directly or indirectly, will be of value to them. Management has the task of reconciling these demands in such a way that it meets, or appears to meet, its responsibilities to these pressures. This necessitates bargaining, the hallmark of management and central to the political process. It takes place between two or more independent parties which are, however, linked by some measure of interdependence, a state which cannot be overstressed for it is perhaps the most fundamental aspect, not only of organisations, but indeed of industrial society at large. We only need to look at the way small groups of workers can bring large organisations and sections of society to a halt, to recognise the critical importance of interdependence.

Bargaining then is a process by which antithetical interests are adjusted so as to bring about an act of 'exchange', involving trade-offs, tacit agreements, wheeling and dealing and compromise.

In stressing the centrality of bargaining it should be remembered that alternatives exist, including coercion, persuasion and manipulation, though it may be argued that even in these some aspect of bargaining is involved.

Bargaining is characterised by interaction between the parties, it involves different types of bargainers with their different theories of bargaining, strategies and tactics and produces different results.

THE NATURE OF BARGAINING

Bargaining may be one of two forms, or indeed a mix of both.

The first is that of distributive bargaining, which is primarily concerned with what share of the pie each party gets. It occurs when there is a scarcity of resources in the firm. It is substantially competitive, with cooperation limited to keeping the bargaining within bounds so as not to lead to a breakdown of relations and to attempts at coercion. This form of bargaining arises from the basic requirement that some agreement must be reached, so that operations in which the parties are involved can be maintained. It represents the setting up of a working relationship in which each party agrees, explicitly or implicitly, to provide certain requisite services, to recognise certain seats of authority, to accept certain responsibilities in respect to others and to share out resources on the assumption that they are fixed. It provides little incentive to the parties to do more than carry out the minimum terms of any agreement which temporarily resolves, or more strictly puts into cold storage, their divergent interests. The parties in distributive bargaining tend to be blinkered in their perception and to concentrate on the willingness, ability and likelihood of others making concessions.

The second type of bargaining is integrative and is concerned with making the pie bigger; all parties gain though no party expects the others to give something for nothing. Its basis lies in the recognition by those involved that no party can achieve its objectives without the others' support. In consequence there is likely to be a measure of cooperation in the pooling of information and ideas, and joint exploration of possible solutions. There is a less blinkered approach with attention given to more cues. It is likely to be slower, more informal and complex. However, it is still a bargaining situation; the different parties may have to make concessions to gain greater rewards, with efforts being made to identify areas of common interest in which they could work together. Even here it will be a matter of compromise, of give and take, since the parties may have differing orders of preference and priority. This form of bargaining is based on the realisation that the better the performance of the individual parts, the better the joint performance and the greater the advantage to all. This recognition of joint-benefit is by no means automatic; much will depend upon the perceptions of the parties involved. To the outsider it may appear obvious that there is general benefit to all parties in working together; this may not be clear to the participants. However, while integrative bargaining may be directed to increasing the size of the pie, it does not necessarily determine how the enlarged pie is to be divided and at this point there will be a return to distributive bargaining.

Unless there is an awareness of these shifts within a sequence of bargaining episodes, inappropriate perceptions, strategies and tactics will be used with unfortunate consequences. Even under favourable conditions there is always the possibility in integrative bargaining of the parties failing to agree on a common area for cooperation, because of fear and uncertainty of the consequences. The fear is based on the recognition that integrative bargaining carries a threat to the authority structure of the organisation, and the uncertainty from a recognition of the persistence of divergent interests. The balance between organisational cooperation and competition is never fixed; it is always liable to move because of the tension which underlies the negotiated order of the firm. For many, integrative bargaining is the ideal with distributive bargaining a poor alternative. On this basis strong pleas are made for the development of integrative bargaining and for a shift from the distributive form. This approach is long on hope and short on reality; it fails to recognise the underlying political nature of organisations.

We can now examine the elements which help to shape the course of the bargaining process. They include:

1. the number of people who are engaged in a particular bargaining situation, whom they represent and their relative experience in negotiation;
2. the question of whether the bargaining is about one-off issues, or is repeated, sequential, serial, multiple or linked;
3. the relative balance of power exhibited by the negotiators in the bargaining process;
4. the visibility of the transactions to others;
5. the nature of the respective stakes of the different parties in the bargaining;
6. the complexity of the issues which are being bargained for;
7. the legitimacy of the issues being negotiated; and
8. the possibility of avoiding or discontinuing bargaining – the existence of alternatives.

During the bargaining process a number of sub-processes co-exist. These include determining the form of the negotiating procedure and the limits within which it operates; in this particular activity the whole question of power surfaces. Bargaining over the rules of the negotiation process is clearly influenced by the power of the participants and other relevant parties. These sub-processes – like the main bargaining – are not neat and tidy, clearly articulated and communicated. Many of these activities are of a testing nature as each party sees what it can get away with, how far it can push the other parties and what is possible given the distribution of power. Here indeed is the art of the possible, the perception of what is and is not attainable, the acceptance that both the building of the bargaining system and the substantive bargaining will lead to compromise, which in some instances will be close to the desired position of one party and some distance from that of the other. The negotiations over procedures, together with the substantive content of the bargaining process, go some way to determining the outcome of the whole process.

With the procedures agreed, there is the possibility of a progressive building of substantive agreements, for basically bargaining is a developmental process. There is an ironing out of residual disagreements even if this is simply an agreement to disagree; there is a trading-off of tasks, issues and commitments. The essence of bargaining is the exchange of commitments which may take a number of forms, such as,

1. the production manager committing himself to increase production, because the sales manager commits himself to increase sales; and
2. the operations manager who commits himself to supply the financial controller with information now, on the understanding that the latter will provide him with information at a future date, and the financial controller commits himself to do just that at the agreed time.

This type of commitment is managerially important for it restricts alternatives. The manufacturing firm that enters into an agreement to hire transport from one distribution firm rather than from others, restricts its freedom of action, unless it breaks its agreement. The breaking of a commitment can be crucial, making the offended party unwilling to enter into another bargaining situation with the culprit unless, of course, it is highly dependent on that firm. This stresses the importance of past performance; if an individual, group or firm has a long record of reliability there is the likelihood that in any new bargaining situation others will be prepared to accept their commitments. If no such record exists, every attempt will be made to build mechanisms or stipulate punishments to ensure fulfilment of commitments. In all these situations the position will be influenced by the presence or absence of alternatives. Numerous alternatives will allow the parties to go elsewhere; few or no alternatives will lead to the acceptance of conditions which would have been rejected if a choice had been available.

An important property of the context of bargaining is the balance of power among the negotiators. When the balance of power between the participants is very unequal, the powerful party may feel free to act independently and, if it wishes, break commitments; in an extreme form of imbalance, the bargaining process contains a substantial element of coercion. However, this form of behaviour may well lead to a realignment of forces, to coalitions of the weaker parties, the aim of which is to curb the strong party before proceeding to bargaining.

The aspect of development in the bargaining process is apparent in the renegotiation of agreements. This may occur because of,

1. the actual violation or failure of implementation of agreements;
2. new issues needing to be explored as they arise; or
3. pressure to renegotiate recurrent issues.

Negotiations may be undertaken with an eye to public impact; they may be unreal, in the sense that the bargainers are going through the motions because they perceive it is necessary in order to placate outside groups. This can occur in the field of international relations when a country agrees to negotiate with another country because of its own electorate, or because of pressure from the international community. In contrast to this public posturing there are many silent bargains and implicit negotiations, where there is little that is visible to external parties. This effort to keep a low profile may arise because the bargainers are aware of the limits within which they operate and which may not be understood or be acceptable to outsiders. Some of these limits are non-negotiable and are relatively fixed, while others are temporary and capable of alteration. If outsiders are aware of these movable limits they can evaluate the performance of the bargainers; they can judge the extent to which the limits have been accepted or modified.

REPRESENTATION IN BARGAINING

This reference to outside parties raises the question of representation. Who is represented? Do they know the negotiations are taking place and if so, do they agree with what is happening? The answer to the latter question depends upon the extent to which the bargainers' negotiating intentions are understood by those represented, and upon the form of relationship that exists between the two groups. Are the bargainers elected, appointed, commanded or are they acting because of their position in the organisation? In much managerial bargaining where the manager negotiates on behalf of his department, it is not always with his staff's knowledge, and often without their approval. The manager may represent more than one interest and if these are in conflict he has the task of reconciling them as far as possible in the course of the negotiations, juggling with differing priorities in the actual bargaining situation and, outside of it, negotiating with the different interests he represents.

In the relationship between the negotiators, the nature of the representation is important. The knowledge of one bargainer that his opponent is not representative of his constituents, produces a different situation and tactics from the position where it is known that the opponent is truly representative. In the former case the knowledge may contribute to the use of tactics aimed at weakening an already weak relationship between the representative and his constituents.

In the search for negotiated solutions the bargainers have to keep looking over their shoulders to consider the extent to which their constituents will accept the result and how it will affect their future relationship. Failure to protect the interests of his staff may mean that a manager loses their future support and makes relations with them more difficult to control. If a manager is negotiating for extra resources for his department and he comes back empty-handed, while his fellow managers come away with substantially extra resources, the members of his department may well judge him to be unsuccessful, especially if this has occurred on other occasions and on other issues. Attempts by managers to keep negotiations quiet in order to avoid evaluation are unlikely, in the long run, to be successful. Ultimately the grapevine will operate and the results will be disclosed. What complicates the situation is that the constituents' evaluation will be influenced not solely by their economic interests, but by what they consider to be 'fair' and 'reasonable' in relation to their overall interests.

In the relationship bargainers are not passive, they can exert intensive effort in attempting to control, manage and manipulate their constituents. They seek to mould consent, so that consent comes down from the top rather than ascending from the bottom. They attempt to promote consent by distributing information selectively and by means of ritualistic and evocative rhetoric, predefine the situation for their constituents.[1] Political leaders of all parties and trade union negotiators are skilled in these tactics, regularly projecting onto their members the demands they want to make.

The relationship of bargainer and constituent can provide a major obstacle to the successful outcome of negotiations, for the pressure from constituents can reduce flexibility and affect the bargaining relationship and the tactics employed. This pressure tends to move the bargaining process towards distributive negotiations and to toughness; it reduces the search for alternative ways to approach and resolve the issue under contention, it reduces the possibility of empathy between the negotiators and inhibits the overall quality of their contribution. This particular pattern of behaviour is likely to arise where the bargainer is not in a strong position *vis-à-vis* his constituents, or where his manipulative skills are limited.

In total there are five major conditions which narrow the negotiator's vision;

First, there is the involvement of the constituents in the planning and actual negotiations.

Second, there is the degree of accountability of the negotiators to their constituents. A number of conditions will influence the significance of accountability; there is the level of contact with constituents, the extent of their knowledge of their representatives and the degree to which they can exert pressure.

Third, there is the extent of the formalisation of their relationship; for example, the degree to which the constituents allow their representatives to use their discretion – the more autonomy, the greater the likelihood of a flexible approach to the negotiations. Formalisation of the relationship can work to protect or expose the representative. It is the attitudes of the parties and the content of the relationship that are critical.

Fourth, there is the question of loyalty between representatives and constituents. Loyalty to the group appears to imply unequivocal acceptance of the views and demands of the constituents, but representatives who demonstrate loyalty over a period of time may be given a freer hand in negotiations. Their bargaining stance can be more pragmatic. Loyalty can generate tension for the representative; in so far as it tends to narrow his vision it may inhibit the resolution of conflict in the bargaining situation; where it leads to increased discretion it may facilitate the alleviation of conflict.

Fifth, there is the extent to which the negotiations are carried on in public. In this situation public stances and postures are liable to be adopted which reduce the opportunity for flexibility. Having taken up a position in public, any retreat from it is likely to be construed as a weakening; to avoid this appearance there is considerable reluctance to move. The extreme example of this, is the public airing on television of demands and counter-demands by unions and management.

It cannot be stressed too strongly that this question of representation is not solely related to the collective bargaining of management with trade unions but is an integral part of inter-management relations. In practice it is not always visible, it lies beneath the surface; it is not always formal, it is part of the ongoing bargaining process. The manager who forgets his representative function is certain to have difficulties with those he manages.

BARGAINING PERCEPTIONS

In any bargaining context the different parties are likely to bring widely different points of view to the negotiations. They may differ in their long-term aims and immediate standards, or agree upon some objectives and differ upon others; the permutations are numerous. These disagreements over goals can be confused and obscured by the language that is used. An apparent agreement may be no agreement at all, for while the parties may agree on the words, they may take away very different meanings, understandings and intentions.

The parties bring to the bargaining arena different views based upon experience, training, function and power, with the result that they may disagree as to the factual situation under negotiation. The problem is further complicated because they have differing hopes and expectations for the future and varying degrees of sympathy and understanding of each other. A sympathetic bargainer may be prepared to listen to his opponent for a longer time than an unsympathetic one; he may try and empathise with his opposite number and in both cases this may, though not inevitably, lead to longer negotiations and to outcomes that are more fully understood. The degree of sympathy displayed can be affected by the weight of the time pressures operating on the bargaining, by the judgement of the relative powers involved and the feasibility of gaining the bargainers' objectives. The differing skills of the parties must also contribute to the results of the negotiations and to the strategies and tactics employed. Finally, account must be taken of the different values of the negotiators.

In all these differences the importance of perception is critical; how do the respective bargainers perceive their opponents, how do unrealistic perceptions affect the present and future relationships of the parties involved? Negotiators observe different aspects, draw different conclusions, and make their own predictions about their opposite numbers' intentions and motives. Under pressure they fall back upon simple perceptions, although the situation may demand complex judgements.

The negotiators' perceptions are affected by their expectations, habits, attitudes, preferences, organisational position and the views of the groups with whom they live and work. Given this complex pattern of causes it is clear why different bargainers will develop dissimilar strategies and tactics.

The fact of differing perceptions complicates an already complex and uncertain bargaining situation. The factors making for this complexity and uncertainty include:

1. the difficulty of appreciating all the issues involved;
2. the piecemeal nature of bargaining;
3. the existence of ambiguous bargaining criteria; and
4. the organisation and manipulation of information.

To understand this complexity is a step towards greater sensitivity to the issues raised in bargaining; to deny it is to bargain in an oversimplistic manner with the likelihood of becoming locked in positions from which it is difficult for the negotiators to extricate themselves.

Determining the nature of the other party or parties is vital if their negotiating tactics are to be anticipated.

1. Knowledge is required not only of their perceptions but also of their impulsiveness, rationality, degree of representativeness and general flexibility. With this knowledge it is possible for a negotiator to set up a self-fulfilling prophecy. If he knows his opponent is impulsive, he can declare that the negotiations are about to break down, submit demands that he knows will be brusquely rejected, and then turn round and say 'I told you so'. Playing the innocent party he can blame the other party, all the while having achieved his own objective – the breakdown of the negotiations.
2. To understand their possible stance it is necessary to know what resources they have,
   a. what tactics they can and will employ;
   b. whether they are principals or subordinates; and
   c. whether they have the power to make a final decision.

This information is needed in order to prepare a plan for the bargaining. The negotiators have to develop an awareness that some acceptable compromise is essential because open warfare will, in all probability, lead to a breakdown in the continuity of relations. Conflict can be pushed so far but no further and prudent negotiators are aware of this.

PLANNING FOR BARGAINING

In planning for effective bargaining there are three stages to identify.

First, there are the objectives of the negotiations; each party should be reasonably clear about its own objectives. When the bargaining party is a coalition in which the members have differing objectives, there has to be prior bargaining in the coalition. If this process is not undertaken the coalition may find itself in disarray when faced with the demands of a united opposition. In addition to clarifying objectives, negotiators need to attempt to identify the issues likely to be raised, and determine what stand should be taken on them and what compromises will be acceptable.

Second, there is the analysis of the issues in terms of their importance to the opposition. Here again knowledge of the opposition is essential.

Third, it is useful to develop and present a major theme; identifying the key issues and key bluffs to be adopted and faced. Bargainers have to be both proactive and reactive. They have to be flexible around a core position. With any negotiating plan it is advisable to set up a series of checkpoints and, if they are not being achieved, to be ready to break off discussions to reappraise the situation. The problem is how to stick to a major issue if severe differences arise and it is inadvisable to break off the negotiations; to maintain the debate there is the need to link the major issue into an offer which is couched in such a way that neither side can afford to dismiss it.

Within this overall approach there is a series of more visible tactical moves. This visibility has its dangers, for an opponent can come to anticipate tactics that are used too often.

Tactics are the means by which the bargainer seeks to change the balance of power between the negotiators. There are four main tactics available, all of them revolving around the issue of dependence.

First, the bargainer may attempt to improve his position by increasing the number of alternatives open to him. This will reduce his dependence on his counterpart and limit the latter's base for influence.

Second, he can decrease the number of options available to his opponent, so increasing the latter's dependence and building up his own power.

Third, the bargainer can decrease the operational significance of his opponent's offerings.

Finally, he can increase the extent to which the opponent values what the bargainer provides.

The bargainer seeks both to manipulate the opponent's perception of him and increase the opponent's dependence on him.

In selecting those tactics which he believes carry the greatest likelihood of success, the bargainer will fit the tactic to the specific nature of the power relationship. A bargainer with few alternatives is vulnerable to tactics aimed at this weakness, and one who attaches greater importance to the results of a bargaining situation than does his opponent, will be more open to manipulation.

Bargaining is part and parcel of the power and dependence relationships within the firm. Concessions are related to the balance of the dependence relationship. The more dependent a bargainer is, the less tough he can afford to be, and conversely the more dependent an opponent is, the tougher the bargainer can be. However, the position rarely remains static and the ability to exercise toughness will change with shifts in dependence. The manager has to avoid being tough when the dependence factor has moved against him, for he may drive the opposition to punitive action.

The effective manager knows how, when and to what extent toughness can be used. He can use it to manipulate information and to contribute to the shaping of his opponent's intentions, attitudes and aspirations. For example, one-sided toughness allied to power is likely to be effective in the early stages of a negotiation, when the aspirations of the parties are to some extent fluid and manipulable, when they have little information on each others' priorities and styles. Initial toughness sets the tone, sends out signals and shapes perceptions. It is part of the communication process in which the respective bargainers seek to create certain impressions, test and evaluate the impressions given by others and assess the resolve and commitment of others. At the core is the fact that the bargainers have incomplete knowledge of each other, and in view of this they will not always act in strict accordance with the dependence relationship. The extent of dependence is tested and explored in the course of the negotiations.

The rules and traditions of an organisation are likely to constrain the bargaining tactics used and there will be a view of what is considered legitimate and proper. Whilst tactics are open to continuous adjustments, these may be only marginal as power relationships are highly resistant to immediate large-scale change. Any attempt at such a change will lead to counteraction to preserve the status quo. This long-term tendency exists because negotiators are concerned not only about the temporary disruption of order, but also about the underlying questions of domination and pressure emanating from different bases of power within and without the organisation. Negotiations are rooted in the realities of power and politics and to fully understand them they have to be seen in the context of technological, economic, political and social factors which, taken together, provide the background for bargaining.

Sanctions are a key dimension in bargaining. The foundation of any organisation is ultimately coercive; coercion being the capacity to punish, or threaten to punish, the other party. Coercion is part of the dependence relationship and its use or threatened use will ultimately unleash an upward spiral of coercive counteraction.

BARGAINING TACTICS

The operational ploys of bargaining take many forms.[2]

The first is bluff, which affirms that the current offer on the table is the last offer, while at the same time implying that there may be a loophole. Each party has to find a way of committing himself to his bluff so that it really does seem to be the final offer. The bluffer has to be convincing; his problem is to avoid over-commitment, making the possibility of deadlock more probable.

Bluff tactics involving commitment to a current offer include:

1. Commitment to a deadline in the absence of any communication. This takes the form of 'If I do not hear from you by X, then I will assume you are not interested.'
2. Commitment to a third party, where a person making the offer suggests that he runs the risk of punishment or loss of favour if he does not stick to the offer. This can take the form of 'I cannot make any further concessions because my chief will be annoyed.'
3. The use of the lackey. A senior manager may have too much authority in a given situation so that he can make concessions if required. To avoid doing this he sends someone with less authority, so that the possibility of making concessions is ruled out, limited or delayed. This ploy provides boundaries; the limited range of the lackey restricts the areas which can be covered in the bargaining. It also softens up an opponent and gives time for assessment; the lackey goes in first and is then followed, if necessary, by the senior.
4. Allegiance to the public, the firm, a principle or policy, or a precedent. This tactic suggests that there is something higher

than the everyday content of the bargaining. Appeal to this higher element makes the opposition look as though it is incapable of taking a higher view. At the same time this commitment can bring rigidity into the situation; when someone contends 'it's a matter of principle' the others in the negotiations can prepare for a long haul.

5. By sheer obstinacy (real or not) a negotiator can seek to convince his opponents that whatever they say, he is not going to move from his position.
6. The use of the alternative, suggesting that there is another way ahead. The proposer of the alternative may be seeking to shift the bargaining into an area that is more agreeable to him, or it can simply be a distraction, a wearing down of the opposition.

Faced with these tactics and associated commitments and having no immediate counter-offer, the opposition can bring into action a series of ploys, including:

1. seeking by one means or another a postponement of the negotiations;
2. feigning misunderstanding so that time is gained to develop a counter-move;
3. raising a different issue;
4. picking at details; and
5. adopting tactics that are identical to those of the other party.

The second major ploy is the threat, involving the conditional bluff – taking the form 'If you do this, I will retaliate.' There is the strong threat where both parties will lose if the threat is carried out, although the one who makes the threat loses least. In the weak threat the party making it stands to lose more, so it must have a loophole. There must be ways of avoiding carrying out the threat; which would mean not merely loss in this particular bargaining but also would put at risk future negotiations. The successful threat is one which convinces others that it will be carried out, and because of this there is no need to proceed and no one gets hurt.

Much negotiation is concerned with the establishment and maintenance of control, often through the development or interpretation of rules. In any negotiations it is unlikely that anyone knows all the rules, much less how they apply. Linked with this lack of knowledge is the fact that rules are not always enforced, and even negotiated informal rules can fall into disuse. A pattern of selective usage operates. Rules are broken when it suits the convenience of interested parties and when there are warrantable exigencies – the rules are stretched to get things done. At the top of an organisation there is often tolerance towards both the extensiveness of the rules and the laxity with which they are applied. It is recognised that too many rules, rigidly enforced, would restrict internal flexibility and limit negotiations. The skilled negotiator uses his knowledge of the rules to strengthen his bargaining position. The rules provide a fall-back position; people may turn a blind eye to them but, when it appears advantageous, someone is liable to remind everyone who is breaking the rule that it exists and could be made operable.

Bargaining is frequently aimed at staking claims and engaging in games of give and take, with the prizes being decisions and rules; for example, laying down where an individual or group will work; who will be colleagues and to whom they will report. Those people who feel threatened by any change which impinges on the existing order will make recurrent demands for fresh negotiation of rules which formerly have been regarded as protective; there may also be demands for explicit rules when someone is not trusted and there is a desire for protection. Rules not only serve to set limits on bargaining, and guide the direction of the negotiations, they frequently provide the content of bargaining.

Bargaining may be covert, involving implicit contracts and understandings. For instance, in the case of changing rules that allocate resources, any explicit negotiation involving open exchange of offers and counter-offers may not be acceptable to those outside the immediate bargaining process, who would be affected by its results. The difficulty with covert bargaining is that it may become overt if one of the parties thinks it can gain by making the negotiations public. An additional complication is that its results often appear more ambiguous and uncertain than those of overt negotiations. Overt bargaining tends to operate more effectively when communication between the parties is reasonably free-flowing and face-to-face. However, communication, even in favourable circumstances, does not necessarily resolve dissent, for it is the content as well as the opportunity to communicate that is important. Overt bargaining also requires the possibility of compromise and mutual consent; that is, the parties must consent to accept the relationship publicly as a bargaining one and take account of the fact that they may have to make concessions openly. Even with this display of openness, bargaining is still a game of information exchange, manipulation and power – the openness simply adds a further dimension.

Demands for open negotiations, freedom of information and the like, generally represent tactics in a power-seeking situation. They represent attempts to shift the distribution of power in the favour of the advocates, if not for those they represent.

In summary, the bargaining relationship can be cast in a number of forms, involving different combinations of covert, overt, integrative and distributive bargaining. They produce formal or informal cooperation or competition, each of which has differing impacts upon the resolution of conflict and of the bargaining process. The extent of these differences will depend upon a variety of contextual factors including structure and resource availability. It is essential that the negotiator is aware of the different forms and of the particular circumstances within which he is negotiating.

THE NEGOTIATORS

Turning to the negotiators themselves, they must be skilled in the novel as well as the routine; they must be able to handle covert and overt bargaining. They must be able to grasp the covert understandings that lie behind the overt agreements.

Where negotiations are covert it may be necessary for them to make overt diversionary moves to distract attention from the real negotiations. For example, in order to conduct sensitive negotiations without the blaze of world publicity there were numerous occasions when Kissinger deliberately gave the impression of being in one place when he was already on his way to somewhere else.[3]

The negotiators must be able to effect trade-offs which are important in achieving agreements and be capable of threatening reprisals without actually breaking off the bargaining. They must be able to handle ambiguity of language and problems of definition; for instance, developing justifications that are political defences to protect covert agreements. In recognising alternatives they have to accept the consequences of choice; that short-term gains may be at the cost of long-term disadvantages.

Within the bargaining processes the negotiator has to balance the favours and concessions being exchanged, avoiding the positive loss; that is, making a concession without getting something in return, for a concession once made is not easily withdrawn. His aim must be that of mutual concessions, and to arrive at that conclusion he must trade efficiently. If a concession has to be made initially it should be small; the negotiator then waits for a limited move in return – all the while using such tactics as the bluff or the threat. The negotiator develops linkages between the different issues under negotiation, so that leverage may be used on one link in order to gain a concession over another.[4] For example, a negotiator may put forward three proposals made up of different building blocks or packages, and then suggest to his opposite number that there may be parts of each set which could be taken and put into a new package. The new arrangement of the blocks gives the proposer some leverage on his opponent; for the package will contain parts which the opponent wants, linked to parts about which he is not enthusiastic.

In all this the negotiator[5] has to consider his opponent's aspiration level (what he hopes to get), and his bargaining level (what he expects to get) and assess these against his own aspiration and bargaining bases.

Because the negotiators have their different sets of priorities, the order in which issues are negotiated is important. There is the initial testing time when the parties are feeling each other out and signals are being sent. One negotiator may seek to reach quick agreement on some relatively unimportant issue and then, having established an optimistic climate, regretfully come to the conclusion that he cannot meet his opposite number's proposals on matters of real substance. Early deadlock is liable to occur where important issues are discussed first, before the negotiators have tested each others' strengths and weaknesses. All this is a matter of skilled agenda building by the negotiators; indeed the agenda may be so crucial that it has to be discussed and settled before substantive negotiations can take place.

The bargainer's approach and use of particular tactics will be influenced by his history, position, ideology and not least by general managerial concepts. In an organisation there are likely to be differing interpretations of these concepts and a manager will need to possess a reserve of stamina if he is to see his own views prevail. Stamina is an essential ingredient in negotiations; often the result a particular bargaining activity will depend upon the ability of one of the parties to hang on longer than anyone else. The degree of doggedness displayed will be influenced by the importance of the issue; that is, how important the bargainer feels it is to exert influence over the outcome.

One bargaining arena where all the skills, tactics and stamina come into play is in the determining of budgets, because it is through budgets that power is allocated and reallocated, in the shape of funds and positions. Budgets are the outcome of political contests rather than the application of rational and neutral decision-making rules.

All the qualities and skills of a negotiator may not prevent the breakdown of bargaining. Failure may occur for any one of a number of reasons.

First, one of the parties wishes this to happen.

Second, there is a lack of political skill and sensitivity at some stage in the bargaining process.

Third, despite large areas of agreement each party is waiting for the other to accept the option on offer.

Fourth, there is the fear that a concession would be regarded as a sign of weakness; this is particularly important at the closing stages of any negotiations. Who is going to make the final concession? Often a small difference between the parties may lead to a breakdown if it means that one side will be seen to have made the final concession.

Fifth, as the negotiations have gone on, the price of yielding has increased in terms of resources and/or reputation.

Finally, negotiations may fail because of strong personal antipathy on the part of one or all of the bargainers.

BARGAINING AND CONFLICT

One of the characteristics of the bargaining process, is conflict, both as a cause of bargaining and as a part of the process. Given the mixed motives and the attendant tension between cooperation and competition, it is always probable that any conflict resolution arising from negotiation will be temporary.

Conflict is the inevitable outcome of interdependence linked with the scarcity of resources. Because of the critical role of conflict in organisational effectiveness, management has to evaluate the impact of conflict on the firm and where possible to influence it through bargaining; hence the importance of negotiating skills. From the outset the manager needs to distinguish between constructive and destructive conflict; conflict is potentially beneficial when it brings about a more effective allocation of political power and economic resources. A significant question here is 'effective' for whom, and the answer will depend upon the goals of the different negotiators and their constituents. In contrast, potentially destructive conflict emerges when there is a failure to recognise the need for some measure of mutuality, and there is such continual coercion by the more powerful groups that the less powerful are either driven from the organisation, or group together to take counter-coercive action.

The problem is to achieve a balance between constructive and destructive conflict, and this raises the important question of how conflict can be managed.

First, it has to be noted that where there is total commitment to a goal, interest or group, conflict is likely to be intensive. Where individuals participate segmentally, where their commitment is divided, conflict is less likely to be destructive. A multiplicity of allegiances tends to constitute a check against the total breakdown of relations and negotiations. Energies are mobilised in many directions and hence it will not be concentrated on one conflict issue. Further, with limited commitment there is less need to block up hostility; because of its diffused nature it is less significant in any one situation and in consequence is less disruptive if expressed. In any organisation there is a need for safety valves; segmental involvement provides just such a mechanism. Where there is rigidity and a demand for absolute loyalty, useful warning signals are smothered.

Second, where there is an external threat there is likely to be pressure to achieve internal unity, to the putting aside of differences and to concentration on the threat. Those who do not respond are liable to be branded as disloyal, with extra pressure being brought to bear upon them. The external threat clearly has its usefulness; if there are major internal problems in an organisation the identification of an external threat can lead to a closing of the ranks and the dropping of demands and claims which threaten that unity. The manufacturing of external threats is a useful tactic for the political manager, and the existence of a highly competitive market can focus managerial attention on the need to reduce differences if the threat is recognised as such. To take another example; it can be argued that the appearance of managerial unity is achieved in part by the existence of trade unions; if the latter did not exist they might have to be invented.

The manager is faced with a number of types of built-in conflict.

First, there is the inter-departmental conflict induced by the operation of the different functions in the organisation. These produce differing orientations which, in turn, lead to the development of differing operational criteria and personal values.

Second, there is the struggle between similar functional units operating in direct competition with one another; that is, units such as production competing for scarce resources. John Brooks writing on 'The Fate of the Edsel' reports how the Mercury division of the Ford Motor Company made things as tough as possible for the new Edsel division of the same company, by undertaking a million dollar (1957), thirty-day advertising drive aimed especially at the 'price conscious buyers' – the very market for which the Edsel car was built. Clearly it was a highly competitive situation between the two divisions, both producing cars for the same company.

Third, there is hierarchical conflict stemming from the various viewpoints of different levels in an organisation.

Within these different types of conflict there are four typical conflict situations. The first is that of win–lose where there are incompatible goals which cannot exist simultaneously – this situation is very difficult to resolve. Second, there is competition over what are the best means for achieving agreed objectives – this is often a conflict over shared dependence or limited resources. Third, there is status incongruence where people feel deprived and see themselves in a second-best position. Fourth, there is the conflict of perceptual differences where people are looking at the same thing differently – for instance, in a firm the production manager and the marketing manager may see the problem of falling sales in very different lights.

Just as there are different forms of conflict there are diverse strategies for conflict resolution.

First, there are those which emphasise the human element in making the organisation work. They stress human skills, reshuffling people, increasing two-way communication, the use of group processes and the clarification of structures. The primary purpose is to increase feedback and minimise structural and personal barriers to communication.

Second, there is the development of structural machinery to control, if not eradicate, conflict. This machinery usually takes the form of committees, procedures and rules.

Third, the stress is on restructuring the organisation to reduce specialist departments and break down barriers through multi-group membership. The aim is to increase decentralisation and mobility across hierarchical and functional boundaries.

The weakness of these strategies is their failure to take account of the essential nature of organisations, of their power structure and of the politics of management. In the last analysis these strategies are cosmetic and are unlikely to have any long-term success.

A crucial factor in this situation is the variety of different attitudes to conflict. Those with power may see conflict being controlled through appropriate job descriptions, detailed specifications or relationships, careful selection of people and the 'right' type of training – largely a hygienic view of conflict. Others stress the value of conflict as a useful way of initiating the search for a solution to a problem; as a springboard for innovation and change; as a way of energising people and directing attention to areas of the firm which are malfunctioning. Managers who see conflict in these terms are more likely to emphasise ways of using conflict and this they will seek to do by absorbing the issues of power, conflict and politics into their thinking and behaviour and treating them as normal, inevitable aspects of organisational life.

To achieve constructive conflict the focus of attention has to be on the distribution of resources and the balance of organisational power; when this is done simplistic solutions are more likely to be rejected. How far conflict can be resolved, modified and made constructive depends on the existing distribution of power and on the readiness of power-holders to restrain their use of power. This constraint will only be achieved if they see that it is in their long-term interest to do so, and that it will prevent the development of countervailing power and the alienation of those with whom they work.

CONCLUSION

The skilled political manager recognises different conflict situations and the factors that contribute to them, and seeks to deal with them using the range of strategies and tactics that are available to him. He will not seek the elimination of conflict, for he recognises it as an inevitable part of the functioning of any organisation; he will look to alleviate it. He will seek to use conflict constructively and prevent it destroying the organisation in which he operates.

6 Structure and Top Management

Management takes place within a framework, a structure which takes a number of forms. There is, first, the formal framework, exemplified in the organisation chart and its attendant rules, regulations and control systems which are themselves the result of negotiations. Then there is the structure that is the result of a further process of negotiation and bargaining which in practice, if not on paper, modifies what is formally laid down. These two structures interact and are influenced by what their members assume them to be, which may be different from what actually exists.[1]

The interaction of the formal structure with the continuing process of negotiation produces the situations in which management operates. In this chapter we will emphasise the 'formal' structure both as a source of power, influencing such questions as who controls the organisation, and the result of power, that is, the outcome of the political process. The central point is that the formal structure is not neutral; it is a tool to be used by the powerful. In consequence, when faced with an organisation structure people need to ask, who has the power to alter it, who is affected by such alterations and how can they effectively react? The formal structure is one critical item on the political agenda, influencing the flow of information in the firm and contributing to those decision-making centres which influence who gets what, when and how. The structure formally delineates who controls the finance, the posts, equipment, promotion, information and expertise. It also influences the visibility of organisation members and consequently affects their ability to influence decisions. This is not to say that the formal organisation is the sole determinant of what happens, but it would be unwise to reject its significance in managerial politics.

Decisions influencing how organisational tasks should be divided and grouped, how many managerial levels there will be in an organisation and what types of relationships shall be defined, have considerable influence on the shaping of power and its associated political processes. Those who have the power to make these structural decisions help shape the future, but it would be unwise to think that they are necessarily of one mind; an organisation structure is the result of bargaining. This early bargaining, which comes to the forefront when there is any discussion of changes, produces a structure which, once established, assumes a certain legitimacy by its very existence. The ensuing allocation of differential access to information and to decision-making helps to perpetuate this established power. Organisation structures are the resolution, at a given time, of the contesting claims for control.

Structural change, whether generated internally, externally or by the emergence of new policies and new forms of information processing, can mean new negotiations and the stirring up of old conflicts. To avoid them there will be pressure to let things be and the contention that any change will be for the worse. In consequence the dissonance between the formal structure and the actual behaviour of organisation members may well increase and produce a further area of unreality and ambiguity, which will be open to political manipulation.

Around the demand for structural change the myth develops that it will lead to an improvement in organisational efficiency and effectiveness. In fact such a myth functions to legitimise the contest for control, and if it is successful the existing legitimacy will be called into question without the political aspects of the change being apparent to the majority of those involved. It is advantageous to those promoting the change if people do not fully understand what is happening. People involved in political behaviour do not and cannot, for their own sakes, provide everyone with the facts because if they did, resistance might be increased. If a manager, seeking a structural change, were to come out into the open and say that he was advocating the change because it would increase his power at the expense of those around him, he would face a hostile reaction, hence his need to argue that the change is for improved organisational efficiency. Paradoxically there may be times when the provision of a great deal of information can achieve the same end –

increasing the power seeker's base. A communication overload can numb the critical faculties of those who have to be persuaded of the usefulness of the change.

Pressure for structural change frequently comes from those who believe that unfreezing and renegotiating the structure will increase their power. This pressure generally comes from outside the dominant coalition, except on those occasions when its members see a structural change as furthering their power.

However, the struggle to negotiate and renegotiate a structure is constrained by a number of factors:

1. There is the recognition, however dimly understood, of mutual interdependence and with it the knowledge that after the struggle the participants will have to live with each other.
2. There are the rules of the game which are established to maintain the survival of the firm, but which also serve to support the already powerful. Because of this the rules themselves may come under attack. From time to time the constraints are tested by one or other of the parties to see if they can be altered to suit their interests. Any consensus on constraints is of a temporary nature, being influenced by factors beyond the control of the contestants as well as by changes in their positions and perceptions. Where the attempt to change the constraints is pushed hard, there is always the possibility that commitments will no longer be maintained; communications will break down and coercion, an everpresent element, will surface.

Structures exist to achieve some set of objectives or goals. Much of the literature on organisational design is based on the notion that structures must be designed to serve the goals of efficiency and effectiveness. Rarely is the question raised as to who will benefit from their attainment. Indeed to speak of the organisation's goal or goals is to assume a degree of consensus and control that is rare. When the distinction is made between the stated and real goals of a firm, a clear difference emerges between what is set down as the goals and what they actually are. They differ, because, like the structure, they are the result of bargaining. The question of what they are and who sets them can only be determined by the analysis of specific firms at specific times. When this is done, it frequently emerges that there is some negotiated agreement on general goals within which there is room for continuing debate, discussion and negotiation, and that the means to achieving whatever goals exist are also subject to power considerations and political processes.

Thus we move away from the view that organisational design can be regarded as an engineering problem, the aim of which is to optimise productivity or profitability with control exercised by rules, evaluation and structure. What is at stake in the bargaining over goals and structure is the central issue of control, and the associated questions of whose preferences and choices are to be served by the firm. The answer that it is the shareholders, owners or managers is inadequate.

When criticising or amending a particular structure it should be asked, what kind of problems are people trying to solve in a specific power and political context when building the structure and what kind of solutions and alternatives are available? What has to be borne in mind is that there is no ideal structure for any given set of goals, problems or situations and it is this very ambiguity which gives participants room to manoeuvre and produce differing structures.

At the same time, an organisation structure is a constraint that makes it possible for people to interact, compete and cooperate. Structures do not directly dictate behaviour, they are merely preconditions for organisational life to develop. They do not integrate the conflicting strategies of those involved; this is accomplished through political behaviour. Structures are frequently regarded as coordinating and control devices but this is to divorce them too sharply from the political processes that operate in and around them. They may facilitate or hinder the possibility of coordination, but that is ultimately the result of human behaviour, of choice, of political activities.

The organisation chart presents a grossly oversimplified picture of an organisation. In the real world there are infinitely graded distinctions barely discernible to the external observer, but very real to the participants. Looking at a chart the observer can mistakenly believe that certain positions are equal, when this is by no means the case to the occupants. The formal chart does not reflect all organisational transactions, only those of a formal nature; it does not reflect the political and social interchanges which form so large a part of organisational life.

Structures are a significant part of organisational politics. It is the awareness of the political use of structure that leads some organisation members to argue that every problem needs a new structure, rather than a minor modification of the existing one – that each new problem calls for a new department, a new expert, rather than the re-education of existing management to cope with the problems that have been identified. The extent to which change will take place will depend upon the power of those who recognise the present structure as a strong source of their power. This is not necessarily the end of the story; faced with the resistance of the establishment, those who seek change may intentionally violate the chart to get things moving and to demonstrate the weakness of the current structure.

One element in the structuring of organisations particularly relevant for political considerations is that of centralisation and decentralisation. The distribution of power between the central and constituent units of a firm is influenced:

1. by the historical ideology of the dominant coalition, that is, how far its members believe in one form of structure rather than another;
2. by the differential control of resources, particularly expertise and local knowledge, by central and peripheral units;
3. by the distribution of task requirements: where are the critical tasks performed?; and
4. by the present distribution of power: what are the sources and extent of power in the centre and at the periphery? How much non-routinised interdependence exists and what are the perceptions of the different groups of others' control of their rewards and punishments? Clearly, the decentralised organisation provides many opportunities for political bargaining and behaviour between the centre and its satellites.

Organisation structures do not exist in a vacuum, they are constrained by that imprecise but important notion of culture. This provides definitions of acceptable frameworks of behaviour in a confused but powerful way and, in doing so, limits the decisions that organisation members make concerning any given structure. Forms of organisation structure are influenced by the educational, industrial, economic, technological, political, legal and social systems of a given society. The influence is indirect in many instances; for example, technology, techniques and innovations are tools to be used, misused or not used by management – the crux of the matter is managerial choice. An important point is that culture is not easily changed; for instance, the decline of British industry is not simply the result of short-term economic factors but of long-term political and social considerations.[2] Given the resistance of culture to rapid change, it is clear that attempts to make British industry absorb and effectively utilise some aspects of Japanese industry are unlikely to produce earth-shattering changes.[3]

At the centre of the discussion of structure there is the question of control. This takes many forms, some apparently more attributable to structure than others but all interacting with it, influencing and being influenced by it.

RULES

In any organisation there are rules, some clearly formalised on paper, some becoming formalised without being part of any written constitution, and some remaining informal and fluid. All can be discarded even without formal prorogation. Some rules arise out of previous conflicts and are aimed at reducing tension; others aim to prevent conflict by indicating what can and what cannot be done. Initially and subsequently they are the result of bargaining and hopefully they confer legitimacy on actions that might otherwise be questioned. Rules act as stated operating procedures, both limiting behaviour and providing freedom, according to their interpretation. They protect the individual from arbitrary action by others; as long as someone has operated according to the rules he has some protection.

Rules cannot cover every eventuality, there is always some element of discretion however constrained; there are always gaps which provide opportunities for non-rule behaviour. Of course rules provide guidelines, of course they limit freedom, and function to homogenise organisational members all of whom may be expected to conform to some general rules, but they do not automate the individual. The individual has some degree of choice. Some managerial work is routine, but the claim made here is that people can and do retain their individuality. To reject this stand is to adopt a pessimistic, plastic view of human beings, and is as distorted an opinion as being over-optimistic.

Rules may be used in an attempt to overcome inadequate motivation and to achieve some degree of order and predictability when commitment cannot be assumed. They can aim at achieving organisational regularity; for example, in assessing the smooth flow of work between departments, the smooth entry and exit of staff; but the persistent question is, for whom do the rules make things regular? The ready-made answer would be management, but given the differentiated nature of management, the answer is not so simple; rather it becomes which managers, indeed which workers and customers? Recognising that discretion in relation to rules generates power, subordinates at any level will attempt to retain or expand their area of discretion. The area of discretion attainable and contested may appear trivial, peripheral and unimportant to their seniors but it is perceived as important to the subordinates. At the same time senior managers may resist any attempt by their subordinates to expand discretion through the manipulation of rules, because they recognise that in spite of the apparent triviality of the contested issue, precedents may be established and subordinate power increased.

Rules have to be applied, and this requires more than simply knowing about them. Their successful application calls for some degree of adjustment, adaptation and interpretation in the light of the ambiguities of a particular situation, and it is through these processes that organisational members seek to achieve their own personal objectives. Rules can be used as resources or stakes in negotiating and bargaining. Formal rules can be bargaining counters to secure informal cooperation; where rules have been supplanted by custom and practice, one or other party can always resuscitate them and work to rule. In doing so the party can claim that it is doing what is laid down, and as rules lay down minimum levels of performance they also indicate what is an acceptance level of behaviour. Strauss has observed that 'even a small number of clearly enumerated rules can be stretched, negotiated, argued as well as ignored or applied at convenient moments. Here as elsewhere (rules) fail to be universal prescriptions.'[4] The strategy of the individual is to manipulate rules to enhance his independence from direct and arbitrary interference from those higher up the organisation. The tendency of people to concern themselves with means rather than ends and, when deemed necessary, stick to the letter of the rules, is often the strategy by which they try to affirm their power positions and their independence.

Regardless of effort, it is impossible to eliminate all sources of uncertainty by multiplying organisational rules and developing a centralised structure. Rules cannot regulate everything and it is around the areas of uncertainty that conflict becomes evident and attempts are made to legislate, or to establish other forms of control of the area. Where there are too many rules in a firm, management may attempt to reduce the number through mechanisation, building the rules into the machine and so depersonalising them. Those who benefit from the rules will resist this type of mechanisation, and if they cannot prevent its introduction they will attempt to gain control over it. At the other end of the spectrum the professional is an example of rule absorption; behavioural rules are built into a professional person's training so that formal organisational rules are less necessary. For example, the teamwork of doctors and nurses in an operating theatre depends less on the existence of formal written rules than upon behaviours developed in training.

Rules are very much part of the political process and as such are often called into question; they are regarded, when politically appropriate, as scapegoats for the troubles of management. The claim is made that there are too many or too few; that no one can act because so many rules make everyone cautious, or that each goes his own way because there are too few rules. These comments reflect a failure to appreciate the use that can be made of rules, or lack of them, in political bargaining within the firm. Rules can be used by managers and workers for their own ends; rules are not neutral.

Similar complaints are made about other aspects of organisation structure, such as the absence or presence of adequate hierarchy; the argument in one case being that hierarchy prevents people developing, they lose their powers of initiative; and in the other case that too little hierarchy leads to too much flexibility with no one knowing what is happening. What really has to be taken into account is that hierarchy is another aspect of organisational structure around which political processes operate; that much of the behaviour attributed to hierarchy is the result of organisational rewards and punishments. Further, the distribution of rewards and punishments is not solely an attribute of organisational structure; it is partly, at least, the result of the bargaining process. Merit is not the only criterion influencing rewards and punishments.

PERSONAL INTERVENTION

Rules provide one form of control; another is through personal intervention by higher levels of management. This may be costly both in time involved and communication overload, as those who intervene do not attend to other pressing concerns and so create a backlog of problems. Information overload also results from their demands for detailed information to enable them to exercise direct control. For example, a chief executive sees problems in one of his divisions and intervenes in its day-to-day working, with the result that he is slow to pick up problems elsewhere in his organisation, makes demands for information which distorts the operation of his management services team and loses sight of the overall strategy of his firm. At the end of the day he withdraws, believing wrongly that he has solved the problems of the ailing division and turns round to find that in the meantime a massive problem has developed in another key division.

Allied to direct intervention by senior management is the resulting centralisation. For reasons of power, personal involvement and centralisation of decisions can be attractive to senior managers. A common device for bringing about this state of affairs is the use of the external threat to create a crisis atmosphere calling for speedy action and decision. Over a period of time a swing effect develops in a firm as it oscillates between centralisation, often springing from some real or imagined external threat, and decentralisation, frequently a response to self-generated information overload. With decentralisation the whole pattern of information-gathering and flows is likely to change. The units who become more heavily involved will demand extra resources in order to undertake the effective collection, analysis and interpretation of information. In general, an increase in peripheral power resulting from decentralisation is likely to be augmented by the additional resources demanded and obtained by the emancipated units.

RECRUITMENT

Another form of control is through recruitment policies and the socialisation of those recruited; the object is control of the

organisation through the network of recruited managers. Ability
and merit are useful attributes, but they are difficult to measure
and do not necessarily produce loyalty, which is a prime
requirement in the establishment of control through management. Too much ability may be seen as a threat to authority and
control. Hiring through the social network minimises the risks of
acquiring a deviant and is consistent with the desire to enhance
control. Naturally firms claim they hire the best, while claiming
that all their appointees are of the same calibre. While this is an
over-optimistic view it reflects the attempts of firms and their
senior managers to homogenise their managers – to get them to
think alike and feel alike. Socialising is part of the manipulative
process exercised by dominant coalitions to maintain their
power. In exerting patronage to acquire commitment, the
dominant coalition is bargaining future resources for present
support; this is evident when it seeks to socialise its management
by giving them a stake in the control process.

Another way to secure uniformity of personnel is through the
production of simple products, requiring basic skills, non-skills
and few specialists; when the latter are required they may be
brought in on a contract basis or, if wholly employed, they may
be sealed off from the main operation. This latter ploy may be
dysfunctional, divorcing the specialist from the sharp end of the
operation, but its value lies in the submerging of visible differences and the creation of opportunities for the main line
production to proceed with limited interruption, and with a
powerful argument against the specialists, 'They do not really
know what it is like here in the kitchen, they cannot stand the
heat.'

Socialisation however is not so clear-cut as those in power
would wish it to be, because organisations are composed of many
different cultures, ideologies, tasks, types of training, backgrounds and new entrants who enter into specific localities
within the firm. They may go through formal induction courses
which are designed to tell them what the organisation does, how
it works and so on, but this is substantially at the formal level.
The real learning takes place elsewhere. In order to survive, the
new entrant has to learn who is really in charge, who has the
really important information and what are the key departments
and dependencies – all those things that are not reflected in the
organisation chart. The existing management plays a key role in

this learning process for they are educators, whether they realise it or not; they provide newcomers and subordinates with cues as to what is and what is not acceptable.

Considered in another way, three types of control can be identified. First, there is the direct, fully obtrusive control, exemplified in the giving of orders and the application of rules, rewards and punishments. Second, there is bureaucratic control in the form of specialisation, standardisation and hierarchy. Finally, there is control of the cognitive premises, which underlie both the making of decisions and the exercise of discretion; through this control the subordinate's range of alternatives is restricted. The premises are found in the 'vocabulary' of the firm, the structure of communications, the language, the style of rules, regulations and standard procedures and in the personnel selection criteria. All these contribute to the internalisation of premises through indoctrination, manipulation and so on. They provide the bases for decisions on future actions and help rationalise the actions that have already been taken. In this sense the thought is not necessarily the father to the deed, the action precedes the thought. Unwittingly the deed is reconstructed because it is believed there must be thought behind it. To admit otherwise would be unnerving, because action appears not to be rationally based. Actions seen in retrospect are given a coherence based upon the internalised premises of managers; the claim is made that some particular set of activities was planned when in fact they were the result of ad hoc decisions taken at particular times. At a personal level managers give their previous careers a planned developmental framework which never existed. Similarly, goals may be merely interpretations of where we have been, not necessarily of where we intended to go.

THE BOARD OF DIRECTORS AND TOP MANAGEMENT

One part of the organisation structure that highlights many of the issues previously discussed is that of top management, including the board of directors.

Organisation structures are many and various; firms exercise choice in the form they adopt and the manner in which they modify and operate it. Nowhere is this more apparent than in top management, where there are a number of varieties of structure for the board and senior management. The board may comprise wholly external part-time directors, or a combination of them with full-time directors with or without executive functions, or simply full-time executive directors. The structure of senior management may also take many forms, rationalised on grounds of theory, practice or persuasion.

The conventional arguments for non-executive directors are, first, that they act as a balancing element between the competing claims of executive directors; second, that being independent they can act both as critics and advisers. Third, they ensure that the long-term interests of the firm are not forgotten, they balance short and long-term considerations, and finally, they can deal with the personal problems of executive directors. The case for the executive director is largely based on his detailed knowledge and understanding of his part of the business. A recognised danger is that he may fail to distinguish between the roles of director and executive and not take a global view of the firm. Michael Edwardes in his restructuring of the B.L. Board opted for a small board, very largely of non-executive directors, on the grounds that strategic debate was easier when numbers were small, nine or ten at most, and that 'it would have been unfair to expect B.L. executives to make decisions about the company at board level which would put their own jobs on the line again and again, and over a considerable period of time.'[5] An underlying consideration may have been a desire to create a board more in tune with his own way of thinking.

Following the line of argument developed in this book, it can be suggested that the executive director will stake claims for his department, the board becoming an arena for negotiations; with the part-time directors, where they exist, involved not only as adjudicators but also as valuable allies to be acquired by the executive directors.

The board of directors provides a microcosm of the wider organisational differences between the formal structure and actual political behaviour, between the stated and the real. The formal basic functions of the board include the following:

1. to establish the longer-term objectives of the company and the strategies by which these can be achieved;
2. to define specific policies on finance, production, personnel,

marketing and so forth, that are to be followed in the implementation of the company's strategy;

3. to decide upon the major organisational structure and to fill key executive positions;
4. to ensure the development of management planning, information and control systems appropriate to the organisation structure and to use these systems effectively to maintain control by the board, at all times, over the results produced by executive management; and
5. to take decisions on such matters as are laid down by law and to reserve to itself any decisions which it does not wish to delegate.[6]

In addition to these formal functions there can be added that of asking discerning questions,[7] with the aim of ensuring that any proposals that are put to the board have been well thought out and that alternatives have been effectively considered.

Many boards perform some of these functions some of the time, others perform all of them some of the time but few, if any, perform all of them all of the time.

So far the board of directors has been considered in formal, almost organisational chart terms. In reality the picture is different, the board in action reflects the need of the firm to deal differentially with various important sectors of the environment; it acts as a boundary spanning unit, relating the firm at its highest levels to the environment. How far it responds to the environment will be a function of its composition, the attitudes of directors and its relationship to top management.

Having placed the board in the context of the firm and its environment we can now turn to its performance – an uncertain area affected by the size of the board, its sub-committee system, its composition, its relationship with top management and the situation of the company at a given time.

Different surveys have suggested that the majority of boards do not take an active part in strategy and policy formulation with the board meetings being simply formal.[8] In some instances non-executive directors sit in on the smaller, regular committee meetings of senior management but this would tend to be exceptional. Decisions are cut and dried at these executive committees and then presented to the full board. The senior management rather than the directors make the bulk of the important decisions; this is true particularly in the area of strategy and policy origination and formulation; the board simply vetoes or confirms decisions taken elsewhere. Only in some limited areas of finance, large-scale capital expenditure, new share issues and dividend does the board exercise a positive approval function, although even this may be tempered by the advice provided by senior management. However, the position is never static and in recent years there have been occasions when powerful institutional investors, such as pension funds, have sought through their board representatives to change the policies and management of firms. In other words the distribution of power in these instances has shifted through movements in the investment policies of large institutions.

Surveys have also shown that executive directors and senior management engage in manipulative strategies aimed at getting proposals through boards; for example, using only generalised estimates of the costs involved in a development and providing the minimum information relating to expected results.[9] This is less startling than may appear at first sight as the relationship between decision, action and results is often ambiguous and uncertain. Senior management aim to control the information that is placed before the board to ensure that 'appropriate' decisions are taken.

Many of the decisions made by the board are of limited importance; it supports its non-decision-making role rather than making the scale of decisions it is formally expected to do. Directors are unlikely to admit too readily to this position, but a study carried out under the aegis of the Department of Employment[10] suggests that while the directors surveyed thought their boards generated policy and made major decisions, it emerged that this was an idealised version of board activity. As in other aspects of organisational life, there exists both an idealised version of what people publicly claim they do, and what actually happens. Much depends on the stage of the life cycle reached by the company and the economic conditions surrounding it; the importance and power of the board is not constant but variable, within limits which are partly of its own making and partly those of others, notably senior management.

It is evident that the manipulative strategies of senior management operate in two stages. First, executive directors meet to decide policy and then second, agree on how it is to be put to the board. The bargaining takes place in the earlier stage when executive directors are involved in trade-offs and commitments. Part of the manipulation process rests in the presentation of one real option – any others are fictions – hence the appearance of consensus and the board's belief that there was agreement. If the board really did generate policy it is highly unlikely that there would be as much agreement as they believe exists; the bargaining, negotiation and trade-offs would move from the executive to board level.

Manipulation of the board takes many forms, such as restricting discussion, vetting board papers and arranging the agenda. In these activities a key figure can be the chairman of the board, for it lies with him to agree the agenda, indicate the importance of different items and guide the discussion; he is part of the power structure of the board and the wider executive arena.

When considering the relationship of the board to senior management it is evident that the key functions of objective setting, strategy and policy-making take place at executive level. These functions are substantially influenced by the type of departmentalisation of top management. This produces the differing areas of special expertise and their relative importance in policy formulation. Each senior manager emphasises the critical significance of his area and the problems with which he has to cope. Their importance will, over time, vary relatively to other departments and be influenced by a complex pattern of factors external and internal to the firm. It is clear there is no one 'correct' set of organisational policies, only talk of policies that will further the goals of some, or all, of the executive participants, who may be forced into a display of unity by outside threats, including the possibility of changes in board personnel which may shift the power distribution between the board and senior management. Michael Edwardes recognised this problem when he wrote 'The restructuring of the board was a vital step, and it had to be done – and was done – in a matter of days, before ranks closed against change. It is always in the first days of a crisis that the situation is fluid; after that the bureaucratic treacle sets again.'[11] No board is permanently captive, it can be triggered into action and, when it asserts itself, seek policy changes that can only be achieved by changes in top management. To forestall this, top management must keep a tight grip on the organisation, knowing who are their supporters. The position is complicated because top management are unlikely to be firmly united, as different members see possibilities as well as threats in any proposed changes. Some will see new top management appointments offering opportunities for progress, for the development of new, more comfortable, managerial styles, for the adoption of ideas which they have advocated in the past but which have been rejected. Others will seek to maintain the status quo, to preserve what power they already have; attempting to take the steam out of any new, possibly threatening policy which the new incoming management might introduce. For them, change is only acceptable if it offers the opportunity to increase their power.

The formulation of policy cannot be divorced from its implementation. The top management originating a policy may also be responsible for its activation. This involves a discretionary element which in turn contributes to the success or failure of policy implementation. Senior management exercises discretion to develop, protect and even thwart a policy inimicable to its interests. The essential untidiness of management and of organisational life is once again apparent as we move away from the clearly defined formal functions of the board and senior management. The notion that boards make policy and management execute it, obscures the subtlety of the relationship.

Surrounding these activities is the segmented environment with its differing interests. Senior management reflects these external interests. The strength of these links will be one of the factors affecting the manner in which the external world is reflected within the firm.

THE CHIEF EXECUTIVE

The formal responsibilities of the chief executive include the profitability of the operation, the growth of the company, its character, its response to change and finally its perpetuation and survival. To fulfil these obligations, using his political skills, he must define the scope of his company's activities, the specific performance criteria, and seek to acquire, conserve and deploy resources among the competing demands of his senior managers. At the same time, he must develop a wide spectrum of policies which relate his firm to the market. If he does not give explicit attention to policy, it will be defined in practice either at lower levels or as a consequence of external events in a series of ad hoc, unrelated decisions which come together to produce some sort of policy. If all management can be said to comprise, in varying degrees, technical, human and conceptual elements, the emphasis for the chief executive must be upon the conceptual, with particular reference to the totality of the firm, the interaction of its departments and its relationship to the external environment. In practice, like all managers, the chief executive is subject to pressures from senior management, customers, shareholders, bankers, suppliers, trade unions and the government, and he has to weigh and balance these pressures in the light of the requirements of the whole organisation. This is what he should do; how far he does it is another matter, being dependent upon his perception of the needs of a specific situation at a given time, the distribution of power in the firm, his own background and experience, the choices he makes between different aspects of his job and whether his preference is for action rather than thought. Overarching all of these is his sensitivity to the art of the possible, to power, conflict and politics.

In this outline of the chief executive there are the following factors to consider:

1. The gulf between the chief executive and his immediate subordinates; his is a unique role, involving responsibility for the whole organisation.
2. His success, and that means the success of his subordinates, will substantially depend upon his sensitivity to the special needs of the different functional areas of the firm, each with its special values and criteria. There is production with its concern for cost reduction, operating efficiency, high degree of certainty and stability; sales, with the emphasis on increasing sales volume, market share and relations with customers; product development with its commitment to high rates of innovation, elegance of design and superior performance.

These, coupled with finance, purchasing, accounting and personnel, lead to differing analyses of shared events and to differing types of power base. All these different specialist functions create procedures aimed at the protection and development of their own positions; they also create functionaries with functions to defend, and constituencies to represent and draw strength from. The situation is rife for political activity and the chief executive has to achieve some measure of balance, knowing that not everybody can be satisfied, that choices have to be made and priorities established. Whatever criteria he stresses most heavily over a period of time will substantially influence the firm's basic orientations for some time ahead and will define its acceptable range of action. In making these choices he acts within a negotiated arena, affected by the current and foreseeable relative power and influence of the different departments, and by his own perspectives.

3. In reaching decisions he has to bear in mind the limitations of the specialist knowledge he is given; that what he decides is best for the total firm is suboptimal from the point of view of some individual managers and their departments; that management of the whole enterprise involves dealing with a great quantity of data, information, activities and events of differing degrees of quality and significance and that among the ensuing patchwork there will be crucial problems and relationships which he must identify. At the same time his role is complementary to the points of view of the individual units. In the light of all these factors he is working in both cooperative and competitive relations with those around him.

This dense pattern of decisions and actions relating to the internal departments has to be linked to the pressures and actions of outside factors. For the chief executive, internal and external factors are inextricably mixed; to lean excessively to one at the expense of the other can have serious consequences for the organisation.

The case of the chief executive links with that of senior management in that much of its political activity is concerned with the subtle skills of control at a distance. The top manager has to find ways of penetrating internal units and external organisations in order to assess what is happening and to influence them so as to gain acceptable responses.

While top management seeks to integrate or coordinate the operations of the firm, paradoxically it is itself not necessarily united. Conflict exists, often in the most potent and significant forms. Decisions are based on a wide variety of criteria, skills, functions and approaches. On occasion age plays a part; older members of senior management will put forward the view that their position on a particular issue is reasonable, while that of younger members is irresponsible, hot-headed and not based on 'what happened last time.' Using the criteria of rationality they aim to disadvantage the younger members and as a by-product take over a promising issue before it becomes the property of rising and potentially powerful managers. Organisational politics is very much concerned with gaining advantages and establishing property rights.

CONCLUSION

In summary, first, the chief executive is involved in a network of organisational members with different competences, skills, values, goals, commitments and degrees of power. The way in which he holds together these different attributes provides an explanation for the specific criteria which have been applied in previous choices and gives some indication of the choices he is likely to make in the future.

Second, the members of his organisation have available to them, immediately or potentially, an aggregation of power which helps shape the alternatives available to the chief executive. Third, these members operate their resources within an environment which provides opportunities and makes demands – it is the combination of these environmental forces which determines, within broad limits, the firm's actions for survival.

Through the chief executive the environment places constraints on what the company should do; the resources available put limits on what it can do, and within these limits the pattern of values, personal competence, influence and power of senior management determine what the firm will do.

Faced with the complexity of his role the following skills contribute to the effectiveness of a chief executive:

1. Conceptualisation – the formation of a total picture of the situation and the pattern of relationships which goes to make up that picture.
2. Perception – the skill to see what is really happening, and sensitivity to the political dimensions of the organisation and its management.
3. Innovation – the ability to think up new developments, or

more realistically the appreciation of the significance of new ideas and proposals when they are put to him.

These three skills are related to reality testing as distinct from functioning; they require the chief executive to face reality and not to fly into utopia.

4. Communication – the skill which contributes to the welding together of management of diverse specialisations and backgrounds into a working, if not harmonious, group.
5. Political skills – relating to others politically in a manner which enhances his actual power to influence and shape not only top management but his external relationships.
6. Decision and action – pulling together all his skills into effective decision and action programmes.

So far the tasks of the chief executive have been discussed in terms of a single individual, but they may be exercised through some form of top management group. This may take the form of ad hoc consultations; semi-formal but part-time executive meetings; full-time executive committees; formalised chief executive cabinets. The last relieves the chief executive of his diverse burden; it brings complementary skills and abilities together to deal more effectively with complex top management tasks, it provides flexibility for both present and developing needs of the business and, finally, it provides a training ground for succession.

It is not necessary to go into all the ramifications of these developments but, in line with the main argument of this book, it will be clear that they all provide many opportunities for political behaviour, power contests and the establishment of areas of negotiation.

The circle can be completed by a return to the relationship of the chief executive and his board, with the following points:

1. Board decisions are only as good as the recommendations upon which they are based and upon the quality of the analyses supporting them.
2. Board decisions are limited by the fact that a variety of executive policy decisions are taken by the chief executive, without reference to the board – the cumulative effect of this is clearly important and reflects again the power dimensions within the relationship of board and chief executive.

3. Almost all of the ongoing implementation of policy depends upon the chief executive's continuous processes of integration, control and motivation; achieved largely through his political skills and his ability to understand the art of the possible, in a changing situation of power and influence.

7 Decision-Making

Decision-making is one of the main functions of management. The classical formulation of the process has been the basis of many approaches to decision-making and problem-solving and is characterised by the following:

1. The manager is faced with a given problem.
2. The rational manager first clarifies his goals, values and objectives and then ranks them in some order of preference.
3. He lists all the possible ways of achieving his goals.
4. He investigates all the important consequences that should follow from each of the alternatives he has developed.
5. He then compares these consequences with his goals.
6. He chooses the alternative with the consequences that most closely match his goals.

Underlying this approach are a number of assumptions.

First, the decision-maker is faced with a problem; this gives the impression that problems come singly to the manager in a clear-cut form. In reality the manager is faced with a complex kaleidoscope of problems to which he gives his own pattern. He defines and formulates problems. Indeed, on occasion, he invents problems when new means or opportunities make new goals possible. (For instance, landing on the moon only became a problem when the technology of space exploration developed.) Between managers there is often room for controversy over what the problems are, and in the majority of cases this cannot be settled by analysis. Here is a point of entry for politics and the so-called irrationalities of decision-making. One apparent irrationality is that the recognition of a problem does not necessarily lead to attempts to resolve it; the parties involved may collude in a manner which prevents resolution. They decide that any practical solution would be too threatening and unsettling.

Second, there is the assumption that there is no limit to the availability of information which flows to the decision-maker.

But information is limited and has to be searched for. The computer may ameliorate this problem while creating another; that of information overload.

Third, it is assumed that the decision-maker has a well-defined preference ordering over possible future situations; that is, he clearly prefers A to B and B to C and C to D. Yet frequently this is not the case; in different times and situations the individual's preferences, their ordering and levels of expectations change. Even at the same time and in the same place an individual's preferences may be uncertain because of his inability to attach cost and benefits clearly to them.

Fourth, it is held that the manager seeks to maximise expected returns from his decisions, yet for many reasons he may accept satisfactory rather than maximum solutions.

Finally, there is a belief in a simple cause-effect relationship, when in fact the number of variables and the varying degrees of uncertainty make the outcomes of decisions much more problematic than would appear from this system.

At the core of this approach to decision-making there is the notion of the rational manager. This underplays the fact that a manager, indeed any human being, has limited rationality. It is an additional misconception to think too much in terms of the individual decision-maker, when normally he is part of a network of relationships which contribute to the overall decision-making process. This questioning of the rationality of management often produces strong reaction for 'there is no norm so central to the existing practice and ideology of management as the norm of rationality'.[1]

In place of the rational decision-maker as outlined in the classical formulation, we could place one of 'bounded' or 'limited' rationality. This explicitly recognises the limited rationality of management; the incomplete knowledge upon which to base decisions or know all the consequences of the available alternatives; the cost of searching for knowledge. Because of the cost of searching for data the manager has, at some time, to call a halt and make a decision on the information available to him. In this sense all decisions are made on incomplete evidence. Not only is the information limited but it is selective; managers hear what they want to hear and read that which reflects their own dispositions, in this they are like everyone else. Of course if a manager wants to avoid reaching a decision he will find it useful to ask for more and more information. In pursuing this tactic he achieves two ends: he gives the appearance of a conscientious decision-maker and he delays the decision. Finally, pressure on the manager normally prevents him sitting down and preparing an exhaustive list of alternatives before making a decision; in general he grossly simplifies the alternatives that are available and selects the first that is satisfactory to him and acceptable to those who have to be convinced.

Given these limitations on rationality, what does the manager do? From the real situation he constructs a simplified model which is built on past experience, prejudices, stereotypes, expectations and highly selective views of the present situation. Most of his responses are routine; he invokes solutions he has used before in situations which appear to him to be similar. Sometimes the routine is inadequate so he conducts a limited search for alternatives along familiar and well-worn paths. He does not examine all possible alternatives, nor does he keep searching for the optimum one. He accepts the satisfactory rather than the optimal, and his standards of what is satisfactory are part of his initial definition of the situation. His standards change with differing experience as solutions are easier or more difficult to find, being raised when solutions are easy and falling when they are harder.

Behaviour based upon bounded rationality takes place within an organisational context which sets out standards and provides information. The premises for decisions are influenced by other managers, some of whom have more or less power than the particular decision-maker. These managers will exert influence in a number of ways:

1. they can contribute to the definition of what is satisfactory behaviour and an acceptable decision;
2. they can encourage the pursuance of sequential and limited search processes that are only mildly innovative;
3. they can structure the situation through the specialisation of activities and roles so that attention is directed to a restricted set of goals and values;
4. they can shape the decision-making process. Joel Barnett as Chief Secretary to the Treasury gives many illustrations of this in his '*Inside the Treasury*'.[2] He particularly underlines the

significance of manipulating time in the decision-making process by various delaying tactics, by the insertion of important items on to the Cabinet agenda at ten minutes to one, when there is little time for discussion and a decision must be reached by one o'clock. Both Lord Boyle and Anthony Crosland stressed the importance of time in coping with decisions.[3] Lord Boyle's willingness to regard arguments as open, created a Ministerial style which resulted in the avoidance of instant decisions. Anthony Crosland created time by tackling one subject at a time and telling his officials that other matters would have to wait;

5. they can channel decision-making behaviour through 'attention directors', that is, rewards and punishments;
6. by the establishment of rules, programmes and control systems they can limit choice in recurring situations and prevent an agonising process of decision-making on each occasion by setting up a series of programmed decisions;
7. they can train and indoctrinate the individual manager to make decisions which have the appearance of independence but which reflect the desires of those with power;
8. by splitting up goals and tasks into programmes that are semi-independent of each other, they can reduce interdependence and restrict the impact of decisions; and
9. they can control the channels of communication and their contents.

By these methods the premises on which decisions are made are shaped, not by the individual decision-maker, but by the complex network of power and influence that surrounds him. It would be taking too static a view to believe that the individual decision-maker is totally shaped by his surroundings; he also makes a contribution, the size of which is influenced by his own power and ability to carry the system with him – he cannot carry decisions simply by virtue of clear thinking.[4]

Decision-making has to be considered within the political framework of the organisation; indeed decisions can be seen as the outcome of political processes rooted in power and influence.

Important as the political context is, it would create a false picture if the individual's contribution was not made clear. In the first place his goals are unlikely to be identical with those of the organisation, they are shaped by his perception of his own interests and those of his department. Consequently in his decision-making he will exhibit a number of biases:

1. In his perception of the problem he will screen out adverse aspects and magnify those favouring his interests; he must not make the matter too black and white as he may be thought to be weighing the scales too obviously in his own favour.

2. Second, in formulating alternatives he will tend to give undue preference to those most favourable to his interests and on which he believes adequate agreement can most easily be reached. So the manager will often stay with a set of alternatives rather than expand it, even though such a development might give him a better choice. Given this position, the order in which the manager assembles and evaluates his alternatives can be extremely important for the ensuing action. The biases that systematically cause him to evaluate certain types of alternative early on in the decision process, will cause these alternatives to be adopted by him more often than they would be if he exhibited no bias. Similarly this would apply in cases of groups' decisions, where the dominant bias would tend to ensure the alternatives were presented in an order which favoured those in power. As simple proposals are usually easier to discuss for obtaining agreement than more complex ones, these tend to be considered first. Where this occurs regularly over a period of time the simple decision may push the organisation into positions that are out of line with its requirements.

When a manager is preparing a decision that requires support from others he will frame his alternatives with them in mind. For example, if they are people who are only marginally concerned but whose voice is influential and who require some quid pro quo for their support, it may be necessary to include something in the alternatives that benefits them even though it does not affect the major issue, or it may be necessary to omit alternatives that harm the interests of powerful individuals even if the firm would benefit. The existence of such 'territorial bargaining' has a number of implications:

1. Managers and their departments will choose alternatives that unduly favour continuation of the existing allocation of resources and power wherever it is propitious to them.

2. Managers will try to exclude marginal effects so as to reduce the amount of agreement required. This will narrow the impact of the decision and hopefully reduce the area of bargaining.
3. The alternatives that are formulated will be affected by the methods of the particular organisation; for example, the way in which the search for information is carried out and by whom; the manner in which information is communicated within the firm.
4. If an initial set of alternatives has been rejected, a manager will either abandon the project, or search for wholly new proposals, or reformulate the rejected ones. If those which have been rejected had significant but insufficient support, the manager is likely to give time and attention to reformulation.
5. He will seek alternatives involving as little uncertainty as possible in order to avoid complications and conflict which might endanger the negotiations. Over a period of time a manager will tend to make decisions that do not take sufficient account of future uncertainties.

All these implications raise political issues requiring political skills. The decision-maker's approach will influence and be influenced by the distribution of power around him.

THE IMPORTANCE OF INFORMATION SEARCH

From what has been said it will be evident that information and the search for it are essential elements in the decision-making process. Decisions are influenced by the willingness or otherwise of the decision-maker(s) to seek out and use information, bearing in mind that the discovery and production of data may adversely upset his present position. Selectivity and bias are everpresent and to avoid them, or at least reduce them, a firm can assign overlapping responsibility for data search to persons with different and conflicting interests or to people unconnected with the particular problem.

What a manager and his department attend to, and hence what information they require, is influenced by their prime responsibility for a narrow set of problems. This encourages parochialism, a trend that is further encouraged by,

1. the selection of information available to the department;
2. the recruitment of personnel;
3. the tenure of the individuals;
4. the pressures exerted upon the department;
5. the distribution of rewards and punishments in the wider organisation; and
6. the attitudes prevailing in the organisation. For example, if a firm is unprogressive it is unlikely to secure the talented direction which might revive it;[5] its decisions will be inward looking, narrow and firmly fixed in the status quo. If information is to be widely sought there is a need to make a conscious effort to look beyond the firm. It can be very dangerous in an organisation if there is widespread acceptance of the view that new ideas must not be allowed to enter. This rejection of innovation can take a number of forms:

   a. There are the mindguards – the gatekeepers who ensure that unpleasant information does not filter through to the decision-makers. This is just a particular example of the general tendency in business and politics to fudge the figures.[6]
   b. There are the illusions of morality, expressed in the belief that what is being done in the firm is essentially moral in contrast to what is happening outside.
   c. There is the stereotyping of opposition, in which the competition is dismissed by caricaturing.
   d. There are the illusions of impregnability, of the belief that because the organisation is large nothing adverse can affect it.

All these factors lead to the distortion of the available information upon which decisions are made. Additional distortion occurs when a manager presents an argument in a way which will show himself and his department in the best possible light. The danger of spreading half-truths and putting forward a steady and immediate flow of uncollaborated facts in order to influence or support a decision, leads to a lack of questioning, to viewing situations in over-simplified terms. This may initially make life easier for the decision-maker and increase his power, while storing up trouble in the long run.

The search for information is a critical activity in the decision process. The shape of the search differs according to the decision stage reached; in the early stages, the search will extend sideways as alternatives are sought, and then forwards as the solving of early problems leads to a concentration on later ones and to the re-examination of possible consequences. As this latter stage is undertaken, solutions may lead to a rethinking of earlier thoughts on possible solutions. A decision which appears to solve a problem will normally produce others. The notion that there is a single solution which will 'solve' a given problem is to misunderstand the complexities and uncertainties involved in the human situation – the entire decision process is uncertain and dynamic and consequently rife for political behaviour.

Facts influencing the extent and nature of the search for solutions include,

1. the conspicuousness of alternatives;
2. dissatisfaction with the available solutions acting as stimulus to further search;
3. the ability of those undertaking the search to recognise cues as to which lines of inquiry are worth pursuing;
4. the readiness to reformulate goals as a result of information collected during the search activity or because of ideas introduced by an innovating group;
5. the restriction of search to areas of the manager's own experience and knowledge; and
6. the ability of those involved to handle large amounts of data.

Search is a cost, involving the investment of both tangible and intangible resources. The cost differences of search can be contrasted in short- and long-term decisions involving capital expenditure. In a short-term decision it may well be assumed that capital equipment will remain unchanged, hence no search will be undertaken in this area. In contrast, in the long-term decision there may be the assumption that capital equipment will have to be replaced and in consequence considerable time will be devoted to a search for information relating to replacement equipment. Capital equipment can be costly both in its own right and in terms of the search that has to be undertaken when it is to be replaced – the replacement of a computer often turns out to be time-consuming, a fact which is well-documented in Pettigrew's *The Politics of Organizational Decision-Making*[7].

Taken together these two factors help to explain the prevalence of routine in large organisations and the fact that it is not possible to change expensive plant every time there is a slightly better equipment design available – the time element in the cost of search is one element militating against speedy change. The relatively low capital cost of new decisions in small organisations may go some way to explaining their greater flexibility, and thus their advantage in situations where frequent decisions are needed.

Another factor in the decision and search process is the pressure of time; under pressure, decisions will be made by relying on less information than would be the case if there were more time. Another possibility is that some managers will exert pressure to close off a search because they do not want more information, as Keynes remarked, 'There is nothing a government [organisation] hates more than to be well-informed; for it makes the process of arriving at decisions much more complicated and difficult.'[8] Search is often limited because decisions are rarely made from a clean slate. The information obtained contains much from the past; the options available are defined significantly in the decision premises; the organisation's capabilities and the location of the decision-makers help shape the appearance of an issue, and both the capabilities and location are the result of earlier decisions.

One powerful factor which does influence search is the previous experience of the manager. Through knowing this it is possible to judge the likely shape of today's decisions and roughly predict how matters will be decided in the future. Of course the progression is not inevitable, but the tendency is there, especially in those firms where the emphasis is on experience, and particularly when promotion and management succession are based on experience. Presented with a complex situation in which he has to make decisions, the manager sees what he is ready to see, and the more complex its structure the more is his perception determined by what is already 'in' the manager and less by what is in the situation.[9]

A further dilemma for the manager is that the need for reliable information may mean involving people at lower levels of the firm. He may well be reluctant to do this as it could undermine his control of the decision process; the gain in information may be at the cost of some loss of power.

THE INTELLIGENCE FUNCTION

Decision-making involves an 'intelligence' function which has three aspects; first, information has to be acquired through search, then analysed, interpreted and finally put into the hands of the decision-makers.[10] Intelligence is not simply storing, indexing and retrieving data; it involves creative elements which combined with its ability to increase or decrease uncertainty, gives those involved organisational power bases. This is not always recognised. For example, for many years both the British and American intelligence services were held in low regard. In consequence 'many men of average or less than average professional competence who were thus detailed for intelligence confirmed the low estimate that had already been made of the value of intelligence work'.[11] As this assessment has changed, antipathy has increased as the power of intelligence has been recognised and because of 'the anti-intellectualism of fighting men'. A similar pattern of developments occurred in business where anti-intellectualism was fuelled by the spasmodic recognition that ordinary knowledge[12] and casual analysis was often sufficient and as good as, if not better than, professional social inquiry for managerial problem-solving. Information specialists, and others engaged in the search for and analysis of information, often overestimate the distinctiveness of the information and analyses they produce for the decision-makers; they underestimate management's use of existing stocks of information as well as the flow of new 'ordinary' knowledge from other managerial sources. Much ordinary language owes its origin to common sense, casual empiricism and thoughtful speculation. Much of this ordinary knowledge comes from experience, from social and political interaction and behaviour. Political interaction is not simply overt bargaining, it builds knowledge through tacit reciprocity; deference to adversaries and forms of mutual adjustment at a distance.

Information specialists and others who provide inputs for decision-making often overstate the conclusiveness of the material they produce. The result is that if their findings are accepted, decisions may be flawed and result in serious practical failings. For example, some social science findings which have been fed into management to provide a basis for managerial decisions and actions, are limited in their application and, when applied widely, are likely to fail or fall short of the expectations that have been raised. It has to be appreciated that something may be conclusive but not authoritative and as such does not warrant action. Much of the failure of specialist knowledge and information relating to non-technical areas is due to non-rational responses to such data; to the inability of such knowledge to cope with normative issues; to its tendency, because of problem definition, to raise more issues than it solves.

The information provided for the decision-makers is often used as a weapon in the political struggle between those involved in making the decision. Since many key problems remain on the firm's agenda for years, the political tactics are complex and there is an evershifting redefinition of the continuing problem. In these cases much of the information demanded by the decision-makers is required in order to display the 'rationality' of their behaviour. Specialist social knowledge can be regarded as part of a ritual to give assurance; people feel better if they make their decisions after the ceremonies of analysis, however inconclusive, have been performed.

Much of the work of the information providers is concerned with uncertainty absorption. Any organisation develops a set of concepts, a classification scheme, a language of its own, all of which facilitate communication. Anything that does not fit easily into this framework is not readily communicated. This is apparent when a body of information is edited and summarised in order to make it fit the existing framework of communication and language. To make it understandable, summaries and conclusions drawn from the raw data are transmitted rather than the raw material. In this situation the manager can disbelieve the information he is given but he cannot check it unless he undertakes the summarising and assessment himself, or he sets up a double checking mechanism. The personnel who handle the raw data have considerable discretion and influence through their absorption of quantities of 'uncertainty'. Decisions are made on the abbreviated information which has been shaped to fit the organisation's communications culture and at the same time is the product of people who have a position to maintain and improve. The power of those who 'smooth' or 'absorb' the data is particularly significant at the boundary of the organisation; for example, the marketing people perceive the market through their own perceptions and the information they transmit is shaped by those perceptions and in line with their power position. They have additional strength because it is even more difficult to check their summarised versions of the outside world, than it is to monitor the information on matters generated by internal departments.

The achievement of agreement in a decision context will be affected by the number of information sources that are utilised and the degree to which uncertainty absorption is centralised in a single unit. Clearly there will be many situations where centralisation is not possible; for instance, where powerful departments are dealing with different sections of the external environment. In this situation there is less likely to be ready agreement, as the information about the environment, especially if the latter is undergoing change, is often imprecise and inaccurate.

UNCERTAINTY

Decisions involve uncertainty, which can be the result of (a) a lack of clear objectives, (b) the long time-gap before there is any definitive feedback on action resulting from former decisions and (c) because of the general variability of causal relations. Faced with uncertainty, managers seek to cope or circumvent it by concentrating on short-term issues and avoiding, as far as possible, long-term strategies.

When decision-making by senior management is made difficult by uncertainty, a number of different tactics exist to counter it.

First, senior management may use experts, believing that they will present an 'objective' view of the situation – this fails to allow for the possibility of political behaviour on the part of the experts.

Second, top management may establish planning procedures, introduce guidelines and strengthen administrative processes. Here there is the possibility of a pathological situation developing, for while firms may need to change, the use of experts and planning procedures may lead them to resist change on the grounds of the objectivity of their behaviour.

Third, they may use contingency decisions, that is, faced with a lack of information, management may take a decision hoping that it will lead to an outcry and to the emergence of information previously hidden within the firm; with this feedback the decision is altered.

Fourth, senior management may undertake additional political activity, aimed at confrontation as a means of clearing the air.

When senior management achieve greater certainty, those at lower levels may experience an increased uncertainty, or loss of power, because the balance of certainty has swung still further away from them. They do not know what is happening, have not been involved and are not in a position to manipulate the new situation.

Faced with uncertainty, decisions may be considered in terms of 'muddling through' or incrementalism.[13] This approach starts from the position that it is not easy to agree on objectives and, in consequence, decisions will be taken without first clarifying objectives. What happens is that, simultaneously, the decision-makers choose an objective as they decide what they will do. The objective arises out of the decision to act. What is more, the choice is made between marginal differences; the decision-makers focus on marginal or incremental issues.

Given this view of decision-making it is not possible to evaluate alternatives in the light of pre-ordained objectives. The test of a 'good' decision is that various people agree on it, and are prepared to go along with it without necessarily agreeing on its complete appropriateness. The analysis of alternatives is drastically limited; in consequence simplification occurs, crucial consequences are not considered, important objectives are neglected and significant values are not discussed. Finally, decisions go through a series of successively marginal, limited comparisons, differing in small degree from policies and actions that are at present in operation. It reduces the number of alternatives to be investigated and simplifies the character of the investigation. In this approach decisions are not made on a once and for all basis but proceed by a series of successive adjustments, invoking objectives that are part of the continuing state of flux.

In this situation, decision is a rough process, achieving limited but acceptable success. The advantages claimed for it are,

1. progression through a series of incremental decisions avoids serious, lasting and large mistakes;
2. the past provides information for the present;

3. it avoids big jumps and never expects a final solution;
4. it allows managers to test previous predictions as they move from one step to another; and
5. it makes it possible to remedy past errors fairly quickly.

The weakness of this approach is that it can lead to overlooking excellent opportunities because they are not suggested by the chain of incrementalism. It has much in common with the politics of compromise and is at some considerable distance from the blueprints of grand planning. In its association with managerial politics it is linked with the distribution of power in the organisation and underlines the weakness of those outside the immediate incremental area – the subtlety of incrementalism helps camouflage what is being decided.

Faced with its shortcomings some have advocated mixed scanning decisions, which seek to combine rational decision making for fundamental issues with incrementalism for less significant decisions. 'Whether or not a series of incremental decisions is, by itself, less effective than a fundamental decision is an open question, but the question is much less important than it appears if we take into account the relationship between fundamental and incremental decisions. ... We suggest that (a) most incremental decisions specify or anticipate fundamental decisions, and (b) the cumulative value of the incremental decisions is greatly affected by the underlying fundamental decisions.'[14] Fundamental decisions are treated to a broad search process which is predominantly concerned with the coverage of alternatives, but limited in its concern for detail. Less significant decisions within the major ones are less concerned with alternatives and concentrate more on details and particularly on consequences. However, in real-life situations, at any level of management, rational decision processes are liable to become distorted by political factors that are not always evident or explicit, and issues are not readily separable into fundamental and incremental categories.

In order to exercise some control over the mass of decisions that have to be taken in an organisation, senior management may use the principle of management by exception. This allows the firm to operate within a framework of assumptions it would be too expensive to question continually, and the automatic reporting of significant deviations at once effectively separates the decisions to review the situation from the substantive decisions which may follow. It reduces the importance of the decision to review by making it routine. It is an example of the wider notion of programmed decision-making. This type of almost automatic decision-making is liable to be less effective than scientific management might believe, as it can drive out unprogrammed, long-term and often critical decision-making; it can discriminate against the less easily measurable and can emphasise those quantitative aspects of performance on which a manager is checked. Much of this is aimed at uncertainty avoidance, that is, procedures are used which emphasise the short-run feedback and play down the future because of the reluctance to base action upon uncertainty. It can also provide a framework behind which political activity carries on.

Despite all the difficulties, decisions are made and their effectiveness is often out of all proportion to the almost random processes that occur when problems are solved. There is always the element of judgement, intuition, rule of thumb, call it what you will, it cannot be analysed. As John Kennedy remarked, 'The essence of ultimate decision remains impenetrable to the observer often indeed to the decider. There will always be the dark and tangled stretches in the decision-making process – mysterious even to those who may be most internally involved.'[15] Clearly the decision-maker has to rely less on learned formulae than on the kind of improvisation learned in practice, the best of decision-makers know more of their craft than they can put into words, they represent 'reflection in action.'

ORGANISATIONAL DECISION-MAKING

Joint decision-making at the organisational level differs from that of the individual manager. In the latter case many of the stages of decision-making are undertaken by the individual and coordinated by him; in the former there is both an organisational division of labour of the parties involved and of the decision process itself.

Because of specialisation within an organisation, various forms of interdependence develop which are played out in the joint decision-making process. The result is a heterogeneity of issues, an absence of clear-cut priorities and the involvement of competing in the processes of raising of issues and the generation of support for them. The scope of an issue and the strength with which it is put forward reflects a unit's perception of how critical it is for survival. Success in furthering a unit's interests in the decision process will be a consequence of the ability to generate support for its demands within the decision-making group and from external sources. The point is illustrated by Barnett, 'When a request for money was considered in isolation, a Minister would find it easier to get backing from other Ministers. It was a different matter when it came to the annual public expenditure hassle in the Cabinet. Then it was every spending Minister for himself, with each fighting for more cash – or fewer cuts – in his or her programme,'[16]

The various steps in the organisational decision/action cycle involve, and are carried out by, many people. This fact adds to the cost of the individual decision – coordination involves cost.

1. There are losses of utility due to errors in the transmission of data, information and other material between the various units in the different stages of the decision. We may consider these stages as: first, the recognition of a problem or opportunity upon which a decision has to be made. When the problem is recognised there is the question of whether to live with it or set going an investigation into the matter. Here it is worth distinguishing between 'Not deciding questions that are not now pertinent, not deciding prematurely, and not making decisions that others should make.'[17] The existence of different interested parties will tend to complicate this initial decision. Investigation will be initiated if the probable solutions are thought to be advantageous to the initiating individual or unit: if the issue seems simple and not disruptive; if it is easily divisible and can be tried out piecemeal and if it is easy to communicate. What is important here is who first identifies the problem or issue, what power they exercise, who decides to proceed with an investigation and who can stop it once it is underway. At this stage some have more concern with investigatory procedures than others; for example, a management services department will attempt to sell the potential seriousness of not tackling the issue and advocate a computer-based solution, indicating its readiness to undertake the investigation and feed in the results to the decision-

making process. At this point there is a two-way or 'mating' process: there are those who are seeking solutions and there are those who have solutions and are looking for problems.

The second stage is intelligence seeking, where there is an awareness of the issue and of the possibility of a solution – here we are back to the question of search and the factors which influence it. The third stage is of designing and testing alternatives. Finally there is the matter of choice, of deciding what will be the best or most appropriate solution in the light of the organisation's goals as perceived through the filter of the goals of the decision-maker. Once the decision is made there is the question of implementation.

This is deliberately a simplified stage model as at each stage decisions are taken, often by different people with different degrees of power, each concerned to order the process in their own interest.

2. At any stage in the decision process and in the communication of the decision to those who have to implement it, there are losses of utility due to distortion. As we have seen, some of this distortion is deliberate, some of it is an almost inevitable result of the communication process with its structural problems, barriers, 'noise' and personal commitments.

3. Resources are involved in the communication activity, not least that of time, and frequently management is unwilling to give the necessary time to communicating its decisions. A manager who has been involved for months in a particular issue becomes so used to the arguments that he assumes people understand the data, the alternatives and the reasons for the final solution, so that when he comes to communicate the decision he has run out of steam, he wants simply to get it over. He assumes that those who have to implement it will understand everything he has to say; he will short circuit his reasoning. The decision having been made, he is off to the next problem. Because of this he fails to take time to put himself in the implementer's position and ask what this will mean to him. The knowledge implicit in the decision, coupled with the authority and power of the individual transmitting it, weighs the scales against the recipient taking up any uncertainties and doubts. In reply to this it might be argued that the recipient ought to challenge the transmitters of the decision, and that he will do so if the appropriate levels of

trust and confidence have been built up between the parties. This is to miss the whole point, that management is largely about power and that power is usually very unevenly spread, so that the recipient of a decision feels in no position to make a challenge; if he does he is liable to be regarded as rocking the boat, as a trouble-maker, as 'dim'. Of course there are firms and occasions when a challenge is made but this is most likely when the disparity in power is not so great that the recipient will be seriously damaged. Senior managers frequently fail to recognise this authority imbalance in their communication system and will believe that because they have called a meeting, announced a decision and asked for comments and received none, all is well. They fail to recognise that because of their position, subordinates are unwilling to challenge them. When different managers have varying degrees of sensitivity to these issues there are likely to be differences in interpretation and understanding on the part of the recipients.

4. In the short run there can be losses of utility due to overloading the communication channels. The more decisions that have to be made, the more that have to be modified, the greater the possibility they will reach the recipient late and delay implementation, or they will reach him in garbled form, or will not be heard or listened to. Information and decision saturation is a modern organisational disease, with a confluence of developments which add to this overload. First, the computer can and frequently does provide too much information. Second, there is the present orthodoxy that people want, and should be given, a great deal of information so that they 'know' what is happening, and if they 'know' it is held they will be more committed; a jump which is by no means certain. Third, there is the real or imagined increase in the rate of change in modern society, which means that many more and complex decisions have to be made and transmitted. In the face of these factors, communication channels are liable to become overloaded and people do not get the basic information they require; in too many firms there is an overdose of interesting information that is not relevant to the individual to whom it is addressed – it is useful to head office but not to plant management. Whether we approve or not, the idea that people must be informed can and in many cases does go too

far. Of course there will be those who cry out that not enough information is available, but the reasons for this demand for information must be put into the context of power, and often the demand for information reflects a demand for power on the part of the few, under cover of the argument for the many.

When different departments or groups of managers come together for the purpose of joint decision-making, some of the problems of the individual decision-maker take on a heightened form. First, uncertainties in knowledge of the present and future environment can lead to demands for more information, investigation, research, analysis and better predictions. Second, where there are uncertainties about appropriate value judgements, arguments arise over the need for the clarification of objectives, goals, policies and values. Third, there are uncertainties about intentions in related fields of activity; there will be a demand for more coordination, for a more comprehensive approach, for more strategic thinking and a redefinition of the problem in more global terms. This point is brought out in a letter from Sir Winston Churchill to Lord Halifax on the Narvik operation,

> I see such immense walls of prevention, all built and building, that I wonder whether any plan will have a chance of climbing over them. Just look at the arguments which have had to be surmounted in the seven weeks we have discussed this Narvik operation.
> First, the objections of the other Economic Departments. ... Secondly, the Joint Planning Committee. Thirdly, the Chiefs of Staff Committee. Fourthly, the insidious argument, "don't spoil the big plan for the sake of the small", when there is really very little chance of the big plan being resolutely attempted. Fifthly, the juridical and moral objections, all gradually worn down. Sixthly, the attitude of neutrals. ... Seventhly, the Cabinet itself, with its many angles of criticism. Eighthly, when all this has been smoothed out, the French have to be consulted. Finally, the Dominions and their consciences have to be squared, they not having gone through the process by which opinion has advanced at home.[18]

The three sets of demands are part and parcel of the political process. They can have the effect of delaying decisions and giving participants the possibility of strengthening their bargaining position, of regrouping within the decision group, of keeping discussions going so that the problems disappear or are transformed, and threats are held at bay. All of these possibilities are covered by the legitimised arguments that 'we want to make the right decisions', 'we want to improve efficiency and effectiveness' and 'it is all for the good of the organisation'.

In terms of the impact of structure upon group decision-making, a variety of factors come into play besides that of the division of labour.

First, there are the organisational positions held by the decision-makers, for this affects the scope, depth and time span of the decisions that can be taken; they will also influence the resources that are available to implement them and help legitimise the decisions in the eyes of those who have to execute them.

Second, there are the relationships of the decision-makers with the external environment. These external contacts may be a source of strength or weakness, requiring them to enter into commitments which powerfully shape the decisions that are made.

Third, the technological basis of an organisation partially influences the degree of socialisation and interdependence within it, and helps shape the pattern and content of decision-making through its contribution to the distribution of power within the firm. Additionally, the use of computers affects decision-making, producing more information more readily; with the result that a wider range of alternatives can be generated and manipulated. Yet it must not be forgotten that it is human beings who programme the computer, set goals, manipulate the information and make the final decision as to which alternative shall be chosen.

Fourth, there is the intelligence activity. The disposition of resources between internal and external intelligence operations will depend upon the importance attached to the respective problems, generated in and out of the organisation. The type of personnel employed in intelligence activities will both affect and be affected by the issues upon which information is required. Facts and figures men will tend to collect one type of intelligence, and qualitatively inclined men will gather another. In both instances there may be dissonance, the intelligence gathered may not fit the essential problem.

Fifth, political activity which is interwoven into the communication and control systems can obstruct the effectiveness of their technical functioning, and hence of the decisions reached.

Finally, there is the factor of chance, which may well influence who rises to powerful positions in the organisation and hence to important decision-making roles.

SPECIAL INTELLIGENCE UNITS

These organisational factors, though not based upon the division of labour between the major functions of the firm, can lead to the separation of the activities of search, analysis and evaluation. For example, while individual departments may wish to develop their own intelligence activities in order to ensure control over them, senior management may decide to establish a centralised intelligence unit. This may occur because the senior decision-makers consider the sources of relevant information to be remote from them in terms of space, technical speciality, or cultural unfamiliarity. Another reason could be that general data is useful to managers working on widely different types of decision and should be available from a common source. Investment has to be made to obtain information through a specialist unit and this represents a 'barrier' fee which senior management may be reluctant to pay, deciding to go along with what they can obtain cheaply, or to join with others in joint information-seeking ventures such as might be found in some types of trade association.

With the establishment of a separate unit to conduct research, analysis and evaluation functions, the problem emerges of the relationship between it and its users. These will be influenced by the unit's relationship with the chief executive and senior management and its desire to augment its own position and power, its monopoly of critical information, its exaggeration of the need for secrecy, its emphasis on those types of information which are likely to contribute to its own significance and its stress on the value of expensive data collection in order that it may obtain a greater share of available resources. The separation of the intelligence function, like that of any specialist unit, has important implications for resource allocation and political behaviour.

The users of the unit may well be ambivalent towards it, seeing it both as a rival for resources and a service to be extensively used. Given the law of free goods it can be overloaded with demands, some of which may be intended to demonstrate its inadequacies with a view to devaluing it, so as to influence future resource allocation and ultimately to capture control of the activity. An example comes from a firm where a new chief executive decided to move divisional budgetary controllers to head office to operate under the financial controller. The divisional managers saw this as a threat to their position and only agreed to the new arrangement on condition that they had direct access to their former budgetary controllers, without reference to the financial controller. With this achieved, the divisional managers made heavy demands on budgetary control, arguing that this was due to their loss of authority over their budgetary controllers. The real reason for their behaviour turned out to be their loss of a useful resource, for they had previously used their budgetary control staff for a wide variety of activities. Faced with heavy demands, the manager of an intelligence unit will seek either to formally price his unit's services or introduce non-pecuniary pricing, such as demanding reciprocal favours, threatening long delays over the requests of non-cooperative users and the development of the red-tape barrier.

Finally, the output of such a unit will be utilised in different ways as each part of the organisation will evaluate it in the light of its own interests; some will exaggerate its important while others will play it down. Scepticism may result, leading decision makers to set up their own intelligence activities, to disregard the information being provided by the unit and to fail to take heed of accurate alarm bells. The setting up of private monitoring systems to check on head office information is a not unknown feature of organisations, where managers are evaluated on the basis of head office information.

THE IMPLEMENTATION OF DECISIONS

There is usually a considerable gap between what is decided and what is actually implemented. Operations are generally blunt instruments; there may be talk of fine tuning but in the end the obstacles to such sensitivity are considerable, as can be seen from the following list:

1. Decisions that demand existing organisational units depart from their established procedures to perform unprogrammed tasks, can rarely be implemented effectively, unless the pay-off for doing so is substantial and clearly identifiable.
2. Decisions that require coordination of the programme of several diverse departments or organisations are rarely accomplished as desired. NASA, with its very large number of contractors and support systems, faced many problems of coordination and had to develop ways of managing diversity.
3. Where an assigned segment of a decision is contrary to the goals of the unit expected to execute it, resistance will be encountered. For example, a production department which has always produced high quality products can find it very difficult to adjust to manufacturing low quality products.
4. Decisions will only be implemented as long as external circumstances do not impose crippling restraints on their activation. The problem here is that these circumstances are frequently outside the control of the managers.
5. For successful implementation there must be adequate time and resources and though assessments and estimates of requirements may be made, these can be found wanting. It is not sufficient to have time and resources available in aggregate, the required combination must be actually available at each stage of implementation. Bottlenecks will develop when essential combinations of resources are not available when needed.
6. Decisions are based upon assumed cause-effect chains. A decision may be ineffective not so much because it is badly implemented, but because of an inadequate understanding, in the decision process, of the problem to be solved, its causes, its cures and its consequences.
7. Implementation is affected by the extent of agreement upon the objectives of the decisions.
8. The original decision cannot always display in specific, complete detail, and in perfect sequence, the tasks to be performed by each implementer. In consequence there will inevitably be some exercise of discretion and improvisation

in the most carefully planned decision, with the result that there is liable to be some modification of the original decision.

9. Implementation depends upon communication, and the many technical, political and social barriers to communication are liable to distort, delay and produce different results from those originally predicted.

10. Implementation rests on the belief that those in authority can and will obtain the necessary obedience; that there will be no resistance to directives at any point in the implementation process. In practice, opposition may not surface but there may well be some form or other of passive resistance.

Idealised conditions for successful implementation quickly explode in the face of organisational power and politics; consequently formal decisions are usually only half-way stations on the path to action. The slippage between decision and action can be substantial because once the decision is taken, the political arena expands and takes on new dimensions.

What, then, emerges as the decision-implementation activity is far removed from the rational management model. What is involved is not simply a decision, it is a range of talking, of more talking and considering and recommending, informing and reinforcing. Decision-making moves spasmodically within a restricted set of possible priorities; it switches from one line to another with a different aspect being considered at different times, with each being given different weight during the process. It gradually arrives at a compromise that will do for the time being, within the present bounds of power and possibility. It muddles through to a satisfactory state. Those with interests at stake use their power to shape the premises upon which the decisions will be made, and lay down the limits of what will be considered.

A decision is arrived at within a power structure in which various interests prefer certain outcomes even before the decision process has begun. There is a possible collection of decision-makers looking for opportunities; solutions look for problems to which they may be the 'right' answer; and there are feelings looking for an issue on which they can come out into the open. Power is present not simply in the decisions but also in the non-decisions; for besides the initiating, vetoing and deciding, there are the dynamics of non-decision-making. Someone decides that a decision is not necessary; his ability to ensure that no decision is taken will depend upon the substantive issue under consideration and his power.

The decision process will involve faulty perceptions, misconceptions, imperfect expectations and inaccurate communications, all of which may be deplored and yet may be the grease that allows decision-makers to cooperate; otherwise their differences would hardly let them coexist. Imprecision may be a prerequisite of cooperation; clarity may impede rather than assist cooperation. Finally, decision-making will not be effective unless there is some reward for the decision-maker in terms of power.

CONCLUSION

It is against this background that we can ask pertinent questions of any decision-making.

1. Who is involved in the particular decision, what are their positions in the organisation and what political games are they likely to play? To what extent are they likely to shift between alternatives: will they attempt to manipulate the situation by putting forward the problem in different guises, will they suggest the setting up of new units and do so as part of a bargaining strategy? What are the existing networks of relations that they are involved in; what are their likes and dislikes and their organisational attachments?
2. What has influenced each participant's stance; what are the interests which have led him to adopt this stance?
3. What determines each participant's impact upon the outcome of the decision-making process; what is his power, his bargaining advantage, his skill and will to use this advantage? Frequently an individual or group have power, but lack the will to use it – they bemoan their position and use the myth of their powerlessness as an excuse for inaction. What are the other participants' perceptions of these attributes?
4. What is the nature of the game being played? How are the participants' stance, influence and moves within it combined to yield decision and action?
5. How is the outcome being affected by the rules of the decision process?

6. What is the outcome, given that it is the result of political behaviour? To what extent do the stated and actual outcomes differ?

This list of questions is a reminder that a decision is not the outcome of an objective, rational process or programme, but of varying degrees of limited rationality. But it would be incorrect to see this as a random and wilful activity. Decisions take place within sets of organisational rules and norms, with given resources, with established patterns and with old decisions giving indications of what may arise and be played out even in a new context.

Faced with this picture, some managers would argue for a reduction in the political element in decision-making. To achieve this the following conditions would have to be met:

1. there would have to be a high level of slack resources; reduction of interdependence among units, and expansion;
2. there would need to be an increase in the degree of homogeneity and agreement through appropriate recruitment, training and rewards policies. The cost could be less adaptability within the organisation; and
3. cooperation and collaboration would have to be increased by stressing the mutual advantages of working together and the enjoyment of exchanging favours.

These conditions are unlikely to be achieved because of the facts of power, competition, rewards and punishments, the overall scarcity of resources and the overwhelming culture of the wider society.

The style of decision-making is clearly subject to many variables, not least the economic and financial state of the firm. For example, at one and the same time when there are financial difficulties, scientific management decision-making is frequently intensified, control systems are tightened up and there is an emphasis on order, but simultaneously, given the scarcity of resources, decision-making often becomes more political.

This chapter has concentrated on management decision-making, but it does not mean that workers do not make decisions which, in aggregate, are of considerable importance. One aspect of worker decision-making, that of participation, will be examined in the next chapter.

8 Participation

Participation has been one of the magnificent obsessions of management since the early 1950s. The pressure for the development of participation came from a number of sources. First, there were behavioural scientists who advocated the development of participative management on the grounds that it would lead to more effective decisions; that if subordinates, whether managers or workers, were consulted or involved in the decision process the quality of the decisions would improve. It would also lead, they argued to a greater commitment to particular decisions and hopefully to the organisation itself. In participative management the outcome, it was claimed, would be 'we' decided, in constrast to the view that 'he' decided, or that with bargaining, 'it' was decided. Further, it was thought that greater involvement would lead to a growth of trust and confidence through the diminution of barriers of communication and of feelings. Finally, participative management would contribute to the development of individuals and facilitate their 'self-actualisation'.

Second, pressure 'for increased participation came from the trade unions who argued that worker involvement (in reality this meant union involvement) would achieve some of the claims of the behavioural scientists and was 'right' in that people should be able to control their own destinies. The power and authority of management to make decisions which curtailed the job prospects of workers should be restricted; power should be more evenly distributed through participation. They argued that the worker did not live by bread alone; that to be fully developed, people in a free society should be able to participate in decision-making as it affected their working environment and the success of the enterprise of which they were a part.

'Participation' – one hurrah word, was linked with another – 'democracy', and the idea of industrial democracy became a notion with powerful emotional connotations.[1]

Third, the idea of participative management and industrial democracy reflected the development, in the wider society, of the view that people should be more involved in the decisions that influence their lives.[2] It is not surprising therefore that the British Institute of Management stated, 'There is plenty of general support for the claim that in a highly developed industrial society there should be more industrial democracy', but it prudently went on to remark 'there is not a great deal of precision about what this means'.[3] This lack of precision is reflected in the fact that the advocates of joint consultation, co-partnership and worker directors frequently do not agree on the mechanisms for operating such programmes. Much of the disagreement centres on the degree of participation and the nature of the involvement of the workers in the decision process. In spite of the differences over the mechanisms for participation, certain notions such as involvement, commitment and human dignity are commonly accepted. More fundamental disagreements on property rights, authority and power, tend to be kept below the surface of discussion. The language of participation is replete with the 'right' words and in consequence is a great beguiler.

A FLAVOUR OF PARTICIPATION

A brief excursion into participative management will provide an example of the flavour of the language. The participative management style involves changes, not only in a manager's dealings with his subordinates, but in his attitudes to them. It is argued that to achieve these changes he will have to:

1. develop a climate of trust between himself and his subordinates;
2. provide as much information as possible to create an open and not secretive atmosphere;
3. adopt a straightforward and honest approach to people;
4. use objective rather than subjective standards of judgement;
5. realise that decisions can affect subordinates' sense of security;
6. provide a supportive attitude towards subordinates;

7. develop a policy orientated towards the potential development of each individual;

8. give subordinates help and assistance rather than simply
issuing directions;

9. adjust the work of the individual to fit his abilities rather
than the other way around; and

10. give subordinates every opportunity to make decisions.[4]

Above all, it is argued, 'participative management is about
stressing the common interest of all who work and prosper
through the success of the enterprise, whilst at the same time
actually making sure that the interests of all are taken into
account'.[5]

The end products are to be improved organisational performance and individual development. The assumption is that they
will go together, 'that members of the organisation at all levels
can best achieve their own goals by directing their efforts toward
the goals of the organisation'.[6]

A main theme of this book is that the common interest is
limited, and it will be the further contention of this chapter that
participation, whether in the form of participative management
or industrial democracy, is part of the power and politics of
organisational life. Specifically what is called participation is
largely covert bargaining, and the personal development that
occurs is in the field of political skills rather than the confidence
building generally advocated.

Participation reflects the interplay of those who are involved;
it provides another arena for negotiation. The perceptions and
expectations of anyone involved in participation will influence
his behaviour and the information that he is willing to provide,
and affect the way in which he interprets the information offered
by other participants. What is more his perceptions, coupled
with his aspirations, will change as a result of experience of the
participative exercise. Participative behaviour will be coloured
by the significance to the individual of the issues being considered, their importance to him in terms of power and influence
and by the state of the environment around the participative
process; for example, whether it is one of crisis or stability.
Furthermore, the rhetoric of participative language intrudes into
the process; creating yardsticks, and influencing expectations
and perceptions.

THE POLITICAL NATURE OF PARTICIPATION

With the scene set, we can examine the political nature of participation. From the outset participation can be seen as a tool that will be used by management or workers, if they think it will help them in the political contest for control over critical contingencies commanded by others. Centralised power, given the feelings aroused by its exercise, suffers from visibility. Paradoxically, participation, particularly if it is widely spread in an organisation, can lead to centralised power and control without the appearance of centralisation. Indeed it may be more powerful because it is less obvious and less responsible. Participation can create the illusion of control by the many, while maintaining the real influence of the few. How does this arise? It occurs because many of the so-called participants are prepared to leave the work to others, leading to a situation where an individual or small group takes on the tasks that are the responsibility of all, with apparent legitimacy. For example, in any participative situation, whether between managers or managers and workers, information gathering will not be widely spread; the task is given to the few, and the many simple react to the data, information or alternatives that have been prepared for them. The few filter the information into the decision and discussion processes of the many. If the few are powerful, and their uniqueness will tend to make them so, they will be in a strong position to shape these processes and their outcomes. In a management-worker participative situation, managers are more likely to have crucial information on key issues at their disposal; so are able to control the form and flow of that information to the participative forum. Power being unequally distributed between the participants means that participation can be a manipulative exercise, in which the weaker are controlled by the stronger. Underlying the process there is a concern with the maintenance or achievement of power and control over the other participants.

In this state of affairs resources are important; the group or individual possessing the most experience or expertise has the opportunity to influence those with fewer of these attributes. The irony is that participation can highlight these capabilities and so fortify the power of the strong *vis-à-vis* the weak. More generally, differences in training, education and social background will also play their part and those who are highly trained may disadvantage those who are not. This is by no means certain, it will be influenced by the bargaining skills of those involved. Another factor affecting the power balance between participants is the increase in 'professional' management. Every management function lays claim to being professional and sustains it through the support of a professional association. This development, while aimed at improving standards, also has the effect of building up a mystique and of giving 'professional' managers a claim to expertise which, they imply, cannot be challenged. Added to this is the rejection, by those who have worked hard to acquire technical knowledge and qualifications, of participation by those who have not gone through a similar educational programme.

The power of those involved in the participative process also depends upon the range of issues upon which they can comment and make decisions. Hence the real power rests with those who define the areas of participation, who suppress the discussion of any issue which challenges their interests and who decide who shall and shall not be participants. Examples of this abound in the field of industrial relations where both management and unions seek to control the agenda of participation, for example there is the trade union which will not allow discussion of collective bargaining issues in joint consultative committees and similar participative mechanisms. Decisions relating to who shall participate and what shall be the agenda of discussion may themselves be the result of prior bargaining. People with power can deploy a number of arguments and tactics against the development or widening of participation: they point to the pressing character of business activities, to the time-consuming nature of participation and the need for speedy decisions (this emphasis on speed is only a partial truth as many decisions are delayed for a wide variety of reasons, not least of a political and technical nature); they can deter participants by developing elaborate decision-making processes. Those involved in the participative exercise can find the decision process is so complex that they are unable to decide anything. Every time they attempt to do so the proposed decision has to be referred elsewhere: the decision process can be arranged so that the participants find themselves at the tail-end when the decision has already been firmed up. Then they can only say 'yes' or 'no', and if they say 'no' they will face powerful arguments as to why they should change their minds. In these circumstances there is the likelihood that those participants who lack power will become frustrated, lose interest and make little or no contribution. This will confirm the powerful in their positions and in their belief that participation is a waste of time.

The hierarchical structure of organisations can be used to help or hinder participation. When senior management is involved it can, if it wishes, supply information, provide guidelines and make decisions to facilitate discussion. When it is absent it can discount decisions made at lower level participative meetings, with the disclaimer that the participants 'did not see the whole picture'.

Formally, management may see participation as a threat to their power even though they join in the widespread acceptance of its rhetoric; to defend their position they will adopt political strategies and tactics of the type already discussed. Management are not alone in their ambivalence, trade unions must evaluate participation in terms of its impact on the power base and take appropriate action to defend their interests, and here a distinction has to be made between the interests of the union with its power system and those of its members.

Participation diffuses decision-making responsibility. Where one person is responsible for a particular decision-making area, others know where to go to express their preferences and exercise influence; where there is diffusion this is less easy. If there is an outcry from the members of a participant's department, his superior can claim that a joint decision was reached through participation; similarly if the workers complain about a decision made through the machinery of industrial democracy, management can turn round and say that the workers' representatives agreed. By providing people with some organisational legitimacy and feeling of involvement it is possible to divert attention from their natural concerns. Where the participative process is frequent, the participants come to identify with each other, and put themselves at risk with the people they represent; so the cry goes out, 'he is no longer one of us'. The 'tyranny' of the large organisation is replaced by the 'tyranny' of the participative group, both for those who are part of it and those who are faced with its decisions. The tyranny experienced by the participants springs form the group pressures to become a 'good' member. For those who have to operate the decisions, the tyranny is that they have been legitimised through participation, by the presence of their own representatives, whether managers or unions.

PARTICIPATION AND POWER

In the decision-making process there are various patterns of power allocation.

1. There are the decisions by superiors, made regardless of the subordinate's wants or needs – basically these are instructions, directions and orders.
2. There is joint decision-making which may be, on occasion, only a form of consultation, with the superior making the final decisions.
3. There is the joint decision, with the superior only using limited influence and delegating authority to his subordinates to make the decision.
4. There is the joint decision where both superior and subordinates seek to achieve agreement through the sharing of authority.

Which of these processes will be utilised will depend upon the relative power and political skills of the parties concerned.

Joint decision-making lies at one end of the continuum, with direction at the other. Between them lie differing forms of delegation; one occurs when the subordinate has 'freedom' but acts according to his superior's general expectations – that is, 'anticipatory reaction'. It might be argued that delegation is more attractive than participation as it encourages achievement, places responsibility clearly and its results are more tangible than those of participation. Whether these are genuine characteristics of delegation is less important than that delegation more easily fits the language of management than participation, carrying with it a greater feeling of autonomy and flexibility. Delegation as a tool of management involves questions of power and control; it is not a neutral practice of effective management.

In the participative process there are likely to be two levels of negotiation or 'implicit bargaining'. First, there is the individual's agreement to abide by the norms established by the participants, in return for acceptance into the participative process; second, there is the implicit bargaining over substantive issues being discussed in the participatory situation. Thus participation sets up an exchange relationship where the various bargaining tactics referred to earlier come into play. This bargaining does not necessarily lead to people working harder, for even if they are happier in the participative arena they are not inevitably more productive. If the only virtue of participation is to make people happier, it is surely possible to provide other ways of achieving this end.

Participative management and industrial democracy can change interaction patterns, set up new relationships and new channels of communication. However, these do not necessarily reduce conflict; to believe that more personal contact will improve relationships is simplistic – more contact may only confirm a participant in his own worst suspicion of others. Similarly the provision of more information can harden people in their existing position, the extra information providing them with further evidence of the 'dubiety', 'inefficiency' and 'instability' of the others.

PARTICIPANT IMPOTENCE

Participation can also be hindered by the imperfect elaboration of company policies, so that no one is quite sure what they are. Consequently discussion of them is liable to be built on shifting sand, resulting in increased decision-making, with the end result being referred elsewhere to those who are supposed to know. Of course it does happen that no one knows what the policy is because it has never been formulated, in which case the ad hoc decision becomes the policy. Difficulties also arise when workers' representatives or lower levels of management do not have the necessary knowledge or know the criteria for acceptable decisions; they can end up making decisions which are rejected by those with the appropriate expertise and understanding. Furthermore, where employee representatives are involved, differing values and interests can reduce them to apparent impotence and unconstructive responses. They may have some difficulty in stating their case because they come up against the 'professional' wall, against those who talk on the assumption, manipulated or otherwise, that other people understand, when they do not and cannot be expected to do so. The latter are then discomfited, their responses are unsatisfactory and a self-fulfilling position has developed. This confirms those who 'know' in their view that it is 'a waste of time talking to these people'. Such an attitude makes relations difficult and increases the element of conflict in participation.

Thus the 'underprivileged' collaborate, even if unwittingly, in their own subordination – power is most effectively exercised when other people are not aware that they are being disadvantaged. Increasing organisational participation may not be really meaningful. Growing participation by organisational members can be offset by growing (or more effective) manipulation by those with power.

Access to the decision arena through participation is not, in itself, sufficient; a crucial ability is recognising issues for discussion and organising around them. We are back to the question of power, in this case the power to place items into the right slot on the agenda of participation. Where the power of any group of participants is limited, the position may develop where they do not accept particular decisions but do not overtly reject them. There is an appearance of consensus but it is no more than rule following, and we know that 'rules are never neutral, they are the embodiment of past political victories'. Here there is no real agreement, merely a lack of questioning. In these circumstances the participants are likely to think participation ineffective, resulting in the maintenance of managerial initiative and prerogative.

Participative managers may be more knowledgable, but when the hierarchical gap is wide, managerial interests and knowledge may be so divergent that the same tensions exist as in employee–management participation. However, where the gap is slight, the knowledge differences may be small, and the political behaviour more sophisticated as the participants know more of each other, of their relative strengths and weaknesses and of the hidden agenda. Given this situation participants may well be guarded in their communications; disclosure of information may be regarded as offering a hostage to fortune which can be used at a later date by one or other of the participants to further his own interests. For example, to involve participants in a small group of issues may lead them to expect involvement over a much wider range of issues. When these expectations are not fulfilled, information gained in the earlier exercises may be used to express frustration, disapproval or simply to exploit a further situation. It may be argued that people ought not to behave in this manner, but the competitive culture, not only of individual organisations but of society itself, contributes to this behaviour. Those who deplore it have to start converting society to new attitudes, standards and behaviour and this in the face of human complexity, of competitive–cooperative ambivalence, consensus searching and conflict.

PROTECTING THE POWERFUL

A critical aspect of the political dimension in participation is that of management ideology – the notion that managers are employed to manage and produce results. While we have seen earlier that in practice it is not as clear cut as this, these beliefs still form part of the management stereotype and are used as a defence of management authority against erosion through participation.

From a managerial viewpoint, effective participation is that which encourages initiative and creativity, while restraining resistance and criticism; it represents an extreme form of manipulation, it makes possible maximum control by those who manage the system with minimum resistance from the participants. Another advantage to management is that participation provides a feedback system, and the more open it is on the side of those with little power the more valuable it is for those in charge; for the weaker participants are likely to give up a substantial part of their informational power base in exchange for marginal concessions of information on the part of the strong. Those without power still do not know all, and the more they involve themselves while others hold back, the more vulnerable they become, whilst the powerful become predominant. If the imbalance beomes too obvious, those who give freely will ultimately become aware of the fact and withhold information, or take other forms of action, to develop a bargaining position. For example, control systems can be manipulated in order to confuse higher management. Marchington and Loveridge show how shop floor workers, who felt they had not been adequately consulted, manipulated the use of raw material in such a way that the firm found itself landed with a stock of a particular raw material the workers thought was of inferior quality. They then demonstrated that this was the case, and the firm had to search around for a quality acceptable to the shop floor.[7]

To prevent this counteraction, those with power can present information in a way that appears to say a great deal when in fact it says little; they can also use the 'secrecy' argument when necessary, justifying this on the grounds that to provide more information would give advance warning of new developments; that it would shake the shareholders' confidence and so on.

The value of discussion as a means of promoting mutual understanding can be greatly overestimated on the grounds that discussion often can and does arouse a conflict atmosphere, producing destructive situations as the participants seek to test each other out while maintaining their own position. This is further aggravated when managers, reluctant to exercise definite leadership because of social and union pressure, pay lip service to participation while using all the available political tactics to ensure the ineffectiveness of participation. For modern management there is an unenviable tension between the belief that managers should manage and the more egalitarian beliefs that have suffused social, educational and political thinking in recent times.

INDUSTRIAL DEMOCRACY

To take the view that it is only management who engage in political behaviour, whether in relation to subordinates, managers or employees, is very much a simplification. As we have already seen, workers and lower levels of management engage in a variety of political tactics, many of which are transferable to the participative situation.

In the case of industrial democracy there is often a clear recognition that participation is about power. While there appear to be very high levels of support for the general principle of industrial democracy, when discussion moves to concrete proposals the objections flower and support is less then wholehearted. This reflects the recognition that industrial democracy is about shifts in the distribution of power within organisations, and goes some way to explain why trade unions may evince more enthusiasm than management. This is underlined when we examine the differing roles of industrial democracy as seen by managers and trade unionists. The former see it as having two functions:

1. educating workers to the facts of life, where the company stands in the market, the problems it faces, its current

performance. Management hopes that this will breed attitudes of 'realism' and a greater commitment to the future fortunes of the organisation.

2. utilising shopfloor experience and expertise in the decision-making process, in the hope that this will lead to better solutions, with workers' involvement giving them better insight into the technical problems faced by management. The fear is that the message may not get across, that consultation may lead to more, rather than less, resistance and to demands for wider consultation. To avoid this, management is more likely to favour an informal participative style coupled with personal contact. However, we have to recognise there is no one consistent management view, much depends upon the level of management; senior management is likely to talk of the need to develop participative styles while lower management, those at the sharp end of industrial relations, will probably see the problems of implementation more clearly. Managers stress that participation ought to be advisory and complementary to management's right to manage and make decisions; it must not be a challenge to that power or a diminution of it. It is claimed that managers have to retain the initiative in decision-making with no abdication of their responsibility for managing.

For the workers, participation on the terms outlined above is an exercise in 'management regaining control by sharing it', and as such is to be resisted. While management seeks informality, workers in general are worried by any scheme in which they would be required to act as individuals rather than as members of unions. Unions provide representation as well as strength; hence there is a concern with formal structure where issues can be bargained over by representatives who will not agree to any decision which their constitutents do not support. Further, they expect management to respond to the demands they put forward and to make comprehensive and timely disclosures of information. These expectations as to how management ought to behave demonstrate once again the existence of differing levels of political discourse, of rhetoric and realism.

The fears of the two groups illustrate their differences. Managers fear the challenge and the opposition to their authority and power, while the workers' representatives fear they will gain little and be seen as the mouthpiece of management. Away from the rhetoric they recognise the political and manipulative nature of participation and seek to counter it; adopting bargaining stances that are overemphatic but serve the purpose of securing the support of their constituents.

What we have at this stage is a series of general notions into which all parties may read whatever they wish. All may agree that participation is a 'good thing', but once the participative process is under way, the underlying issues of power and conflict begin to surface. This is not to say that on every topic there will be disagreement, but very often an area of agreement overlaps an area of conflict. For example, agreement that there should be more investment can develop into conflict if the result of the new technology will be the deskilling of skilled workers. Important contradictions emerge within the views of management and workers. Managers stress areas of common interest where they believe no bargaining is required, while retaining the right to manage on these very same issues. The workers' representatives seek an extension of influence in the decision-making process, but fear incorporation into management-dominated decision-making. Paradoxically this can lead to acceptance of unilateral managerial control.

THE UNIONS AND UNITY

Behind the workers' views lie the concerns of the unions. While managers tend to look upon negotiation and participation as distinct activities, union officials prefer to see participation largely in terms of negotiation. Collective bargaining has traditionally provided the means through which unions enhance their power and influence in industry, and it is collective bargaining, suitably strengthened and extended, that most union officials favour as a form of employee participation. Through collective bargaining worker solidarity is maintained, the risk of isolation is lessened and the freedom of management to act unilaterally is restricted.

For unions, unity is required if workers are to negotiate successfully with management. Any innovation which is thought likely to weaken that unity is regarded with suspicion and hostility. The management emphasis on increased worker commitment to the firm through participation, cannot be wholeheartedly accepted by the unions as it implies a weakening of commitment to union policies and practices. 'Unity is Strength' and no man can serve two masters; unions recognise that participation could weaken their power base and so it must be resisted, if not openly, certainly covertly. This appears to be going against the union argument for a greater say in industry; hence unions need to argue for involvement through forms which ensure union control of those who represent the members. Those who are involved in the participative process must, in the unions' view, be wholly indoctrinated into union ways of thinking; they must be people who will not be compromised into failing to represent the workers effectively. They are there to represent the workers' interests and not to become involved in discussions and activities which might be detrimental to union members. The stress on representation gives the game away, it accurately states the position that what is involved is power: that there is a power struggle between management and the unions and indeed, on occasion, between the unions themselves. This may be deplored, but to do so is to fail to recognise the nature of a trade union: a trade union exists for the benefit of its members, not for the benefit of the firm, industry or country. It is a self-interest organisation, as are many forms of organisation. Its members judge it by its ability to produce results, that is, to ensure members retain their jobs with wage increases of sufficient size to guarantee, at worst, no loss of rank in the earnings ladder and, at best, a rise up that ladder. Any participation which produces results that run counter to these criteria is not acceptable to the members who, in the final analysis, can say 'you are paid to protect us and not to help managers manage us'. There is an us–them situation in industry and attempts to blur this are likely to further complicate an already complex relationship. Any successful bridging of this gap will probably be of a temporary nature.

The adversarial view of industrial relations is deeply etched in the minds of managers and trade union officials, indeed one might almost say that both parties need it. A clearly identifiable opponent is useful both for uniting the ranks and for allocating responsibilities for present problems. With their ready recognition of the power dimension, trade unions are concerned to extend the scope of collective bargaining as a better way of achieving greater workers' participation in company affairs, than through systems of participation. What they are concerned with is 'union' participation and with it an extension of the power of the unions and of control by the unions of their members. The more extensive the range of issues dealt with directly by the unions, the less opportunity for members to look outside their union, in particular to their firm. It also means that members receive information on this widened range of issues predominantly from the unions, which, like any other organisation, structure and present information in a form which suits the unions' perception of an issue. It ensures that the workers' lack of interest in areas other than those which directly affect them, a habit to be found in all walks of life and on all topics, should not be used by management as a means of manipulating workers; the unions see themselves as protecting workers from their own apathy. Further, the unions recognise their own skills in negotiating and would not want to see these weakened through the development of other types of worker-management relationship. In fact this is unlikely to happen, as even in the different types of participation the basic process is one of tacit negotiation and bargaining. It simply means that there is an adjustment of union bargaining skills, not an abandonment of them. Another aspect of this situation is that bargaining skills are scarce resources and their owners have no desire to see developments which would reduce the value of those skills – they provide a power base. Trade union officials and negotiators have no desire to see their power eroded.

A EUROPEAN VIEW

A survey of industrial democracy, 'In Europe', openly written in a spirit of optimism, points to the rapid development of European industrial democracy which 'is changing the distribution of power and influence towards equality between the various groups of employees'. However it goes on to admit that the process could be viewed more pessimistically:

> the systems for participation which are covered by this study, also act as a part of the managerial control system. Decisions are more easily accepted by employees. The participative bodies in themselves have an effect on employees' attitudes,

irrespective of the effect of influence and involvement. The legitimacy of the establishment is increasing, possibly without any change in the distribution of power. Or the levels may be come closer in terms of power, but the hierarchy still remains ... systems for participation, whether they are within or outside the management hierarchy, do not challenge this hierarchy, but might rather reinforce it. In total, this could mean that increased participation is a defensive measure, a necessity for providing internal stability in a period of rapid restructuring ... it is quite possible that what is really happening in the enterprises covered by the study is a process whereby the employees are being led towards something over which they have very little control ... only the presence of unions with links outside the enterprise was likely to create a counterweight to management dominance and expertise.[8]

Put in another way the study goes on to state that 'in spite of the seemingly elaborate systems for employee representation in several of the twelve countries ... the effects on the distribution of power and level of industrial involvement are mild, and generally we conclude that industrial democracy is still in an embryonic state'.

I have quoted at length from this study because participation and industrial democracy are major examples of the gap between rhetoric and practice. What emerges is a highly political activity, a management tool to be used to restrain criticism from workers, unions and the wider society. For the unions it is only useful if it is fully under their control. For both management and unions it is only acceptable if it does not undermine their respective power positions. For both, their power depends upon apathy, upon the limited interest that human beings evince for wider issues. Participation is a way of perpetuating, not reducing, that apathy; it places power in the hands of the active participants and provides an arena in which the contest is waged over the distribution of that power.

CONCLUSION

This chapter is not an advocacy of non-participation; it is an argument for the recognition of the political nature of participation, of its power implications and of the existence of forms of participation which are more regularly recognised as based upon negotiation. It would be better to recognise frankly the nature of participation, whatever its form, than to perpetuate the double-speak of participation. Participative management styles and industrial democracy represent different forms of manipulation pursued by managers, unions and workers.

9 Change

Some people make change;
Some people watch change being made;
Some people don't seem to know that things are changing.[1]

Change is a fact of managerial life, for some it is a challenge, for others a threat; for some it comes from within the organisation, for others it enters from the world outside. Whatever the circumstance it is linked with power and politics.

Environmental change is the result of one or many of the following causes:

1. fluctuations in the market due to alterations in the competitive structure;
2. shifts in government policies;
3. technological developments;
4. the general industrial, economic and commercial outlook;
5. changes in trade union activity; or
6. movements in the general views of society.

Simply to list these general possibilities is to draw attention to the fact that change comes to management from all quarters which are differentially capable of control by the organisation.

The first critical fact is that these changes will be perceived by management at different levels of the organisation and representing diverse functions. The same change will be viewed differently, depending upon whether the manager is a senior executive or a lower level manager; whether he is in production, sales or finance. Some managers at the same level and operating in the same function will see the same change as providing an opportunity and others will see it as threatening. These differences will be partly related to the perceived impact of the change upon the distribution of power in the organisation.

Similarly, an internally generated change will be viewed by those affected by it in terms of its meanings for their power bases

173

and position. One thing is clear – those promoting the change will do so in the belief that it will benefit them in terms of power.

The change, wherever originated, will lead to any one or combination of the following: the introduction of new methods, new machinery or new technology; new and different personnel; a different organisational structure; a redistribution of finance, resources or tasks. The same change may mean for one department an increase in the resources available to it, greater freedom, readier access to top management; while for another it may mean the very opposite. Much will depend upon the nature of the change and the amount of slack existing within the organisation. Change will tend to create internal uncertainty and, in coping, individuals and units may generate still further uncertainty. This will be aggravated by the tendency of those units initiating the change to be aggressive and imperialistic, claiming more resources and behaving in a manner to justify the innovation they are sponsoring or developing.

When a decision involves a major change, or, for that matter, a small change that is important to lower levels of management and staff, the political process leading up to it is likely to be highly active. In this type of situation any technical change will be as much influenced by political factors and motivations as by technical considerations.

Small changes should never be underestimated; many marginal changes when taken together may represent a major shift in a firm's style and operations. For this reason managers should pay attention to the implications of proposed minor changes and fit them into the context of other changes that are underway. A change may be seen to have very different implications from those originally perceived when it is put into a change context.

Around the fact of change has grown a cluster of myths which play an important part in the political process.

1. It is widely held that managers welcome change while workers resist it. In practice, resistance to change expressed in 'trained incapacity' – the ability to ignore cues and signals when change is difficult and dangerous – is a general characteristic of those who are threatened. To suggest that managers are absolved from this particular human attribute is a convenient piece of managerial ideology. It is useful when attributing blame for the rejection of change, but it hardly fits the reality.

2. The problems of change are held to centre around job security, when it is the distribution of power that is critical. The deskilling of work is likely to be resisted less on the grounds of alienation than because a routine job is more easily controlled, its operator has less power and is easily replaced.
3. There is the myth that change proceeds in one direction, that is, from conception to implementation, when in practice the change process is reiterative, shuttling backwards and forwards through the stages of change.
4. There is the belief that a really good idea is the best guarantee of success, but the intrinsic 'goodness' of an idea is no guarantee; an idea has to be sponsored by those who have the power to do so and, even if accepted after being pushed and pulled in the political process, there remains the key problem of implementation.

COSTS OF CHANGE

Given the political and power aspects of change, it is perhaps not surprising that so many changes take more time and cost more than was originally expected. These time and cost factors are influenced by the following:

1. Plans for change are often incomplete, with too little account being taken of contagion, that is, with inadequate attention being paid to the range of people who will be affected. As a result, unexpected resistance develops and steps have to retraced to cope with the unforeseen developments. Added to this, the social organisation of management and workers is based upon existing technology, methods and structure and these groups have invested time and energy in these aspects of the firm. When planning a change it is unwise to underestimate the significance of peoples' job investment.
2. Change may be delayed because of the subject's symbolic nature; the outward sign may seem unimportant to those initiating the change, but be of considerable importance to those affected by it. For example, moving someone's office from proximity to a key manager's office may have repercussions which go far beyond the fact of the move. The resistance

to such a move should not be interpreted simply in terms of status and dismissed on these grounds, but in terms of power, based upon visibility; on acquiring knowledge through proximity and on the chance, often important, that one's views might be called for when formally this could not happen. The chance meeting in the corridor may provide the opportunity to be asked for one's views.

3. Change may be protracted because undue euphoria, based upon over-exaggeration, has been built up. Budgets may have been attached on the basis of anticipated major gains resulting from the change, rather than the marginal improvements that are most probable. Delay can arise from exaggerated ideas of reality, so that when faced with actuality, the change has to be reformulated, modified amd even in extreme cases abandoned. Now this process of readjustment will bring political activity involving those who, because they initially espoused the change with enthusiasm, have benefited from the consequent resource allocation. They will be reluctant to forgo any of their acquired gains and will seek to substantiate their initial claims, often on the basis that others have not cooperated or that totally new factors have emerged to change the situation; they will reiterate that they can, of course, cope with the new situation.

4. The emergence of unanticipated costs can delay the change. These costs may be administrative with the change destroying established routines, customs and practices; opening the way for plundering, for groups to try to fill the vacuum so as to gain power and exercise control. The costs may arise because some critical factor has been omitted and suddenly emerges. The oversight can be due to any one of a number of factors, such as the desire of the innovating group to get the change underway quickly in order to justify itself and its claims to acquire resources. Such a group may seek speedy action to prevent others introducing changes which will push its own proposals down the list of priorities – to avoid this a pre-emptive strike is undertaken. Among other factors raising costs is the unforeseen eruption of complaint or protest: a particular individual or group is mistakenly expected to remain quiescent, but once the change is under way the sleeping manager or unit comes to life and begins organising forces in support of its cause,[2] entering into coalitions and

generally seeking to reopen the whole question of the advisability of the change. Here the self-fulfilling prophecy comes into play – a group opposed to a change who either failed to prevent its introduction or who initially did not offer resistance, can protest that it will not work. If, then, the group or individual is involved in the implementation of the change, it can behave in such a way that ensures failure.

All these unanticipated problems can reduce flexibility, as the different parties are liable to become frozen in their positions of defence or offence. Where the change is delayed, where there is a gap between the intended result of the change and the actuality, there is likely to be pressure from senior management to produce quicker and 'better' results. This in itself can make political trade-offs difficult to achieve and result in lower organisational levels becoming increasingly defensive.

CONTROLLING ENVIRONMENTAL UNCERTAINTY

Faced with the consequences of change, organisations will seek to manage environmental uncertainty and change in such a way as to avoid having to make significant structural, human and technological responses. Competition can be an obvious source of environmental uncertainty and faced with it firms can either fight by becoming more efficient and more effective, or seek to enter into arrangements with competitors to limit the scope and severity of any change. In the achievement of this latter state of affairs the professional managers employed in different firms may utilise the informal collective structures and networks of which they are part. In addition to the informal arrangements there are the formal linkages, which may be developed to structure interorganisational behaviour. These formal linkages may take the extreme form of mergers, which result in the new organisation having more of its critical sources of uncertainty and change within its own boundaries and hence subject to internal control. One adverse consequence of this may be the development of internal crises, arising from what are now internal sources of uncertainty and change. The problems of change move from being external to internal, and an additional cost can be loss of flexibility.

Another organisational development is that of the joint venture, where two or more firms come together to undertake some common activity or to operate in a complementary manner. For example, large firms find it difficult to develop entrepreneurially and, in consequence, are ready to link up with small, entrepreneurially-minded firms who have not the resource capacity to fully develop their ideas. These moves are taken in the name of efficiency, but they are essentially a means of reducing uncertainty and controlling change, so as to prevent shifts in the distribution of power within and between firms. Another device for reducing uncertainty is that of cooption; for example, through interlocking directorates. By involving outsiders in the firm it is hoped to influence them and reduce the possibility of them initiating outside developments which could create uncertainty for the firm – they represent an early warning system for the firm. The cost here is that they become party to what is happening in the firm.[3]

The firm may diversify in the hope that it can control more efficiently the various sources of uncertainty by reducing the significance of each of them. In practice there may be some increase in uncertainty because of the problems of coordinating diverse activities.

Other tactics for increasing control include long-term contracts to freeze relationships and conditions for a given period of time. These long-term contracts are examples of the process of reciprocal exchange which helps to create mutual dependence and hopefully, in consequence, produces some measure of stability. The cost here is that the firms involved lose some of their freedom of action. What is clear is that all these uncertainty reducing strategies involve costs which, in the long-run, may be more onerous than simply living with uncertainty.

To cope with changes in markets there are a number of strategies available:

1. There is buffering. For purposes of efficiency a manufacturing organisation will seek to operate as if the market for its products absorbed them at a continuous and constant rate, and that the raw materials and semi-finished parts which it requires for the manufacture of its products flow in on a continuous basis. However, neither assumption is likely to hold good; the market is liable to vary in its capacity to absorb the products and the suppliers of raw materials will

vary in their ability to supply continuously at the right time, in the right quantities and qualities, in the right place and at the right price. To overcome these uncertainties and the changes associated with them, firms will buffer by stockpiling materials and supplies, maintaining warehouse stocks to cope with a fluctuating customer market. This buffering process enables the manufacturing operation to be maintained on a relatively continuous basis. While the firm reduces the costs of fluctuations in its operations, it faces the cost of holding stocks of materials at one end of its operations and of 'finished' products at the other.

2. In contrast to buffering there is the strategy of smoothing, which is an attempt to reduce market fluctuations through the use of discounts, special promotions and sales.

3. Other strategies include, anticipating environmental changes, planning a stable production with necessary adjustments at the end of the planning period, and of rationing output among customers.[4]

ORGANISATIONAL STABILITY

The counter to change is the development of processes to maintain organisational stability. It is stability, not change, which is descriptive of the power distribution in most organisations. The stabilisation of power arises from several processes:

1. Commitments to decisions and policies already adopted, tend to cause managers to persist in courses of action long after they have outlived their usefulness. This is very much in evidence when the results of decisions do not come up to expectations. The manager seeks to justify the decision, puts more resources into its implementation and continues to do so even when it is clear that the original decision was mistaken – it is an example of 'investment in managerial ego' and of the 'snowball' effect. Once some big, multi-faceted development has moved even a few inches down the production mountain, the weight of it begins to increase by geometrical progression, and in no time at all the snowball, soon to become an avalanche, is unstoppable in psychological terms. Once the landslide has begun nobody is capable of seeing it straight, they are hypnotized by their own commitment.[5]

Organisational commitment involves binding the individual to decisions so that consistent beliefs develop, ensuring that similar decisions will be taken in the future. For commitment to develop along these lines, a manager has to have, or believe he has, choice. Commitment is related to the extent to which choice is made public; publicity makes it difficult to revoke and so the decision is defended as right. An additional support for this committed behaviour is the belief that managers must act consistently; failure to do so is regarded as bad management and indicative of an indecisive approach. Further, it is difficult to admit mistakes if there is a widespread view that managers do not, or should not. If things go wrong in this no-mistake climate scapegoats have to be found; other managers, uncontrollable events, unions or whatever is to hand. Problems are seen in terms of control and implementation breakdowns and arise because of the lack of energy and ambition on the part of others or insufficient resources. It is left to Drucker to observe that he would never employ anyone as a manager who claimed he had never made a mistake.[6] In managerial mythology there is a failure to recognise that mistakes can be used for future learning and as a basis for improved performance.

Commitment illustrates a managerial dilemma; too much of it can lead to disastrous results, too little of it to wayward performance.

Committed resistance to change can lead to more formalisation of control. The resisters argue that successful implementation of existing operations needs more staff, information resources and more sophisticated information systems – all of which reinforce the status quo. Commitment can be a word for the protection of personal and unit interests.

2. The maintenance of stability is furthered by the institutionalisation of beliefs and practices. Organisational rules, processes and beliefs about the organisational world and the wider society come to be accepted unquestioningly and acquire an objective reality. The firm develops a 'theory' about itself which suffuses the organisation. This process of institutionalisation is underpinned by the assumption that organisations are rational, stable and authoritative; notions which help to legitimise present practices, structures and the distribution of power. The prevailing attitude is likely to be one of 'dynamic

conservatism': 'this is the way things have always been done, and will be and should be.' Thus there emerges a regularity of behaviour which is not explicitly questioned, although within and around that regularity, political pressures are at work. In organisations there is a tendency to fight to remain the same – it is this attribute which is at the core of 'dynamic conservatism'. This stability is liable to be challenged if the costs of adherence to established values and systems become overwhelming. Under these circumstances a great deal of political activity will take place, aimed at modifying without revolutionising the present position.

Institutionalism is, in part, a response to external threats which are met by counter-arguments aimed at reinforcing the dominant organisational beliefs and by a tendency to tighten control within the firm. In turn, these aspects lead to the enhancement of the domination of those already in control. When this occurs 'The more the organisation might appear to need change because of manifest performance problems, the less likely change is to occur.'[7] While essentially a barrier to change, institutionalisation ensures that degree of stability which enables routine operations to be performed.

3. Stability is further enhanced by the ability of the very powerful to obtain still more power and ensure their own perpetuation. They must have enough power to be able to prevent other power seekers upsetting the prevailing stability of the organisation. The powerful can frequently obtain resources others cannot get, and many of these resources, in turn, provide the base for future power. The possessor of power has greater ability to control others and, if necessary, to absorb them. Power, used with foresight, provides its possessor with the capacity to attract the best and brightest people, thereby increasing his power and weakening others in the internal competition for ability. Taken together, the ability to attract talent, resources and information, increases the ability of the powerful to cope with critical contingencies. The stability of the rest of the firm is more dependent upon the wishes of the increasingly powerful. The ability of the less powerful to organise a new base, from which to challenge the authority of the energetically powerful, is increasingly threatened. It is very much a case of 'to him that hath shall be given'.

It may be argued that stability is necessary on the grounds that any new operations carry risks for all concerned, creating fresh uncertainties and involving the possible loss of influence for some members of the firm. Rather than face these prospects, the argument goes, 'let us stay as we are, and if this is not wholly possible let us keep the changes to the minimum and preferably at the margin. If we do something we can give the impression that we are responding to pressures for change'. Incrementalism will again be the order of the day; there will be some slips in power but these will be kept to a minimum. The main thrust of this is of course, that those with power retain it.

Combining management's commitment to decisions, with the institutionalisation of beliefs and practices, and the self-perpetuation of power, makes change in the distribution of power difficult.

ORGANISATIONAL STRUCTURE AND CHANGE

Another focal point in any discussion of change is that of organisational structure. It is clear from earlier discussion that structure is both a source of power and the result of power and hence a key factor in the political process. However, contests over structure are constrained by the mutual dependencies of the parties involved; they have to live together and within the rules of the game. In spite of these constraints some managers will seek to change the rules to make more room for manoeuvre, and will exploit the source of structural change. These occur for a variety of reasons;

1. the development of new fashions in management thinking;
2. the emergence of new styles and functions of management;
3. new technology; and
4. changes in strategy – a firm decides to enter a new market with its existing products, or to develop a new product.

Key questions around the development of new units are concerned with their location in the structure, the degree of authority they will possess, their control and to whom will they report.

1. What are their distinctive competences?
2. Who leads them?
3. What will be the competence of the staff, and where will they come from?

The answers to these questions will indicate the present distribution of power and the impact of structural change upon that distribution. For a development of this point, there is the example of a firm which had three main operating divisions, each headed by a senior manager who reported directly to the chief executive. The decision was made to develop a new product line which was very similar to one in an existing operating division. One development would have been to place the new product line under the present head of the appropriate product division. In terms of power this would have increased the power of that division, bringing it new activities, new resources, new personnel and new technology. In actuality this did not occur; the new product line was set up in a separate division with its head reporting directly to the chief executive. The chief executive was a recent appointment to the company and his decision gained him a supporter, whilst ensuring that the present head of the existing product division did not become more powerful. These facts were submerged in the argument that the new arrangements would not disrupt the current operations; that efficiency would be increased and that the chief executive would be involved in an important new development in the company. The decision was also a signal to the organisation of the uncertain relations between the chief executive and the head of the existing product division. The outcome was that an increasingly disgruntly senior manager found it more and more difficult to communicate with his chief executive and he finally left the company.

Another structural aspect of change concerns its organisation within the firm, for instance whether it is located in some formal Research and Development or planning unit, or spread throughout the firm. If it is the former, the efficiency of the special unit will depend upon its accessibility to senior management, its understanding of the significance of the power distribution and of the implications of its proposals for that distribution. If it is the latter, it will depend upon the manner in which the firm encourages innovation and change and this, in turn, will depend upon the management style; which is related to the recruitment, training and reward systems it employs.

Faced with the need for a structural change, an organisation may set up new operating units to avoid the disruption of existing ones and because of anticipated strong resistance. The creation of these new units does not always signify the presence of innovative behaviour; they may only be established for political purposes. One certain problem is that with the creation of a new unit there will be the question of its integration into the existing structure and this will be affected by the political forces within the firm.

At the structural level of individual positions, change in the content of a position can have important implications for the distribution of power between individual managers. For example, if a manager has had the authority to make appointments to his staff and it is decided that in future this shall be done by a new section of personnel, working in conjunction with the present appointer, the power position of the latter will be weakened. His subordinates will no longer see him as the source of their appointment and in consequence he will have to find other ways of binding them to him.

Changes in structure are a response to pressing demands, created by external and internal parties interested in the organisation. One way of dealing with the internal demands is the creation of sub-units or the delegation of minor responsibilities; that is, by amending the authority of a position so as to constrain the demands – a further example of the 'absorption of protest'. All of these changes can be rationalised retrospectively as part of the overall planning process of the company; planning is not the immediate cause of the changes.

Alterations in organisational structure are demanded by those who seek to improve their power position, while such reorganisation is resisted by those in control, unless it is to their obvious advantage.

These claims and counterclaims over reorganisation are couched in the language of rationality, efficiency and improved performance; they can be seen as part of the process of legitimising the struggle for control. This political view of restructuring reduces the emphasis on planned structural change; rather is structural change seen as a response to power pressure. Planning is a rationalisation of structural changes rather than a guide to such amendments. The central issue is that of control. The basic question is, 'Who controls the organisation?' and the answer places any proposed structural change in context and indicates who is likely to benefit from it.

TECHNOLOGICAL CHANGE

A source of change which may or may not lead to structural alterations is technology in the form of, for example, methods, tools and machinery. It would be incorrect to talk of technology, structure and human beliefs as separate entities; they interact upon each other. New technology, whether 'hard' or 'soft' ware, does not enter into a vacuum, it displaces or modifies existing technology and in doing so begins a chain reaction in structure and human beliefs and behaviour. At the same time both structure and beliefs influence the choice of technology, the way in which it fits into the present framework and the manner in which it is employed.

The introduction of a new technology can have far-reaching consequences, leading to a restructuring of the firm, to the introduction of new skills, which raises the question of whether the existing workforce can and should be retrained and whether the required skills can and should be brought into the firm. If the former is decided, there is the question of who does the training; if it is the personnel department, it will be liable to seek additional resources for the training and redeployment of its existing staff. There is also the question of the competence of the existing management to manage the new technology, with further questions of training and promotion. Clearly if the changes are restricted to one section of the firm's operations its influence upon the rest may be limited, but even so account must again be taken of the 'contagion factor', that is the ripple or domino effect of even minor changes. But what is minor? Some managers may indeed see a particular change as 'minor' while others see it as 'major'. Where the changes are indeed 'major' the whole structure, skill and behavioural aspects of the firm may be changed and with them the distribution of power and the activity of politics.

CHANGE AND ORGANISATIONAL ETHOS

The introduction of innovation involves a number of steps. First, there is the new idea, as perceived by the individual manager or unit, placed in the context not simply of increasing efficiency, but of the reality of power. Second, there is the communication of the new idea to others, with questions of presentation and manipulation. Then the new idea will operate in a framework of beliefs, structure and technology and the process, from conception to implementation, will take time. The time factor is crucial, as the idea is liable to undergo modification when different people adapt it to suit their own perceptions of how it will affect them.

How any change will develop will be influenced by the major managerial ethos of the firm; the parochial firm is self-satisfied in its isolation and is confined within self-imposed, narrow limits:

1. the adaptive firm is receptive to new ideas but often relies on other firms to provide them; and
2. the technically progressive firm is neither parochial nor parasitic on others' developments, but seeks to create its own products and processes.[8]

These different types of firms reflect different relations with the environment and, as we saw earlier, much change is brought into the firm through environmental change. New types of raw material, new equipment, new processes, new economic conditions, new competitors and new customer behaviour will all affect the operation of the firm, bringing in their wake a wide variety of changes. In reverse, the development of a new product, a decision to restructure, to introduce new machinery and new products will alter relations with the relevant segments of the environment and change the power relations between the firm and its stakeholders.

To facilitate change it is necessary to recognise the interdependence of structure, technology and beliefs and to identify the power factor within and around this framework. Given the emphasis in this book it is not too difficult to identify the major sources of resistance, if one understands the ideology and interests of those involved and estimates their awareness and power to influence the change.

The skills required to cope with change are substantially political:

1. the ability to accept the need for endless give and take;
2. the readiness to bargain, knowing that there are no precise answers and that any change which is introduced to solve one problem will at some stage produce other problems; and
3. the capabilities of exhorting, urging, cajoling and brow-beating, that is, the skilful use of different forms of pressure behind which is the ultimate threat of coercion. Apposite to the whole question of change are the remarks of Anthony Crosland who, when asked how a Secretary of State gets enough resources for his service, answered;

> By persuading, arguing, cajoling, exploiting his political position, being a bloody nuisance in Cabinet. Above all by being persistent. Obviously success depends on a whole mixture of factors, a lot of them a matter of luck – your relations with the Chancellor; your standing in the Cabinet; the way the rest of the Cabinet feels towards the education service; whether you can exhaust your colleagues before they exhaust you. It's an endless tactical battle which requires determination, cunning and occasional unscrupulousness.[9]

A manager bringing about a change must have the capacity to face unpleasant realities, notably that people will resist change for reasons which appear to him trivial, selfish or unethical. He has to know how to slow down the pace and even do nothing if he recognises that the forces aligned against him are at the moment too powerful; in which case he may need to seek a coalition with those who are presently uncommitted, demonstrating the virtues of his proposed change to opinion leaders and to those with power.

THE PRESENTATION OF CHANGE

In considering the presentation of a change to his colleagues a manager needs to evaluate it against three tests of feasibility.

1. The technical one – can it be done?
2. The economic – is it worth doing?
3. The operational – will it be used?

If the answer to any of these is 'no', he will need to think of a different solution to the one he is considering. The need to think in these terms arises because those opposed to his proposals will be very ready to ask these questions from their own standpoint and in relation to how the proposals affect their power bases. Failure to think through these basic questions can leave the manager vulnerable with his standing weakened.

In order to improve the chances of getting the proposed change accepted the manager may use any of the following tactics:

1. Seek out quick success so as to provide an easy reward for the participants in the change, in other words, go for the easy parts first.

2. Take advantage of 'natural' occurrences to modify change if there is resistance; discover some factor that makes it possible to alter the proposals without loss of face.

3. Go with the grain – utilise as much of the status and power systems as possible, incorporating elements of previously accepted arrangements into the new proposals.

4. Stress structural modifications such as location, controls and the division of labour, rather than 'conversion' or attitudinal changes. Too often the stress is on changing people's attitudes and basic nature, rather than on changing their behaviour through political pay-offs, rewards and structure.

5. Use ceremony to gain recognition both for the profundity and the legitimacy of the various elements of change.

6. Give assurances that those affected will not be hurt. Whether these will be accepted will depend in part upon the previous history of similar assurances and in part upon the perceptions of those affected by the change.

7. Be realistic about the length of time required for adaptation while recognising that the longer the time span, the greater the probability of modification.

8. Managers and employees who feel threatened need substantial support; there needs to be a moratorium on critical evaluation.

9. Expect to have to deal with three different situations at the same time; the old methods, the in-between-not-certain and the new methods.

10. Be prepared for the unexpected, it may help or hinder the change.[10]

The problems of change are not simply of communication, personality and irrationality but of substance; that is, the break-up of established power bases, of vital routines.

AWKWARD QUESTIONS

It will be evident that change involves political processes, notably bargaining. Who needs to be convinced? What is his present power? What are the advantages/disadvantages of the change to him? How is the former to be made to seem more significant than the latter? How can this be made clear to him? What objections could he make and how can they be overcome?

Faced with a proposed change in operations a manager can raise some of the following awkward questions:

1. Will the new method be obsolete before it is paid for?
2. Will the existing plant last long enough to wait for still better methods to be developed?
3. Are costs, expected returns, determined by some temporary distortion of the market?
4. Will the new process cause labour difficulties and managerial problems?
5. What are the risks of innovating compared to the risks of not doing so?
6. Is the project to be financed from outside the firm and what will be the cost, in dependence as well as financial terms?
7. Can it be managed by the present management or will they have to be brought from outside? What will be the cost in power and financial terms?
8. If successful will it contribute to long-term stability? What will be the consequences of success for the power distribution within the firm?
9. Is technical progress in other fields likely to improve its prospects?
10. Are competing firms interested in the new methods? If they are, what will be the consequences of their interest?
11. Will the output be sold to receptive or unreceptive markets, to old or new customers?
12. What is the worst possible outcome of this development, what is the best?

The questions outlined above are, on the surface, about efficiency and effectiveness, but beneath lies the hidden agenda of power: who gets what, when and in what form, as a result of this change? How does it affect the bases of power? How does it affect relations with others?

Attitudes to change are influenced by loyalty to one's own sub-unit and to the persons proposing or making the change, and that loyalty will be based upon a mixture of personal and political considerations, of knowing what has to be given and what received. These attitudes to change will be significantly influenced by the firm's policies for recruitment, training, promotion and rewards.

When people feel threatened they will often seek to retrench and emphasize the benefits of existing arrangements. The threat of change concentrates the mind wonderfully; practices once queried by those who operate them suddenly become efficient and irreplaceable if the new arrangements will disadvantageously disturb the existing power pattern. Conversely, practices long-held to be essential are likely to be speedily discarded if the change brings clearly perceived advantages.

The political process that change involves, moves away from the belief that those in authority decide and subordinates accept. It is also some distance from the acceptance of change through participation, involvement and commitment. Both of these approaches are oversimplified; they fail to see that a certain amount of conflict is the inescapable accompaniment of the individual's freedom of choice, including the freedom to accept or reject change. It should be clear that change which adversely affects people will not become acceptable by trying to plan on a participative basis, as if it were a mutual problem. Too much has been expected of participation: realistically it is a means of confronting the political issues involved in change, not of smoothing out differences through talk of consensus and common goals. If there is a failure to recognise that participation is an exercise in bargaining, it will prove to be largely unfruitful; expectations will not be met and the effectiveness of its inherent bargaining will be hindered.

REACTION TO CHANGE

Negotiations for change involve obtaining appropriate support and, if the change is accepted, having the capacity to make the necessary pay-offs not only to those who support it, but also to the powerful who could prevent it operating effectively, and to those who could have blocked it earlier and only let it go because of some promise of future pay-offs. Those who are required to implement change can respond in a number of different ways:

1. they can accept and set the change in motion;
2. they can refuse, take no action and wait and see;
3. they can ask for more information on the grounds that they cannot implement the change without it;
4. they can refer their concern about the change to higher authority;
5. they can enter into a coalition to fight the proposals on the grounds of not being consulted; and
6. they can collude; they can appear to be implementing the change without doing so.

Political behaviour is likely to be a special feature of large-scale innovative decisions, when they threaten the existing pattern of resource sharing and when the existing distribution of power is endangered. The resource problem is highlighted when new specialisations are a part of the innovative package. These new specialists tend to be more expansionist than their established colleagues as they have to prove themselves; they will also take advantage of the honeymoon period when they are liable to have an easier hearing from senior management than those who have been around for some time.

To bring about large-scale change often requires the alteration of the premises of management decision-making. Rather than attempting the difficult task of changing senior management values directly, an indirect approach can be more successful. One method is to change the experience of people who have access to top management posts; rapidly promoting people who have had deviant rather than conventional career lines. This will upset those on the traditional career ladder and there may even be some loss of efficiency, as those with established competence will still be following the traditional pattern. Another critical way of changing basic premises is through the introduction of a new chief executive who, seeking to underline his new approach to his board and senior management, will be ready to bring in those who follow his line of thought if the present management do not accept his style.

CONCLUSION

Faced with the issues raised in this chapter it may be felt that change is very problematic, and so it is. However, it can be achieved if there is effective targetting of those who support the current systems and operations, so that political pressure can be brought to bear on them. Style of personnel, rewards and budgets can affect major changes over time, but in the short-term the forces of inertia, resistance and conservatism make effective, directed change uncommon. Cosmetic changes most certainly do take place but often they are only skimming the surface, they do not basically change the direction of the firm.

If change is to have a chance it must satisfy the following conditions:

1. It must have the support and understanding of the appropriate top management and be of central concern to them.
2. It has to be preceded by a careful diagnosis of the existing situation, notably the power and political aspects.
3. There has to be discussion on a bargaining basis of the problem and/or proposed changes with those who are affected. If these discussions show that the opposition is too strong, then it will be appropriate to break off until sufficient support has been gained. If opposition is limited, then concessions can be built into the change to obtain the required support.
4. The technological, structural and human aspects of the proposal must be reconsidered in the light of the bargaining.
5. Consideration must be given to the training and management development required to make the change effective.
6. A negotiated understanding has to be reached with all parties, with acceptance that, over time, the original change will lose its shape. In the light of this it will come as no surprise if the monitoring and evaluation of the change throw up deviations, some of which will be significant.

In conclusion, it can be said that managers are often unprepared for the conflict generated by change. This arises in part from the urge to believe that change is simple; that managers are forward-looking, confident about the future and believe in inevitable progress; that change will work, and that encouraging initiative at lower levels of the firm will be good for it and them. With this stress on change there goes a belief in management's ability to make changes. The reality is that change can threaten managers, introduce disturbing questions of power and initiate the break-down of accustomed and efficiency-related routines.

10 Management Succession, Promotion and Education

Structure, technology and human behaviour interact in the political process, at the centre of which is management. This chapter examines some of the processes and tactics involved in the selection, promotion, succession and training of managers.

One of the important factors in the political process is the management career ladder, involving such questions as who is recruited and promoted, and how they are brought into the firm and advanced. Surrounding these questions is the management philosophy of the organisation, which undoubtedly influences the activities mentioned above. At the same time the philosophy may be a source of discrepancy, of not getting a match between the manager and his job. For example, given the emphasis in management philosophy on the need for more creativity and initiative, many firms seek to recruit people with these qualities and to train the existing managers to develop these attributes. Yet very often the tasks the managers have to perform do not require creativity and initiative on the lines indicated. Additionally, many managers who call for greater initiative on the part of their subordinates have little or no desire for this to happen, because it can create uncertainty and apparently weaken their power. Again we have the tension between rhetoric and reality.

Another factor in the process is the environment; a source of uncertainty, constraint and contingency which in consequence affects the distribution of power and control in the firm. In turn it impacts upon the selection and removal of managers, their behaviour and the structure in which they operate. This chain of events is itself uncertain, the relationships reflect loose couplings and are influenced by the political processes in the firm.

The selection and tenure of managers reflects the distribution of power within a firm. In terms of efficiency the tenure and removal of managers should be related to the ability to cope with critical problems, but it is more likely to depend upon the power of those concerned. To fail, when possessing power, will not necessarily lead to removal, to fail without power, is to be at risk. Similarly in the selection of personnel, it may be expected that those most capable of dealing with the current problems of the firm will be appointed; however this is by no means certain. Those in power will tend to select people who fit in with their views, people who may or may not be capable. Personal survival and support may well be the hidden criteria of selection.

THE CHIEF EXECUTIVE AND SENIOR MANAGEMENT

Management appointment and succession are political processes of contested capability where the contest is resolved by the power of the contestants.

The appointment of senior management is important but that of chief executive outstandingly so; this selection is highly political, reflecting internal power conditions. His selection sets off a series of actions aimed at solidifying and institutionalising his power, and these actions have important consequences for current senior management. He has a number of options open to him,

1. he may bring in new personnel from outside;
2. he may create new positions rather than get rid of the present incumbents;
3. he may promote existing managers sideways;
4. he may develop new sources of information and external support.

If the new executive is an internal appointee, this strategic replacement activity may be less necessary, or at least less obvious. The outcome of these tactics can be the creation of resistance to the new appointees and of a high level of political activity, much of it aimed at protecting existing positions and cutting down to size the incomers.

The change of chief executive may be the result of some crisis which cannot be resolved in the existing framework. The firm may be suffering from 'circular stagnation' – it is in a rut because it lacks imaginative and entrepreneurial types and it lacks them because it remains in a rut. The precipitating crisis which breaks such a situation may be such that a chief executive is appointed who gives new ideas an airing and translates them into profitable action; the firm grows and attracts more resilient management and the firm grows still more. Such shifts are liable to be traumatic and splinter the old power bases: however over time there will be a regrouping and the new will begin to freeze. At the basis of this is the tendency towards an organisational cycle in which firms develop, grow mature and decline; the decline will be arrested through new ideas, new personnel and new activities but the halting of decline carriers with it the seeds of future ossification.

Management selection and succession are factors in organisational change. The extent to which change is possible depends upon the perception of the appointees and successors, their power and ability to increase that power and to deal with the internal and external constraints.

There are three main factors underlying recruitment and selection to chief executive and senior management levels.

1. There is the distribution of power.
2. There is the extent to which there is agreement about the necessary criteria of successful performance at senior levels of management. This is an ambiguous area and its definition will be influenced by the location and power of those involved in the selection process. This ambiguity rests in part upon the fact that experience at one level of management does not necessarily produce effective learning for management at a more senior level – the more a promotion demands strategic and critical decisions rather than tactical or routine ones, the less transferable does the experience become. Indeed it is for this reason that in many organisations it is unlikely that promotion from within will produce enough adequate senior management. This was a problem which faced Michael Edwardes at British Leyland where he undertook a major reshuffle of management, moving 'staff' types out of the 'line' jobs into which they had been previously placed.[1] Another reason for ambiguity is that senior management calls for skills, knowledge and aptitudes which can only be stated in general terms and measured imprecisely, if at all. Additionally, the political skills required become more sophisticated, as

the balancing of demands and the nature of control becomes more complex.

3. There is the question of the career channels of 'standard' and 'deviant' executive leadership, that is to say, the extent to which a firm operates on a standard well-known career plan or recruits talent wherever it is to be found.

In management succession the critical political outcome of promotion is the potential for increased power. Once installed there is the opportunity to obtain resources, guide decisions and, especially, to exercise discretion. It is in the area of discretion that the manager's political range can develop, hence the aim must be to occupy jobs with increasing areas of discretion and the opportunity to exercise it. However, there can be occasions when a manager may decide not to use his discretion because he sees that it is in his interest not to do so. His reluctance may be due to his firm's management style as expressed in the organisation structure and assessment criteria – the more serious the consequence of error the more are managers likely to evade discretion and seek power in other ways. There is a difference between the position of those managers in early ceiling operations, who have little or no recognised discretion, and those in high ceiling occupations. In the former case power leverage may come through collective, coalition activity or by the individual seeking to move out of that occuption. In the latter, the manager is visible to his colleagues and his power is in part built upon his relations with them and upon his ability to use his discretion to solve organisational problems.

When assessing performance against multiple and incompatible criteria, senior management can produce a systematic bias through the exercise of discretion. When workloads exceed capacity and the manager has choice, there is the temptation to undertake the tasks which are liable to enhance his reputation with his superiors. For example, where workloads fluctuate and he is assessed on the maintenance of a steady workflow the manager will, if he is politically sensitive, stockpile; where there are alternatives he will report successes and suppress evidence of failure. Faced with this, senior management often sets up new monitoring and control systems administered by existing or new departments, who then negotiate with those being evaluated in order to obtain the information upon which the evaluation takes place.

In considering management selection, succession and promotion, it should be remembered that organisations are places where people compete for advancement and are rivals for organisational rewards, yet at the same time have to cooperate. The organisation chart is both a control system and a career ladder upon which few will succeed, as is the case in the wider society.

The political view of promotion runs counter to the common belief that promotion goes to those who perform best and is the result of rational, non-political behaviour. This belief is important, as it helps to maintain the legitimacy of the firm's internal labour market and helps to assuage the feelings of those who do less well than others in the promotion stakes; there is at least the appearance of fair competition for all. The belief in the efficacy of hard work and good performance is widely held and forms part of organisational ideology. Yet the truth is that this view is inadequate, in being incomplete. Of great importance is the ability and political skill of managers being in the right place at the right time. This entails the establishment of contacts, of identifying and linking into significant social networks, of fitting in; of possessing an appropriate social background – of ancestry, membership of clubs and of 'political' affiliations – this relates to all levels and not simply to senior management; and of being in the right department with the right leader. As the power of different units changes, so do career prospects within them, hence the need to be sensitive to departmental ratings in the organisation and aware of any planned development of the company's markets, sales and growth areas generally and, where possible, to be able to shift between departments at the right time.

When thinking of career development through the political process, it should be remembered that power ploys and strategies are subject to various forms of social control: the need to live together – the existence of one manager's privileges depends to a large extent on others' privileges, agreement of the need for a minimum level of efficiency and the requirement of some stability in individual and group relationships. Within these constraints, mutual accommodation is the result of various trials of strength, of time – of knowing when to move, when to become visible. There are different stages in everyone's career; old avenues close off and new choices open. In this there is the element of luck, of chance. Planned career development, either by the firm or by the individual, is largely a chimera; uncertainties, chance events, uncontrollable developments, all contribute to making formal career development a fragile concept. For the individual, a programmed career development is often post facto, a rationalisation after the event. For the organisation, planned career development is a part of the superstructure of rationality so necessary to give it legitimacy. One aspect of the chance factor is that development depends upon appropriate vacancies and these cannot always be guaranteed; they depend upon a degree of human and organisational stability that is difficult to contemplate except in a frozen system. Planned vacancies reflect a programmed development of a company's operations that is not possible to forecast accurately in a changing economic, social and political environment.

Managerial promotion is also the result of present location in the organisation structure, and the all-important ability to build support. As one executive remarked, 'Life in a large organisation is pretty much like politics. A fellow gets along pretty much on what kind of organisation he has been able to gather around him. As far as I am concerned the lone wolf with no friends will get nowhere, either in business or politics.'[2] Support building needs a realistic appreciation of the availability of sponsors and of the viability of existing information networks. Support and information are key elements in the politics of promotion.

MANAGEMENT TRAINING AND DEVELOPMENT

Coupled with succession and promotion are the activities of management training and development. Given the theme of this book, it is argued that too much current training and development is based upon human relations, human resources, structural and scientific management models and that too little attention is paid to political skills. What often occurs is that managers are 'taught' or 'learn' through a variety of techniques how they ought to behave outside the context of actual behaviour; they are developed to become creative and innovative but only so long as they stay within the boundaries laid down by those in power.

They are trained in leadership skills without being expected to challenge the present leaders. The main thrust is disguised manipulation.

Another strand is based on learning new and sophisticated techniques, numerical and statistical procedures, the belief that there are best and optimal answers to managerial problems and that there are ideal organisation structures designed around the new techniques. As a result, managers are desensitised to issues involving uncertain multiple goals and to the use of data for political ends, such as the restriction of argument and explanation. There is a failure to recognise that techniques and structures are tools in the political process; they are there to be used for the purpose of increasing power while at the same time being useful bases of power. Within this strand there is the development of information technology with its overtones of greater rationality in decision-making, and the reduction, if not the elimination of judgement. There is an unwillingness to recognise that information gathering and its processing and use, are highly powerful and political activities.

The result of such training is the development of people who are useful allies of politically oriented managers, for in coalitions their specialised knowledge and techniques can give useful support while remaining politically ineffective and insensitive to the games that are being played.[3] Technocrats provide important support for the management politician.

The emphasis needs to shift to a more political appreciation of the process of management and of the techniques, tactics and strategies that are used. In terms of skills the stress should shift to developing negotiating and bargaining skills, to the recognition of these as highly important attributes of leadership. Attention should also focus on the conflict model of organisations, with concern moving from conflict resolution, to conflict amelioration. Decision-making should be seen less as a technical procedure and more as a political process, as indeed should resource allocation. Risk-taking becomes recognised as part of the political process and is allied to elements of chance as an acceptable part of management. In all these aspects there is the recognition that part of management is a mystery and attempts to remove that element, to make it wholly rational, is to move still further from the manager as a human being of considerable complexity. Judgement and intuition are part both of the mystery and of the political process.

This is not a frontal attack on the rationality of management, but an argument for the recognition of the limitations of that approach. It is also an argument for acceptance of the power and political dimensions of management, and involves the view that managers should become more analytically sensitive. It is frequently assumed that by nature all managers are rational thinkers and skilled in analysis, and that all that is needed is more data and better techniques: this is far from the truth. The need is to improve analysis; recognising, first, that it involves a political dimension and second, that one of the key factors to be analysed is that of power, exhibited through political activity.

Thus the implications for management education are:

1. the need to bring the conflict element of management into the open, accepting that conflict is not to be deplored. This recognition would lead to the development of a more complete picture of organisational and managerial behaviour; bringing into perspective the balance between conflict and consensus, conflict management and resolution, and at the same time underlining the continuous and open-ended nature of conflict.
2. managers should be educated to recognise the limitations of the rational approach to certain management processes; for example, decision-making, strategy and policy making.

In this way the limitations of 'conversion' education with its strong stress on developing participation, consultation, trust and confidence would also be put into perspective. The process of decision-making, change and leadership would be interpreted through a political approach using political skills. The gap between rhetoric and reality would be narrowed and the tension between what is propagated and what happens in organisations would be reduced.

Further, the significance of 'ordinary' knowledge would be reinstated. Casual empiricism, thoughtful speculation and analysis would be recognised as complementary to professional social knowledge and not superseded by it. The language of management education would be less rarified and more grounded in managerial experience.[4]

CONCLUSION

At the centre of management there are theories which are themselves political tools. First there are academic theories devised to facilitate and support management – they are constructs, frameworks for thinking and not always applicable to managerial practice. Second, every manager develops his own theories which guide his everyday activities; they are the application of ideas, propositions and intuitions which may be difficult to articulate, being improvisations learned in action. Finally, there are those espoused theories which managers use to justify and describe their behaviour. In practice the three often become interwoven.[5] What is important is that theories of one sort or another are part of the practice of management and as such part of the political process. Management training and education should aim to increase understanding of this fact and of its importance. The interplay of theories and power in political activity needs to be understood.

11 Interorganisational Relationships

Power, conflict and managerial politics are characteristics not only of the internal operation of the firm, but of its relationships with the· world in which it operates. In these relationships management has to keep the firm at the centre of several necessary streams of action and as these are variable and mobile, the hub itself is both transient and difficult to control. At the same time managers have to act in such a way as to satisfy their sense of order and control: through the manipulation of environmental constraints, through the processing of demands environmentally generated and through the management of relationships to meet the short-term requirement of certainty and the long-term desire for freedom from dependence and commitment. These activities come together in the quest for survival.

The components of the environment which generate uncertainty, sustain demands, represent constraints and provide the context for organisational activity, include:

1. culture; the values, beliefs and ideologies which go to make up the basis for and justification of action.
2. technology; the level of scientific and technological development in the wider society.
3. education; the standards of literacy, sophistication and bias.
4. politics; the climate and culture of the political system at national and local level.
5. law; the legal system and the government framework of which it is a part.
6. demography; the distribution of age and sex, the pattern of births and deaths. The significance of this can be seen in the impact of the 'baby boomers' (56 million Americans from 25 to 39 years of age) upon the American economic and political scene in the 1980s.[1]

7. industry; the framework within which the firm exists and the prevailing state of the economy at any given time. The privatisation policy of the British government of the early 1980s has had a ripple effect on the rest of the economy, shifting resources, changing competitive patterns and challenging the balance of private and public enterprise in an industrial society.
8. society; the class structure and social institutions, including trade unions.

Some of these components are more important than others to the firm's functioning at a given time. The problem for management is not simply the complexity generated by the interaction of the components, but their dynamic nature.

ENVIRONMENTAL DIFFERENCES

The general framework of components outlined above can readily be made more specific and as such are of direct concern to a manager: customers; competitors; local and national government with those departments which directly impinge on industry and commerce; sources of finance, banks and financial institutions; technology relevant to a given operational process. These components can be further classified in the following terms:

1. their degree of homogeneity; for example, the inputs from suppliers may be very varied or similar; the customer markets may differ greatly or little; what is clear is that these differences will have an impact upon the strategic choice of the organisation. It is necessary to note that the complexity of the environment need not of itself generate uncertainty.
2. their stability and instability; that is, the degree of change among the components. The variability is the result of the frequency, scale and irregularity of changes in the overall pattern.
3. the extent to which the components are unified or segmented; for example, whether there is a single market or a number of markets all with the same characteristics, and
4. the degree of hostility and benignity of the environment. This raises the question of the degree of threat, arising from the environment, to the attainment of the firm's goals.[2]

These dimensions are highly important to the management of a firm in that they,

1. directly impinge on the internal political processes of the firm, providing constraints and opportunities within which these processes work;
2. relate to different levels in the organisation and to different decision-making units at those levels;
3. mean that managers who deal with different segments of the environment may face different combinations of the above dimensions; and
4. affect organisation structure and the operations that are performed within it.

The complexity of inputs and outputs of a firm, influences the level of individual skills needed by management in its transactions within the environment.

The environment is a storehouse of resources for the individual firm; if its resources are scarce, the firm may decide to move to richer environments, develop more efficient operations which require fewer resources or establish closer links with other firms in order to jointly cope with the problem. In constrast, in a rich environment where resources are plentiful, the firm may not feel under pressure to increase its efficiency or to forge closer links with others.

In many senses the environment is enacted, that is to say, managers give meanings to environmental events after they have occurred. 'The human creates the environment to which the system then adapts. The human being does not react to an environment, he enacts it.'[3]

Associated with the environment and its pattern of different components, both generalised and particular, there is the question of uncertainty.

First, given the differences in perception, personalities, information systems and forecasting capabilities, what is uncertain to one organisation may be certain to another. Added to which, if a firm has a surplus of resources it can afford to be less immediately responsive to resource uncertainties.

Second, firms faced with uncertainty are still evaluated against criteria of efficiency. The central problem is one of coping or of appearing to do so. To deal with the uncertainty, various tactics will be employed and positions and departments established.

Third, firms faced wtih uncertainty tend to develop particular patterns of behaviour, they move to satisficing and 'disjointed incrementalism' rather than formal planning and rational decision making. They embark upon a process of short-run adaptive reactions underneath a cover of formal planning and control systems.

Fourth, uncertainty arises in decision-making when,

1. there is a lack of environmental information and knowledge which could mean that a firm does not know how much it would lose if a particular decision was incorrect; and
2. there is inability to assign probabilities with any degree of confidence as to the outcome of a particular decision.

In addition to considering the uncertainty factor relating to the different environmental components, there is the need to focus on individual differences between organisational members, and the interests they represent. The external uncertainties and the internal differences interact upon each other to produce particular strategies, policies, structures and behaviours.

All this is not to suggest that a passive attitude must be taken towards uncertainty; it can be controlled and mitigated through the existence in the firm of slack, through loosely coupled internal systems which tend to localise the effects of uncertainty, and through forecasting, surveillance and managing the environment. In terms of power and politics, those who have the skills to cope with and manage uncertainty for others in the organisation have a power base to exploit internally.

ORGANISATIONS IN THE ENVIRONMENT

A firm operates in an environment which contains other organisations and institutions. The relationships that arise between that central firm and the others can be regarded as the network of an organisational 'set', and are influenced by the following:

1. the connections of the boundary personnel, that is, those members of the various organisations who relate their own organisations to the central firm, and the members of that firm who relate it to its set;
2. the two-way flow of information between the firm and the surrounding organisations;

3. the flow of products and services to and from the firm;
4. the flow of personnel between the firms in the set;
5. the structure, authority and power of the boundary spanning units in their organisations;
6. the input and output sets, that is, the relations of the central firm to the various organisations who provide it with the operationally essential resources and to others who accept its outputs;
7. the number of organisations in the sets;
8. the external organisations against which the firm compares its performance and those institutions which provide it with its values and goals; and
9. the overlap in membership of the central firm and other organisations, for example, employees who are trade unionists; specialists who are members of professional associations.

In an organisation set there are liable to be a number of sources of instability arising from, differing and changing patterns of interaction between the central firm and the others in the set; differences in power among those involved in the set; differences in the insulation of internal activity from visibility to others, so that deviant behaviour is not easily detected; differences in the visibility of members' conflicting demands upon the central firm and a reluctance of others to reduce demands and, finally, differences in access to support from outside the set.

In the set a number of activities can impact upon the firm.

First, conflict between other members of the set may reduce pressure on the central firm. This conflict may be fuelled by the central firm in order to ease pressure on itself and hopefully to increase its power within the set.

Second, groups of firms may form temporary alliances for limited purposes, for example, resource scarcity may lead to coordinated action.

Third, all organisations in a set are linked by specific types of relationships and these form various networks.

Coordinated action by groups of organisations in a set is affected by a number of factors which include the following:

1. The number of organisations in the coordinated action. Where there are many there is likely to be greater formalisation, more planning and a greater need for executive action by the organisation acting as the leader. There is a need to

monitor the behaviour of the members of the group to detect deviance.

2. The leadership within the coordinated group. Arguably the more concentrated the power in the hands of one organisation, the easier it is to coordinate the actions of the group; for example, Marks and Spencer and its suppliers. The powerful organisation acts as a substitute for detailed plans and lines of authority.

3. Where the firms acting together have similar values and attitudes, there is less need for formalisation and strong authority.

4. The impact of other coordinated groups, producing the effect of countervailing power.

At this stage the organisation set should be distinguished from the wider social context in which it is embedded. Each organisation in a set has its own organisation set, and as the interconnectedness with other sets increases so does interdependence, although not necessarily uncertainty.

Relationships within a set involve specialisation out of which arises exchange and dependence. From the individual organisation's viewpoint, its effectiveness rests on its ability to exploit its environment in obtaining resources and markets while at the same time maintaining an autonomous bargaining position.

The relationship between the central firm and its surrounding set is characterised by:

First, the formalisation of agreements and structural arrangements.

Second, the level of intensity which indicates the amount of investment an organisation has, in its relations and activities with others; the amount of resources involved and the frequency of interaction it is prepared to undertake.

Third, reciprocity, which refers to the degree of symmetry in the relations; where there is sustained assymmetry there is likely to be a dependent relationship.

Finally, standardisation, that is, the degree of standardisation of the organisations involved, and to the procedural arrangements between them.

Clearly these dimensions interact upon each other, for example, intensity of interaction and organisation size will affect standardisation.

Maintaining interdependence, while avoiding unwanted dependence and loss of autonomy, requires political skills of the highest order. The outcome of consistently attempting to achieve these differing aims can lead to built-in contradictions, as compromises are made between maintaining autonomy and yielding to external constraints. Managers have then to learn to live with the outcome of their compromises.

THE BOUNDARY SPANNING ACTIVITY

Central to these many and varied activities is the boundary spanning unit, which is specifically concerned with mediating between the firm and the different components in the environment. Examples of boundary spanning units include the personnel function, the marketing and sales function, the supplies function and finance.

The activities of the boundary spanning unit include:

1. The management of information, that is, information processing, the selection, filtering and summarising of data coming into the firm and directing it to the relevant organisational sub-units. In this activity there is a duality of purpose, it acts to absorb uncertainty while preventing ossification, through searching for new ideas and knowledge. In the process of distributing information a boundary spanning unit may break down a problem, so that relatively independent individuals possess different pieces of the information which the boundary spanning unit possesses in its entirety. This increases the unit's power.

   This activity of information processing is complicated by the fact that there are numerous boundary spanning units in a firm; providing information, representing different interests and pursuing separate and potentially conflicting courses of action. The solution of problems will often require the involvement of different levels of management and specialists from a variety of functional units, all drawing directly or indirectly upon environmental data, much of it processed by boundary personnel. Boundary spanning units have a strong base in their control over information into the decision-making process of the firm. Of course the flow of information is not all one way, boundary spanning units also process the information that goes out from the firm to its constituents in the environment, and this flow is managed to facilitate the firm's attempt to influence and control the different sectors of the environment.

2. Boundary spanning units have external representative functions including acquiring and disposing of resources which are directly linked with the work flow of the firm. They manage and improve the political legitimacy of the organisation through mediating, bargaining and negotiating. They also seek to maintain and develop an effective image of the firm. Their power here lies in part in the fact that they generally have the face to face contact with customers, suppliers and so forth; they establish personal links which can become a power base in their dealings with internal sections of their organisation.

The crucial problem for a firm's boundary spanning units is one of adjustment to constraints and contingencies not controlled by the firm. In the end their ability to reduce constraints and manage contingencies gives them leverage in their firm. Their skill lies in managing situations over which they have little or no formal control.

Boundary personnel and their departments occupy positions of potential power. Their relationships with internal and external individuals, units and organisations provide linkages and points of entry into internal and external networks. The number of boundary personnel, their quality and education, their position in the organisational hierarchy and their values, play an important part in influencing internal and external relationships. Because the boundary spanning personnel of organisations in a set will differ inevitably in quality, education, expertise and power, the distribution of power between firms within a set will be influenced by these differences. Those firms whose boundary personnel are less effective will be at a disadvantage. Thus it is critical to recruit personnel of the appropriate calibre and skills, notably political, at all levels of boundary spanning; to train them to think in terms of that particular organisation and by one means or another build up their support, because there is always the risk that they will identify more with those outside than with their parent firm. At the same time it must be recognised that they have to straddle the boundaries of the firm in order to design effective networks and increase organisational effectiveness.

Boundary spanning personnel deal with different segments of the environment and their perception of the sector they are scanning will be influenced by a number of factors, including,

1. their attitude to their unit's goals;
2. differences in time orientation – some are concerned with long-term and others with short-term considerations;
3. differing interpersonal orientations; some concentrate on getting the job done, others are more concerned with maintaining relationships; and
4. the formality of the structure of their unit, its levels of hierarchy, its degree of formality and its rewards and control systems.

Because of these boundary spanning differences the integration of a firm's views of the environment is not automatically achieved through the working of its hierarchy. Integrative devices, involving a considerable political element, will be required.

As with other managerial personnel, boundary spanning managers are concerned to develop their power base so as to influence internal and external issues. In addition to the tactics already discussed, they can develop alliances with external elements in order to enhance the interests of each, without necessarily serving the interests of their own organisation. Boundary personnel have a strong tendency to identify with the external; faced with this possibility the firm can reduce the discretion of its boundary personnel by setting up limiting rules and by requiring decisions to be cleared at higher levels in the firm.

Clearly the boundary position can be of critical importance in determining the distribution of power within the firm. Where environments are dynamic, complex and differentiated, the relevant boundary positions will tend to reflect those conditions. This may not always appear to be the case, as equivalence between boundary positions and environmental conditions may be slow to develop if it requires basic changes in the existing power structure.

When the different segments of the environment are stable, there is less likely to be a need for monitoring, and possibly fewer boundary positions will be needed than in an unstable environment. This depends upon whether the rate of change is constant or variable, and whether the differences in change are substantial or not. If the firm operates in a rich environment where resources are readily available, there may be fewer boundary positions than in a lean environment where the search for scarce resources and information is critical.

The formalisation of boundary roles will be influenced by the technology and markets of the firm. Where a firm provides the same services for large numbers of customers the boundary positions may be routinised; where there are long production runs to a stable market there will be a large volume of standardised transactions, contributing to routine activity and to control by rule. In contrast, heterogeneous, unstable environments, face critical contingencies. In this situation boundary spanning personnel will be able to exercise discretion and, if they are successful, acquire power. In all these alternatives the fact of power is never far away; boundary spanning personnel will always be seeking to establish themselves in activities which will provide them with a solid power base. The fact that they span the firm and the environment gives them an initial point from which they can build power. In many respects they have the opportunity to be managerial manipulators par excellence. Of course it has to be remembered that the links between environment, boundary spanning activity and internal operations are problematic and not deterministic; the various relationships outlined above are possibilities not certainties, factors of chance, history and current power, to name but a few, may all contribute to different patterns of development.

ORGANISATIONAL COUPLING

Another aspect of the network of linkages in an organisational set is that of coupling which is both an internal and external feature of organisations. Coupling may be tight or loose. Where the individual organisation is internally tightly coupled, that is, where there is a high level of dependence between the different parts, any disturbance is liable to spread rapidly and destroy stability. Conversely loose internal coupling will tend to produce a limited area of disturbance.

Similarly external networks can be tightly or loosely coupled and the extent to which this occurs will depend upon the strength of ties, the regulatory functions, the scope and diversity of organisations in the set, the persistence of the network and its success.[4] The organisational issues raised by different degrees of network coupling can be illustrated by considering the advantages and disadvantages of internal and external loose coupling.

The advantages of loose coupling include the following:

1. It allows an organisation and its different parts to persist and evolve independently of others in the network.
2. It provides an organisation with selective sensing mechanisms; that is, there will be a plurality of organisational parts testing and monitoring the environment.
3. It allows local adaptation of organisational sub-units facing an environment that, in aggregate, poses conflicting demands.
4. It permits the retention of a greater number of mutations and novel solutions than do tightly coupled systems.
5. A breakdown is confined to one part so that it does not affect the rest of the organisation. It may lead to some duplication of effort but this would reduce the uncertainty that could exist if no such duplications existed.
6. It permits greater self-determination.
7. It is relatively inexpensive so long as self-coordination occurs in the network.

Against these possible advantages has to be placed a corresponding list of disadvantages:

1. Loose coupling is not selective in what is perpetuated and may lead to the retention of out-of-date traditions.
2. The heightened sensitivity may expose an organisation to the influence of transitory factors in the environment.
3. It may prevent the diffusion of desirable changes in the network.
4. It may be difficult for the network members to help each other in time of difficulty.
5. Members are more on their own in dealing with hostile environments.

Clearly the different types of coupling affect the extent and style of political activity that is undertaken both internally and externally. One important factor influencing the type of coupling that develops will be the power distribution in a network, reflected in the extent to which joint decision-making between units and organisations takes place.

THE LINKING PIN FIRM

In a set or network there will tend to emerge a linking pin organisation which has a central integrating role and which achieves, through its centrality, a position of power. Where the linking pin organisation acts in a specialist capacity it will become still more powerful because it can, for instance, cut costs for others and provide them with an advantage over those who do not use the link. Dominant, high status organisations generally occupy this role because they manoeuvre into the central position through manipulating interorganisational relations. This manipulation may take the form of developing a non-competitive marketing structure to eliminate threats to the dominant firm, through bureaucratic pressures and the organising dependencies. In addition manipulation may occur through kinship links between members of the different firms, resource control and increasing the multiplicity of relationships, hereby giving the central organisation the opportunity to hedge and to divide its potential opponents. An example of a linking pin organisation in a business network is that of a bank, with its control of financial resources and its specialist skills. Where no linking pin organisation emerges there is likely to be a multiplicity of relationships, as the organisations in the network have to treat with each other rather than through a central intermediary.[5]

Within a network, organisations are concerned with survival and evaluation. Firms are evaluated by the stakeholders who are members of their organisation set, and are tested on the different dimensions of efficiency, effectiveness and social reference. How then do organisations create the impression that they are operating in a satisfactory manner?

First, by demonstrating historical improvement; for example, growth is regarded as a sign of health so a firm will stress any activity which shows growth – output, sales or profits.

Second, by seeking to score favourably in relation to comparable organisations.

Third, a firm may not be able to demonstrate improvement on all the criteria of the stakeholders, so it will seek to hold fast on some and show improvement on those of direct interest to the environmental elements upon which it is most dependent. Where the stakeholders lack the technical ability to evaluate the organisation it will seek an extrinsic measure, for example, prestige.[6]

Ultimately survival depends on the acquisition of resources and these will be forthcoming if the organisation meets the appropriate criteria. However, an organisation's ability to succeed is influenced by a number of factors such as, its perception and interpretation of the environment, and the attention it pays to the relevant sector. In turn these will be affected by its readiness to search for information and ideas and the efficacy of its information system. Its ability to succeed will also be influenced by its skills in coping with and responding to constraints – which are often the result of prior decisions – knowing that behind every constraint there is an interest group.

Thus survival derives from the management of the demands of the environmental interest groups, upon which the organisation depends for resources and support. It has to provide inducements, manipulate and even coerce; it has to have the political skills to manage competing demands from different stakeholders, knowing that to favour one may upset the others. Usually it cannot respond to every demand so must decide to whom it will react; depending in part upon the internal power structure of the other organisations and in part upon its ability to identify those who have the power to damage it. All of this will be influenced by the extent to which it is tightly, or loosely coupled to those upon whom it depends.

One of the means by which an organisation controls its environment is through the development of 'distinctive competence'. This means the firm establishes its own 'domain' through its range of products and services and the population of customers it serves. It also involves the suppliers and others who provide it with support. Its domain has to be negotiated and is in consequence highly political.

Because interdependence is a factor in this political activity, matters rarely proceed as quickly and in the exact form as anticipated by the negotiators.

The relationships so far described are political and dynamic; the less powerful will seek to reduce the relative power of the strong. Yet in this situation of potential conflict, the organisations involved must be aware of the nature of their interdependence, and of the need to take each other into account if they are to achieve their goals. They need to distinguish between the subjective and objective perceptions of the environment, its variability, its complexity and its illiberality. If these distinctions are not made, the result may well be incongruity between events and perceptions, in which case certain organisational responses will be inappropriate, with decisions being based upon invalid premises.

JOINT VENTURES

To cope with some environmental problems, firms enter into joint decision-making and action. Joint decision-making involves issues of power and politics.

First, the potential decision-makers recognise their interdependence. They see that consolidated decisions can lead to an increase in joint resources, albeit with a reduction in autonomy. In the light of the tension between costs and benefits, joint decision-making between firms will involve negotiation and political activity.

Second, the technologies of joint decision-making, that is, the pattern of information exchange and the structure of authority, have political implications for the managers concerned. Three critical issues have to be considered,

1. whether authority for joint decision-making will be centralised or decentralised;
2. whether there will be information centralisation or decentralisation; and
3. whether information will be freely available or rationed.

Managerial attitudes to interorganisational decision-making will be influenced by the outcomes of the process; if these threaten their own power bases they will be reluctant to proceed; stressing the possibility that any united action is unlikely to produce the desired results, and that previous attempts at joint decision-making have not been successful. If they are unable to prevent joint decision-making being undertaken they can fall back upon many of the tactics discussed in these pages.

The greater the number of joint programmes a firm has, the more its decision-making is constrained through obligations, commitments and communication obstacles and the greater the degree of its interorganisational dependence. The more joint programmes that a firm develops, the greater will be the complexity of its external relationships and the greater the impact upon its own internal structuring. Yet all is not lost; a multiplicity of programmes can provide the opportunity for political activity, for hedging, fudging and trade-offs.

Those who work closely in joint ventures will be in a position to regulate the flow of information in and out of their organisations. Information is a crucial variable in the operation of any firm and, in this case, close ties with other organisations may provide advance information of impending externally-induced changes in the input and output transactions of the firm. These changes will influence the search for and activation of more advantageous input and output transactions and will have an impact upon the available memory store of environmental interchanges.

The acquisition of information is only one step in the process of linking a firm to its environment. Once the information enters the firm it has to be organised and transmitted to the appropriate units, so as to produce a response to the environment. That response will be partly the result of the way the information is handled, which in turn will be the result of the existing power distribution in the organisation.

In terms of information an organisation may misread or not perceive its dependencies; for example, firms frequently respond to external demands by stressing greater internal efficiency, when the demands actually relate to some aspect of the firm's product. This is the result of (a) the selective principle – people are trained to see some things but not others and (b) the commitment of firms to the past, to traditions, mythologies and rituals.

Much information entering a firm relates to demands generated by stakeholders. These demands have to be managed, with firms identifying their significance and that of the interest groups making them. Not all interest groups are equally important, they vary in the extent to which they control resources critical to the functioning of the firm at a given time.

Faced with demands an organisation can adapt, modify, change or seek to manage them. Yet whatever strategy it uses it will never be able to wholly escape from some dependence upon the environment and as present demands are dealt with, new ones will be made.

CONCLUSION

Managers will endeavour to influence and control environmental demands using a number of different tactics.

1. They can seek to satisfy some part of a demand so that the relevant interest group will not push others.
2. They can attempt to influence the demanding organisation's definition of what is satisfactory, then claim the demand has been met. If this ploy is successful they are in a position to manage the demands made upon them.
3. A firm's control of communications influences the demands another organisation makes.
4. The creation of uncertainty provides an opportunity to control the formulation of demands, by creating the impression that the firm has knowledge which the other organisation requires.

The ability of a firm to manage environmental demands will be influenced by its visibility to demand-generating organisations. Of course one way to avoid being faced with demands is not to possess the capacity to comply with them. In addition to those cases where a firm has neither the physical nor technological capacity to comply with demands, there are legal and social constraints. Legal constraints forbid certain activities on the part of organisations and social constraints create a framework of guidelines as to what can and cannot be done.

Faced with the environmental complexity discussed, it is evident that organisational disasters are liable to occur for a number of reasons, including false assumptions, poor communications, cultural lag, misplaced optimism or pessimism and a large number of errors. It can be said that 'large-scale failures can only be produced if time and resources are devoted to them'.[7] To counter these upsets managers have to use their political skills. Interorganisational relations have many of the political features of the internal relations within a firm, but with the added dimension that control is less easy; requiring more political ability if it is to be exercised effectively.

12 Policy and Strategy

Policies are the bench marks from which business plans are constructed; they lay down guidelines for present and future action.

Policies are generated in a number of ways all of which involve a political element.

First, there is orginated policy, in which top management focuses upon overall objectives and develops guidelines for subordinates. This policy may be broad in scope; allowing key subordinates to give it clearer definition and to exercise discretion. In some instances it may be promulgated so thoroughly that it leaves apparently little room for discretion; but this is misleading as any policy statement has to be interpreted, which means there is room for the exercise of power. It would be incorrect to think that all originated policy is made at the top levels; it can be made at any level so long as it provides guidance for subordinates. It is not necessarily imposed by command; it may be achieved through unobtrusive suggestions. What is evident is that its making, interpretation and execution all offer the opportunity for political activity, using the tactics discussed earlier.

Second, there is appealed policy, where exceptional cases are passed up the hierarchy for decisions to be made – in this way a form of common law is established, precedents are developed to guide future activities. As a result of its piecemeal development it is often incomplete, uncoordinated and confused; demonstrating the difficulty of knowing exactly what policies exist. Appealed policy may be the result of leaving loose ends and large areas of policy making to chance. It also raises the question as to whether subordinates have understood the formal policy. Clearly, appealed policy is highly political, as its formulation derives from a policy vacuum over which there is the possibility of political manoeuvring – it rests upon a basis of power, as its formulation derives from the exercise of discretion and the existence of organisational uncertainty.

Third, there is implied policy, which grows from actions which people see about them and believe to be based upon some constituted policy. It raises the question of the distinction between real and stated policy; for example, between a stated policy of producing high quality products and what actually happens – management's acceptance of large quantities of shoddy work. This occurs because management has not, or believes it has not, the authority to secure compliance to the stated policy; is not committed to it; or because there is no such policy. In these cases managers develop their own guidelines with an eye to their own power position.

Fourth, there is externally imposed policy, arising from the pressure exercised by external bodies such as government, trade associations, and trade unions. These pressures may be directly or indirectly exerted and are based on the authority and power of the parties concerned.[1]

Policies more towards plans and in an organisation three types of plans can exist: operational, administrative or strategic; all three involve political considerations. This chapter will focus mainly on strategic planning, on corporate strategy.

The task of the organisational strategist is to adapt the firm to its environment through a series of objectives, policies and plans, while at the same time seeking to modify the environment. Firm and environment interact upon each other.

From the outset there is the problem of defining the objectives of the organisation. They are never as clear-cut as they appear. They are the result of a complex pattern of forces operating internally and externally, they are essentially a product of organisational political processes – of the company's information and search systems, the power structure in and around the firm and the perceptions and values of the decision-makers and the interests they represent.

In the process of the firm's adapting to the environment, recognition of opportunity plays an important part; that is, the degree of awareness of the environment and of the segments which have particular relevance for the firm, and of the various types of strategy that are available; such as increasing volume sales, expanding markets, moving into new geographical areas, product diversification, vertical integration and horizontal mergers. Behind these factors is the basic concept of the business as a match between a given product group and a given market;

essentially the identification of a market niche. Defining a business involves,

1. a definition of its product(s);
2. the identification of its market(s): it cannot appeal to all customers so there has to be a critical strategic choice of customer target and of tactics. Failure to recognise shifts in the customer target can be disastrous, witness cooperative retailing and the old Woolworths; and
3. an explicit understanding of the connection between the two.

Put in another way, firms create their environments by making choices of markets, products, technologies and the desired scale of operations. The choices are set within the political system and power distribution of the firm and is constrained,

1. by existing knowledge of resources;
2. by managerial beliefs;
3. by the perceptions of the dominant coalition;
4. by the way the organisation has been previously structured to cope with different parts of the environment; and
5. by such dynamic constraints as productive capacity, price initiatives, competitors' research break-throughs, shifts in the basis of competition and the entry of new competitors.

The choices that emerge out of this welter of factors shape the structure and processes of the firm. How do these choices emerge? Why is one particular choice made rather than another? The answer lies in the power and political skills of those involved. What is certain is that these decisions are significant for the future. Once they have been made operational through structure and processes, they constrain future choices; they make it difficult to pursue activities outside the normal sphere of operations.

POLITICS AND STRATEGIC CHOICE

Strategy and strategic choice are essentially political. Although most strategic planning models are basically rational,[2] uncertainty in human behaviour vitiates much of the supposed rationality. As a result, conflict, uncertainty and power are inevitable components of the strategy and planning process.

Any organisation is faced with powerful internal and external groups, who make demands which have to be met if support is to be maintained, and so further constraints emerge. Where the demands are conflicting a number of consequences follow: there is compromise – broad policy commitments are generated so that different groups can see some scope for achieving their goals – the incompatible are able to co-exist; sequential attention is paid to demands – attention is paid to one while the rest are held in abeyance.

Political action is both a constraint and lubricant on strategy; in both delaying and facilitating the execution of major decisions, it exemplifies its own duality. It is through political processes that demands are articulated, negotiated and progressed.

The making of policy and strategy is both an intellectual activity and an institutional process[3] shaped by the perceptions, attention and attitudes of decision-makers and by the information flows that connect them to their environment. The institutional processes operate within and upon the political and structural framework of the organisation.

From this perspective, policy innovation is less a product of new ideas than of political conflict; its shape reflects bargains between established political interests. This emerges clearly if the phases of policy making are considered, for at each phase influence and power are at work:

1. awareness – how are policy makers made aware of the situation and the problems that affect them?
2. salience – why is the situation and its problems considered significant?
3. definitions of a problem – among the differing conceptions of a problem which predominates?
4. specification of alternatives – what courses of action are considered and why are some excluded?
5. why is one particular course of action chosen?

The critical point is that the problem revealed is not necessarily the problem solved; it depends upon the response of the various interest groups.

In all stages there is a negotiating process involving, first, the giving and seeking of information, the mapping of power relations and the discovery of zones of agreement. Second, there is the pursuance, rationalisation and consolidation of one position and, third, there is the making of agreements, involving terms and implicit commitments.

The phases seldom occur strictly in the order outlined, but all are essential and need to be distinguished for analytical purposes. What is important is the recognition that each phase is open to political influence. In organisations the logical sequence is upset; policy making and strategic planning is, in actuality, dynamic and iterative. The clear sequence is not possible because of the extended duration of the planning process, the technical unknowns, the changing balance of power, expectations and requirements among interest groups. In the light of these factors the need for reappraisal of plans is an inevitable feature of managerial life. Regularisation, routinisation and standardisation, so much parts of traditional management, are not adequate to meet changes that, by their nature, are not clear-cut. For example, new technology creates its own problems; it frequently imposes long lead times, which make it difficult to assess progress when no quantifiable result is readily available, when different managerial groups need some evidence of developments, and employees have to be provided with some organisational sense. New technology complicates planning – obsolescence is an ever-present threat and technical experts persistently seek modifications which lead to delays and creeping sophistication.

Counter to much received wisdom, new polyorganisations can hardly operate on computers or on the basis of neat engineering plans; they represent large-scale political systems involving ingenuity, improvisation and negotiation – the development of American space technology was characterised by these factors.[4] Human values, confrontation and compromise are indispensable to the management of polyorganisations. Most forecasts on the enduring effects of new technology and new organisational forms tend to be misleading if not wrong. For example, management by objectives, so popular in the 1960s and 1970s, turned out to have limited application; similarly matrix organisational forms have had a chequered career. Indeed the history of management practice is a long story of developments which were of limited success.

The politics and bargaining that occur over the formulation of organisational objectives also permeate the making of plans, policies and strategies; the view that these activities are in some sense removed from the day-to-day life of the firm is naïve. The recent emphasis on highly elaborate quantitative planning techniques can be misleading, in that their advocates can be in the position of having 'solutions' that are looking for problems. Another limitation on rationality is that of long lead times which result in the emergence of incremental decisions, most often made before the results of prior decisions are known. Planning rarely, if ever, works out as projected.[5]

Strategic planning, interorganisational relations and negotiations cannot be separated. As a planning project develops, new considerations and applications emerge which have to be fed back into the development process, thus making the planning process continuous and adaptive.

Planning and organisation structure affect each other. The planners' position in the structure affects their power and authority, while plans determine the balance of power through the allocation of resources and selection of courses of action – they identify the beneficiaries, both potential and actual.

THE PLANNERS

The place of formal planners in the political arena of the firm can be significant. A listing of their possible functions will give some indication of their political role:

1. designing the planning system;
2. selling ideas to the chief executive and senior management. The relationship between top management and planners is political in every sense, one of the trade-offs being the support the planners receive against the additional information base provided for senior management;
3. building up personal contacts in the firm and persuading line management to accept planning. Persuasion, manipulation, negotiation and coalition building all figure in the network that is developed;
4. helping operating managers to plan and at the same time to challenge their ideas;
5. coordinating total planning activities on a continuous basis;
6. monitoring all programmes.

But their very existence raises the question, who shall plan?

The planners or the doers, or both together? There is no clear answer. What is evident is that planning provides a power base over which conflict can be expected. In recent years there has been something of a swing away from large, full-time planning groups towards a stress on the need for operating managers to be much more involved.[6] The reasons for this are partly the imbalance that developed, with firms overloaded with specialist staff, and partly a response to economic conditions. Less readily admitted, but none the less a factor, is that company planners can experience difficulties in establishing strategic planning, they represent a threat to the existing distribution of power and influence, they can lead to the disclosure of weaknesses in operational management and they can become a political weapon used by different factions within senior management.

Planners are often the middlemen between the intellectual and managerial world and their importance is most evident in their awareness of new problems, opportunities and solutions. The image they project is not necessarily in line with actuality, but it can be politically powerful. By themselves their knowledge and techniques are not power, they have to be harnessed to more powerful organisational forces if the direction of the organisation is to be changed.

Planners tend to concentrate on the technical aspects of planning, emphasising the quantifiable and avoiding the political dimension. Yet the basic role of the strategic planner is political, involving the creation of a forum for bargaining where the interests of the organisation's parts are explicitly considered in relation to the whole. Such a forum requires relevant information systems and explicit criteria if the political process is to be kept within acceptable bounds, and if political defeat is to be accepted as being more than arbitrary. Proposals in the arena need to be formally justified, by reference to the normative rules of the company, that is, they are acceptable justifications for action. Technical grounds are not a sufficient basis; the culture of the individual firm has to be taken into account. At the same time top management prefers decisions to be seen as rationally grounded; in consequence the debate within the forum is likely to be carried on at diverse levels. A further complication is that of reaching agreement on evaluative criteria – different groups evaluate the planning proposals by using criteria favourable to themselves. In addition, uncertainty is injected into the discussion when future technical developments are difficult to forecast.

Ordering of information in the forum is also made difficult by the propensity of interested groups to introduce new information, and further uncertainty is generated by problems arising out of the relations of different levels and functions of management. In all these circumstances anyone who introduces proposals for reducing uncertainty is likely to increase his own power position.

Some writers, such as Mintzberg[7], argue that planners play a relatively minor role in strategy making. This evaluation is based on,

1. the view that the planners' programmes can only be loose and ill-defined. In most cases the important work is left to the operating managers and in practice the planner frequently 'muddles through' in spite of the facade of statistics and other aids; and
2. the fact that the information necessary for strategy making flows directly to the managers rather than the planners. Much of the information on problems, opportunities, pressures, values and opinions is unavailable to the planner and this means, in effect, that he operates politically blind.

The two extremes of organisational strategy making are 'muddling through', and integrated strategy, one judgemental and the other programmed. In reality, organisations use different mixtures of these approaches, depending on the situation in hand. Where there is no articulated strategic choice, 'muddling through' takes pride of place and gradually, by force of events and piecemeal decisions, some sort of strategy emerges.

The planners represent only one of the many groups who can influence the planning, policy process. Among these groups there is no simple hierarchy and while management is central, it is itself pluralistic. The managerial structure influences the type of demands and the way in which they are initiated. Whatever the origin of a policy proposal, it has to survive the initial selection process. Not all possible policy issues that are brought into play have an equal chance of survival; much depends upon where the power really lies.

PLANNING AND BOUNDED PLURALISM

Bounded pluralism is of the essence of organisation; that is to say the multiple process of strategy making occurs within the limits set by the dominant coalition, which is itself a pluralistic grouping. During the making of a particular strategy the power of different interest groups changes. For example, a major interest group may be denied access to the policy making process of a firm by the dominant coalition, which determines the agenda and who will debate it. Faced with this situation the major interest group may itself enter into a coalition so that with the resulting additional power it can force a hearing. One power ploy is met by another.

Every strategic decision must strike a balance between the many conflicting values, objectives and criteria of the different interest groups, with the result that it will be suboptimal from any single viewpoint. Every decision affecting the total enterprise is likely to have negative consequences for some of its parts, and in the knowledge of this each part will endeavour to obtain results favourable to itself.

These conflicting pressures limit strategic choice, placing constraints on what the firm can and cannot do. The availability of resources puts further limits on what the firm does and within these limits the values, competence and influence of key members determine the firm's actions.

In view of these factors some managers throw up their hands and declare that it is impossible or not worth developing a strategy; but strategy cannot be avoided, it will emerge from the actual performance of members of the firm. The reluctance to articulate strategy is strengthened by the recognition that its development means questioning the future validity of the bases of present success and failure. It challenges the existing distribution of resources, the present product range and the current markets, all of which contribute to the existing framework of power.

The development of strategy is affected by the structure in which it is formulated and it in turn affects the structure. While it is argued that structure follows strategy[8] and that failure to harmonise the two will end in failure of implementation, neither of these arguments is necessarily true. In the first instance it can be said that a given strategy is the result of the present structure or, perhaps more accurately, is the result of the prevailing power distribution, one of whose components is the structure. Structure may remain unchanged when the new strategic developments are not strong enough to require a structural alteration, or because management is unaware of the need for a new structure. This apparent failure of awareness may be because management is too involved in day-to-day management problems; has failed to understand the structural implications of a new strategy or because it sees that such a change would threaten its power. If strategic change is not too great, effectiveness may not be impaired by the dissonance between structure and strategy, given the ability of management to make incremental adjustments without covert formal changes in structure, operations and behaviour.

At this stage it is evident that corporate planning has the following characteristics – it is reiterative; it will involve the major centres of power in the firm; it is experiential, so that managers learn from experience and it is conceptual, allowing for the formation of new concepts regarding the relationship of an organisation to its environment.

Before examining further the different stages of policy and strategy making there are certain key points to be made:

1. Any policy tends to be complex, involving such sequences as setting out to achieve objectives X, X1, X2 ... under conditions Y, Y1, Y2. These factors complicate the various planning stages up to and including that of implementation.
2. Any new policy is established within the context of existing policies and strategies.
3. Scarcity and control of finance tend to set limits to policy development.
4. Change resulting from policy decisions is a protracted time and cost consuming process, which will result in changes in the decisions already taken.
5. Some implementation problems arise from policies and strategies which are expressed in general and unclear terms.[9] This situation provides opportunities for political activity, as different managers interpret the diffused goals to meet their own power positions. The oft derided ambiguity in goals arises for several reasons:
   a. the policy makers are not sure what they want;
   b. there is a lack of political consensus, leading to a lack of agreement amongst implementers;
   c. the adoption of administrative procedures which are explicitly designed to obscure the situation; and
   d. the intrinsic difficulty of specifying some policy goals.

THE PLANNING PROCESS

The overall policy formulation and implementation process, with its different stages, can be analysed in the context of the political nature of management.

Policies and strategies are initiated through perceived changes in the environment. These can be technological or industrial changes, or competitors' behaviour; market changes; shifts in government policy; alterations in economic and financial conditions. They may be initiated by stakeholders dissatisfied with the results when evaluated against their own criteria. Whether the particular stakeholder's view is noticed will depend upon his power. These changes are also perceived by the firm's management, who see them either as a threat or an opportunity, relative to their operations and power. Internal pressures, such as the arrival of a new chief executive or a new type of specialist, may act as precipitating events, generating policy changes.

It is critical who perceives these changes and pressures and who generates ideas, whether it is top management, a planning unit or different functional and operational divisions of the firm. Initiation depends upon managers' perception of the significance of the changes and pressures, of the power of the groups pressing the changes, of the opportunities and threats the changes pose and whether the change is seen as feasible, legitimate and widely supported.

The perceived opportunities and threats can lead to innovation, new fields of action and development, alteration in the scale or range of existing provision or to new ways of doing something already produced. All these possibilities clearly raise issues of power and politics. For example, an upward change in the scale or range of existing products can mean additional resources, which can increase the power base of the department involved. A decision to cut out present methods of producing a particular line and replace them with new technology, can shift power from those with past power to those involved with the new technology.

Demands generated for the development of new policies, or the adaptation of existing ones, have to gain support through fostering a belief in the existence of a common good, or by indicating the pay-offs to those who are prepared to support the demand. In a firm it is likely that there will be a queue of demands which have to be regulated, with some people in the organisation acting as gatekeepers to determine priorities. Here is the first in a long line of selective decisions. Norms, rules and precedents develop over time, helping to determine the kinds of demands that are acceptable. Rules, constraints and precedents are not restricted to the initiation stage but are operative all through the policy making process, defining the limits within which political action takes place and policies are made. These constraints are not neutral, they do not favour all equally and, because of this, those who wish to push their demands may have to seek to change the rules and other constraints.

At this stage there is a reduction process in which demands are modified through compromise, generated by those making the demands and those who determine whether they shall go ahead. Similar demands may be grouped, because few issues remain unrelated to others. Problems and solutions link and overlap as they are being continually matched and associated, so that any one demand tends to become part of a pattern of demands. The manipulation of demands is an important political tactic, with success often depending upon the ability to present a demand either with or separate from other demands. Managers may try to fuse certain demands in an attempt to win allies, or strive to keep them apart to avoid unwanted ones. How demands are managed, separated or brought together, will have a significant impact on the scope of debate and conflict that develops round them.

Managerial groups who operate from a strong power base may adopt a tactic of limiting links when putting forward a demand, while a group with a weak base will tend to adopt a tactic of expansion – seeking to increase its linkages with other demands. Any demand which solves more than one problem is more likely to pass the gatekeeper than one which has a narrow application, though again it will depend upon the power of those pressing the demands. There is a limit to bringing demands together because the end result can be an open-ended programme which is not easy to control. Yet the association and separation of demands remains important:

1. Because it is possible to modify the legitimacy of one demand by linking or divorcing it from demands of different degrees of legitimacy.
2. It is closely related to the process of demand regulation, that is, to the process of seeking an economy of remedies – it affects calculations and feasibilities.

3. It provides a means of influencing the scope of argument about a demand.

What is likely to develop is a programme of disjointed incrementalism; only demands whose known and expected consequences differ incrementally from the status quo will be likely to go ahead. In all these aspects there is the association of demands, problems and solutions; new problems kindle interest in old solutions, while attractive, available solutions may advance the priority of the problems with which they cope and the demands to which they can be applied.

An old demand may be resurrected and accepted because it links with a current crisis; information relating to it has become more readily available and it has been found to be feasible.

The initiation stage may be regarded as the first in a process which ultimately leads to the production of a policy or strategy.[10] Any logical model for policy making inadvertently draws attention to the ordering of political activities; its very presentation points to the idea that different groups at different times are more likely to be connected with one stage rather than another. The logical planning process is short on the political dimension, on the dynamics of policy formulation: it is a model, and as such should not be taken for real.[11] In the logical progression through the different stages, policy content and process need to be distinguished, yet it would be incorrect to consider them as entirely separate entities – they interact.

It helps to know where the initiation lies in making a policy demand and where the authority lies to approve or veto it. In the absence of overt direction, the existing power structure determines which demands go forward and in doing so determines the organisation's strategic direction and emphasis. If the forces for perpetuating a particular structural and strategic form are very strong, the organisation is unlikely to accede to any demands which involve basic changes in its strategic position.

INFORMATION AND POLICY MAKING

After the initiation stage when a particular demand has obtained a place on the policy agenda, the policy-makers will require further information,

1. to understand the nature and magnitude of the issues raised by the demand;
2. to formulate alternative methods of coping, that is, seeking to resolve a problem without recourse to a change of policy;
3. to assess how the firm is presently operating, to survey its present strengths and weaknesses;
4. to facilitate the transmission of any newly agreed policy to those who have to implement it; and
5. to assess the consequences of that policy in action.

Information and data are essential ingredients of policy making. Yet the paradox is that organisations exist to suppress information, some is screened in, but most in screened out. The very structure of organisations, the units, the levels – the hierarchy, is designed to reduce data and information to manageable and manipulable proportions. In whatever direction they turn, the policy makers find that information error is endemic. If they look to original sources they are easily overwhelmed; if they rely on what they are given they are liable to be misled.[12] In the light of this it is critical for the policy makers to be aware of who collects the data and assembles it, where it comes from and how much time has been allowed for search. In considering these factors they have not to be misled into thinking that because some of information comes from a computer it will be neutral – it is a mistake to think that the computer purifies the data it processes.

Management requires guidelines for search while at the same time seeking to protect their personal positions. Wherever possible managers will narrow the range of issues upon which search has to be undertaken so that they can use data which is available and within their control. New data may throw up disconcerting problems. In spite of this there may be occasions when managers will want to widen the search because they believe that by doing so they will protect their positions.

Faced with uncertainty, the policy makers may call for more data – the raw material of information – at any stage of the policy making process. This demand for additional data is often a demand for false certainty, and the development of formal policy and strategy making procedures may encourage this demand. Yet there is no advantage and much error in making decisions more precise than the subject matter to which they refer.[13]

Uncertainty is not ignorance, it can be knowledge. The desire for precision leads to an emphasis on quantification, but a seemingly precise forecast often hides uncertainties and can provide less information than a seemingly imprecise one. In the strategy making process there is the temptation to give more weight to the measurable than the non-quantifiable. It is in the light of this distortion that increased interest has been shown in the use of scenarios with their mixture of quantifiable and non-quantifiable components.[14] When managers are asked to commit themselves to the future they are liable to seek a nonexistent certainty and dangerously believe they have achieved it. Overcommitment then can lead to,

1. decisions that do not reflect the possibility of error in the data upon which they are based;
2. an overconfidence which produces excessive commitment to future action; and
3. a reluctance to take new decisions in the light of new data which challenges the existing position.

Excessive certainty can be engendered because questions leading to a search for data are not always framed in an objective manner, they are constructed under the powerful influence of political values. In consequence the data collected and the information produced can reflect the values built into the original question. Questions designed to produce a desired answer can build up confidence in a given position and lead to overcommitment. Ultimately this means that strategy is influenced by planners' theories and values as much as by the new data.

There are four major determinants of the manpower, time and money that an organisation allocates to data collection and information development in the strategy making process.

1. The degree of conflict and competition in the external environment.
2. The degree of dependence on internal support.
3. The extent to which internal and external operations are believed to be rationalised.
4. The size and structure of the organisation, its heterogeneity of membership, diversity of goals and centralisation of authority.

The more dependent the firm is on different segments of the environment, the greater the likelihood that it will use 'contact men' and external experts. The more dependent it is on internal support, the greater will be its use of internal communication systems and communications experts. The more a firm sees its environment and internal activities as predictable, the more it will concentrate on 'facts and figures' men who supply data and, in doing so, seek to mobilise support. They introduce, it might be claimed, a rational, responsible bias, a more conscious examination of alternatives and long-range consequences. They act to depoliticise management and in doing so shape the verbal environment of the firm. Their activity is in essence political.

When environmental facts become self-convincing symbols, the arguments, propaganda and stereotypes based upon them and captured in felicitous dogmas can, for years, remain impervious to new evidence. Stereotyped oversimplifications can be fatal for organisations.

So the quality of organisational data and information available to strategy makers is influenced,

1. by hierarchy and hierarchical loyalty;
2. by specialists who represent a powerful source of information distortion. The primary cost of specialisation is the specialists' parochial intelligence, which is often misleading and sometimes irrelevant. To combat this, top management and strategy makers can examine multiple sources of data and stimulate competition between those providing it. President Roosevelt recognised the value of this; doubting the flexibility and inventiveness of the established departments of government, he set up new agencies, making a point of keeping their authority incomplete and overlapping in order to ensure a steady flow of diverse information and advice, and in particular keeping power securely in his own hands.[15] The gains of calculated competition can be lost if top management insulates itself from the squabbles of subordinates and forces rival departments to settle their differences out of sight. The results are likely to be 'agreement by exhaustion'; blurring of policy discord and an overstatement of agreements with rivals on behalf of an 'ultimate consensus'. Sharp questions, cogent arguments, minority positions and the clear balancing of

gains and losses are hidden from the view of top management; and

3. by structural concerns; policies of centralisation are attainable only if there is delegation, but they are coordinated only if there is centralisation. A balance has to be struck between the centralisation and decentralisation of different elements of the organisation. Out of this balance will come a workable set of trade-offs of gains and losses.

Views of the 'intelligence' function affect its organisation, recruitment base and quality. Management may demand all the facts, require quick estimates, ask questions that stimulate the imagination, give shape to major strategy alternatives and point the general direction desired. In making these different requests, management determines the style of the intelligence function. Winston Churchill's use of the minute, a dictated note containing a question, or a series of questions were used to acquire information, to initiate discussion, and to propose schemes and stratagems. From these minutes Churchill expected to learn what was happening over the full range of his responsibilities, and to probe every area of potential war policy and action.[16] Churchill's minute was a basic device which shaped the flow of information around him, his Ministry and Cabinet.

Those who collect data and formulate information have many opportunities to influence policy in ways far removed from the formal policy making process. They can crystallise policy options, sharpen the definition of a problem when its specificity is low, fill the vacuum when senior management is busy and time is short and use official pronouncements as levers to push their own views. Subtle political behaviour is an important component of their more obvious activities.

As organisations grow, so the intelligence function tends to change and with it, its political and power implications. It is likely to become more formalised, to move from concern with ideological to technical questions, to shift from less to more routine. Organisation myths relating to intelligence become more fixed and there is a shift from the most to the least urgent. All these elements tend to reduce relevance and timeliness of intelligence. Intelligence failures are built into complex organisations; restructuring can only partially reduce them as more depends upon management understanding of the nature of data and information, its significance in different conditions and its part in the politics of management. Among the facts that managers have to face is that, the more they find out about what might be done, the harder it is to make the choice.

ALTERNATIVES

With information gathered, the next stage is the formulation of policy alternatives. Underlying this activity is the fact that those responsible for the generation of alternatives will seek to protect their interest and to present options in a way that is favourable to them. However, those devising the alternatives are themselves subject to pressures, including deadlines arising from crises or set by those in power. Pressure can be used to manipulate the options that emerge. Where there is pressure of time, information is liable to be based on less data and ready-made alternatives will be the order of the day. At the same time those compiling the alternatives will obtain data from different sources, especially internal departments who are aware that the data being gathered could be used to analyse their strengths and weaknesses. Inevitably they will take care to emphasise the strengths and underplay the weaknesses, unless more will be gained by reversing this stance. It may be that some of those who search for data will also be involved in defining the alternatives, thus reducing the possible communication gaps that might otherwise exist between the data collectors and the strategy formulators.

DECISION TIME

Then there is the consideration of the alternatives and a decision in the light of the main objectives as they are perceived by the dominant decision-makers. The question to be faced now is, what does top management want to do? There may well be a gap between what senior management wants and the alternatives that emerge from a formal policy making process. In practice, consideration of alternative strategies and policies will be influenced by the preferences of the chief executive and senior management, who have to approve and contribute to the development of any strategy. The rational output of the policy process is modified by the political pressures of senior managers. It will be evident that the composition of the policy making group is all important; their respective power and concern for the defence of their interests, and their readiness or otherwise to join coalitions within the group will influence the decision that emerges.

IMPLEMENTATION AND EVALUATION

When a decision has been reached it has to be implemented, translating it from generalities to operational detail – here the opportunity for political behaviour through the interpretation function is apparent.

First, implementation involves the design of the organisation structure, raising the question of what impact the newly accepted policy will have upon the existing structure and who will design the structural alternatives if any are required.

Second, there has to be effective administration of the processes and systems through which the policy is implemented.

Third, there is leadership to build up commitment through negotiation; to defend the policy and to set the climate in which the policy will operate. Implementation may be seen as a threat to existing power bases and, in consequence, efforts will be made to modify it. Its implementation may differ substantially from what was originally defined by the policy makers.

While formulation of policy has to be analytically separated from implementation, in practice they are interwoven, for the results of implementation are fed back through evaluation into the formulation stages. This feedback may be subject to time lag, especially if the information reflects adversely upon the key implementation group involved. What we have at the implementation stage is a series of processes involving measurement, evaluation, motivation, control and individual development.

One writer[17] notes that 'Business organisations also serve as the stage upon which the conflicts of individuality are played out for many people. On the one hand, there seems to be a demand for conformity and identification with organisations that threatens the very essence of individuality – the sense of one's personal impact upon events. On the other hand, organisations provide ample room for individuals to assert themselves and express their unique style of performance. The point is that organisations do not provide individuality as a gift. It has to be gained and even fought for while sustaining one's involvement and responsibility.' In other words, when managers move towards action they face personal and organisational challenges in substantive guise. The substance plays a part, but not necessarily a central part, in the outcome of negotiations concerning planning and resource allocation choices. The key point is that a plan or policy is not merely a manipulation of economic data, it is an argument for something a network of managers wants to do because it will be in their self-interest to do so.

The job of top management is to keep self-interest and corporate interest, so far as it can be said to exist, in some alignment. On the surface their managers implement strategy and policy within the scope of their jobs as they have been defined and against which they are measured, but at a deeper level they will seek to modify the context and results of their jobs in order to improve their position in the political arena. The implementation of a policy or plan depends upon the way in which different managers, at the several levels of the firm, interpret what is required of them, in the light of their assessment of the potential impact of the policy upon their performance and political base. The way that performance is measured will have a critical influence on the way the managers define and activate it.

The evaluation of the success or failure of a policy is not a simple matter; much depends upon the point of view of the evaluator, his power and that of the managers being evaluated. The success or failure of a particular policy may be related to the initial predisposition of the manager to the policy he has implemented: here the self-fulfilling prophecy may well operate. If a manager does not believe in a given policy he can implement it so that it is unsuccessful, and then claim justification for his initial scepticism. The result may not be produced by any crude sabotage but by a lack of commitment, which is transmitted to his subordinates and leads to actions which hinder the implementation of the policy.

During the implementation stage delays can occur, objects are modified, some parts of the policy receive more atten-

tion than others. Additionally few implementation programmes are left to run their course unaffected by still newer
policies. The acceptance or rejection of a policy by those who
have to implement it rests upon whether it is profitable to them,
what effect it will have upon their commitment to an existing
activity in which they have invested and developed organisational skills and capabilities. Where these are threatened every effort
will be made to obscure their obsolescence, with organisational
inertia and managerial ego playing supporting roles.[18]

The relationship of one policy to another further complicates
judgement on success or failure. A policy which may seem to fail
may in fact facilitate another, higher priority, policy. The
problems of policy evaluation often begin with the selection of
unattainable goals, and with the use of language directed to
making people feel better rather than causing events to occur.

The difficulty of implementating policy can lie in the proliferation of veto and clearance points, so that implementation is
delayed and support for the policy erodes, or there is a technological breakthrough which invalidates it. Overall, policy implementation has a tendency to run down, as the advantages to be
gained from it become less significant in the light of other
developments in the organisation. Incentives to ensure implementation and its continuation can be subject to diminishing
returns and will lose favour if they threaten general political
values, such as fairness and equity.

Policy implementation emerges as an activity that is not
separable from policy formulation and day-to-day management,
indeed the inevitable discretion allows for policy making in the
implementation process; 'policy is being made as it is administered, and administered as it is being made'. Policy is made in
the implementation stage – because managers attempt to simplify it,

1. because of the 'centre-periphery' relationship, that is, the
   belief of field management that the centre does not understand the problems of the field, so that any policy emanating
   from the centre has to be adapted to meet local conditions;
2. because of the characteristics of the implementing departments; and
3. because of the essentially dynamic nature of all the interrela-
   tionships involved.

CONCLUSION

Policy-making is complex; there is a multiplicity of managers seeking to influence the final outcome, there is the making of deals and compromises so that the eventual end-result – action – may not be wholly satisfactory to any single party. Processes that create strategy and policy also create uncertainty all along the line, not least in the implementation stage. Emerging from conflict and compromise, policies are inevitably vulnerable to shifts in the balance of organisational and individual interests. Particularly is this the case when implementers see policy as a form of control, which has to be subverted if it encroaches on their own bases of power. The key factor is that policy is mediated through managers, and the failure of central policy makers to comprehend the values, perceptions and motivations of the implementing managers leads to an 'appreciation gap'. The problem is augmented by a number of complicating factors, such as whether the strategy or policy is implemented within the same organisation, in the same geographical region, or by semi-autonomous units in the same or different regions. Policy making and implementation may occur at different organisational levels and distances, in and across organisations – a policy may be developed at the top of one organisation, implemented at a lower level in the same organisation, with impact upon the top management of another. Within this and other networks there is ample room for political activity.

Strategy making does not take place in a vacuum; it emeges as the result not only of internal political behaviour but of external activity. With this in mind, firms develop offensive and defensive strategies, the aim of which is to exploit opponents' weaknesses and erode their strengths so as to inhibit their retaliatory capacity.

In considering an opponent's position it is necessary to analyse the political dimensions of their activities, that is,

1. identify the basis of the dominant coalition within its organisation's political structure;
2. consider the major demands that are made upon the dominant coalition from within that political structure;
3. identify the discretion structure and the level of the people who exercise discretion;

4. study the opposing the organisation's major rules, procedures, policies and programmes;
5. identify the major monitoring and control systems employed
   by the opposition; and
6. check out the information system and determine how long it
   takes for information to reach the position where counter
   proposals and responses can be instigated.

All this comes down to the need for effective intelligence when
developing strategies and policies. Know your opponent is a
dictum applicable to both internal and external politics.

In the final analysis interorganisational relations, strategic
planning and policy making involve essentially political behaviour based upon power. The effective firm and its managers
are well aware that this is the case and behave accordingly.

Conclusion

This book was written from experience grounded in the view that political behaviour, being an essential and inevitable part of human activity, is a major feature of management.

In so far as it runs counter to much current management thinking it was necessary to sketch briefly some of the important strands of that thinking. Not least it had to be argued that organisations are pluralist in character and that to act on any other assumption would contribute to managerial problems.

Given the pluralist view it was inevitable that questions of power, conflict and the associated activity of bargaining had to be examined. Instead of regarding conflict as undesirable, power as unmentionable and bargaining as questionable, it was suggested that effective management required skill in handling power, coping with conflict and in negotiating. All of these benefit from managerial sensitivity to the political nature of management.

The ubiquitous nature of organisational politics was demonstrated by reference to various managerial ideas and practices, and the significance of language, information and structure clearly emerged. These factors and associated ideas, such as the nature of dependence, need to be understood if managerial effectiveness is to be increased, specifically if reality is to make progress against rhetoric. The wide variety of political strategies and tactics available to management have been demonstrated to further facilitate the recognition and practice of political behaviour. It has been the aim of this book to introduce a new strand of reality to help further the development of effective management.

Notes and References

INTRODUCTION

1. K. O. Morgan, *Labour in Power 1945–1951* (Oxford University Press, 1984) p.viii.
2. R. T. Pascale and A. G. Athos, *The Art of Japanese Management* (Harmondsworth: Penguin, 1982) p. 105.

CHAPTER 1 MANAGEMENT MANIFESTATIONS

1. I. Berlin, *Russian Thinkers* (London: Hogarth Press, 1978) p. 22.
2. W. Brown, *Exploration in Management* (London: Heinemann, 1960) p. 24.
3. S. Zuckerman, *From Apes to Warlords 1904–46* (London: Hamish Hamilton, 1978) pp. 220–45.
4. J. Ellis, *Cassino: a Hollow Victory* (London: Andre Deutsch, 1984) p. 409.
5. T. E. Stephenson, 'The Longevity of Classical Theory', *Management International Review*, no. 6. (1968) 77–84.
6. T. E. Stephenson, 'Organisation Development: a Critique', *The Journal of Management Studies* vol. 12, no. 3. (1975) 249–65.
7. C. Argyris, *Management and Organizational Development* (New York: McGraw-Hill, 1971) p. 13.
8. E. H. Carr, *What is History?* (Harmondsworth: Penguin, 1964).
9. A. Gouldner, 'Metaphysical Pathos and the Theory of Bureaucracy', in A. Etzioni (ed.) *Complex Organizations* (New York: Holt, Rinehart & Winston, 1964) pp. 71–82.
10. G. Stanford, 'Openness as Manipulation', *Social Change*, vol. 2, no. 3. (1972)

CHAPTER 2 MANAGEMENT IN ACTION

1. A. Fox, *Industrial Sociology and Industrial Relations* (London: HMSO, 1966) pp. 3–4; G. Burrell and G. Morgan, *Sociological Paradigms and Organisational Analysis* (London: Heinemann, 1979) ch. 5.
2. J. Woodward, *Industrial Organization* (Oxford University Press, 1980) p. 255.
3. R. V. Jones, *Most Secret War* (London: Hamish Hamilton, 1978).

243

4. M. Kogan, *The Politics of Education* (Harmondsworth: Penguin, 1971) p. 103.
5. H. Mintzberg, *The Nature of Managerial Work* (New York: Harper & Row, 1973) ch. 3.
6. Ibid., p. 51.
7. L. Sayles, *Managerial Behavior* (New York: McGraw-Hill, 1964) chs 5, 6, 7.
8. W. Brown, *Piecework Bargaining* (London: Heinemann, 1973) p. 107.
9. R. Stewart, *Choices for the Manager* (London: McGraw-Hill, 1982) ch. 1.
10. J. Child and B. Partridge, *Lost Managers* (Cambridge University Press, 1982) p. 111.
11. E. Mumford and A. Pettigrew, *Implementing Strategic Decisions* (London: Longmans, 1975) p. 164.
12. G. Strauss, 'Tactics of Lateral Relationship: the Purchasing Agent', *Administrative Science Quarterly*, vol. 6, no. 4. (1962) pp. 161–86.
13. M. Gilbert, *Finest Hour: Winston S. Churchill 1939–1941* (London: Heinemann, 1983) p. 322.
14. Lord Armstrong, 'The Individual, the Enterprise and the State: a Personal View', in R. I. Tricker (ed.), *The Individual, the Enterprise, and the State* (London: Associated Business Programmes, 1977) p. 32.

CHAPTER 3   THE POLITICS OF MANAGEMENT

1. J. Pfeffer, *Power in Organizations* (Boston: Pitman, 1981) p. 337.
2. Z. Brzezinski, *Power and Principle* (London: Weidenfeld & Nicolson, 1983) p. 22.
3. R. Lewin, *The Other Ultra* (London: Hutchinson, 1982) p. 61.
4. J. S. Boswell, *Business Policies in the Making* (London: Allen & Unwin, 1983) pp. 8–13.
5. M. Dalton, *Men Who Manage* (New York: John Wiley, 1959) ch. 3.
6. F. M. Cornford, *Microcosmographia Academica* (London: Bowes & Bowes, 1908).
7. H. Kissinger, *The White House Years* (London: Weidenfeld & Nicholson and Michael Joseph, 1979) p. 43.
8. L. Sayles, *Leadership* (New York: McGraw-Hill, 1979) pp. 95–6.
9. R. Stewart, *Choices for the Manager* (London: McGraw-Hill, 1982).
10. E. H. Carr, *The Twenty Years' Crisis 1919–1939* (London: Macmillan, 1946) p. 96.

CHAPTER 4   POWER

1. T. Eccles, *Under New Management* (London: Pan, 1981) pp. 113–15.
2. S. McLachlan, *The National Freight Buy-Out* (London: Macmillan, 1983) pp. 112–16.
3. K. Done, 'Olympia Sales Falsely Inflated by Staff over 5 years to 1981', *Financial Times*, 19 August 1982.
4. T. Burns, 'On the Plurality of Social Systems' in J. R. Lawrence (ed.)

Operational Research and the Social Sciences (London: Tavistock, 1966) ch. 12.
5. H. Leavitt, *Organisations in the Future* (New York: Praeger, 1975) p. 196. -
6. J. Pfeffer, *Power In Organizations* (Boston: Pitman, 1981)
7. R. E. Sherwood, *The White House Papers of Harry L. Hopkins* vol. 1. (London: Eyre & Spottiswoode, 1948) p. 3.
8. R. Dahrendorf, *Essays on the Theory of Society* (Standford University Press, 1968).

CHAPTER 5 BARGAINING AND CONFLICT

1. E. Etzioni-Halevy, *Political Manipulation and Adminstrative Power* (London: Routledge & Kegan Paul, 1979) p. 7.
2. S. Bacharach and E. J. Lawler, *Power and Politics in Organisations* (San Francisco: Jossey-Bass, 1980) pp. 156–7; S. Bacharach and E. J. Lawler, *Bargaining* (San Francisco: Jossey-Bass, 1981) pp. 42–3, 47, chs 3, 5, 6; I. C. MacMillan, *Strategy Formulation: Political Concepts* (St Paul: West, 1978) pp. 29–49.
3. M. and B. Kalib, *Kissinger* (London: Hutchinson, 1974) For various examples, notably a secret visit to China.
4. H. Kissinger, *The White House Years* (London: Weidenfeld & Nicolson and Michael Joseph, 1979) pp. 129–30.
   See Z. Brzezinski, *Power and Principle* (London: Weidenfeld & Nicholson, 1983) for numerous examples.
5. MacMillan, ibid., pp. 30–2.

CHAPTER 6 STRUCTURE AND TOP MANAGEMENT

1. W. Brown, *Exploration In Management* (London: Heinemann, 1960).
2. M. J. Wiener, *English Culture and the Decline of the Industrial Spirit, 1850–1980* (Cambridge University Press, 1981).
3. S. Prakask Sethi *et al.*, *The False Promise of the Japanse Miracle* (1984).
4. A. Strauss *et al.*, 'The Hospital and Its Negotiated Order' in G. Salaman and K. Thompson (eds) *People and Organisations* (London: Longmans, 1973) pp. 306–8.
5. M. Edwardes, *Back from the Brink* (London: Collins, 1983) pp. 49–50.
6. H. Parker *et al.*, *Effective Boardroom Management* (London: B.I.M., 1971) p. 13.
7. H. Koontz and C. O'Donnell, *Principles of Management*, 4th edn (New York: McGraw-Hill, 1968) p. 394.
8. B.I.M. *The Board of Directors* (London: B.I.M. 1972)
9. R. E. Pahl and J. T. Winkler, 'The Economic Elite: Theory and Practice' in P. Stanworth & A. Giddens (eds) *Elites and Power in British Society* (Cambridge University Press, 1974)
10. C. Brookes, *Boards of Directors in British Industry* (London: Department of Employment, 1979) pp. 44–7.
11. M. Edwardes, ibid., p. 50.

CHAPTER 7 DECISION-MAKING

1. J. Pfeffer, *Power in Organizations* (Boston: Pitman, 1981) p. 10.
2. J. Barnett, *Inside the Treasury* (London: André Deutsch, 1982).
3. M. Kogan, *The Politics of Education* (Harmondsworth; Penguin, 1971) pp. 95 and 155.
4. Ibid., p. 30.
5. C. F. Carter and B. R. Williams, *Industry and Technical Progress* (London: Oxford University Press, 1957) p. 115.
6. Barnett, ibid., p. 21.
7. A. M. Pettigrew, *The Politics of Organizational Decision-Making* (London: Tavistock, 1973).
8. K. G. Banting, *Poverty, Politics and Policy* (London: Macmillan, 1979) p. 149.
9. Pettigrew, ibid., p. 195.
10. F. H. Hinsley *et al.*, *British Intelligence in the Second World War*, vol. 1. (London: HMSO, 1979) p. 4.
11. Ibid., p. 10.
12. C. E. Lindblom and D. K. Cohen, *Usable Knowledge* (New Haven, Conn.: Yale University Press, 1979) p. 12.
13. C. E. Lindblom, 'The Science of "Muddling Through"' in H. I. Ansoff, (ed.), *Business Strategy* (Harmondsworth: Penguin, 1969) pp. 41–60.
14. A. Etzioni, *The Active Society* (New York: The Free Press, 1968) p. 289.
15. J. F. Kennedy in G. T. Allison, *The Essence of Decision* (Boston, Mass.: Little, Brown, 1971).
16. Barnett, ibid., p. 40.
17. C. I. Barnard, *The Functions of the Executive* (Cambridge, Mass.,: Harvard University Press, 1958) p. 194.
18. M. Gilbert, *Finest Hour: Winston S. Churchill 1939–41* (London: Heinemann, 1983) p. 133.

CHAPTER 8 PARTICIPATION

1. The notion of industrial democracy has a long history but only surfaced as a major management concern in the 1950s.
2. T. E. Stephenson, 'The Tinge of Politics in Management', *The Times Review of Industry*, July 1959, p. 64.
3. B.I.M. *Industrial Democracy: Some Implications for Management* (London: B.I.M., 1968) p. 8.
4. P. A. Reilley, *Participation, Democracy and Control* (London: B.I.M., 1979) p. 38.
5. Ibid., p. 40.
6. D. McGregor, *The Professional Manager* (New York: McGraw-Hill, 1967) p. 13.
7. M. Marchington and R. Loveridge, 'Non-participation: the Management View', in *Journal of Management Studies*, vol. 16, no. 2 (1979) p. 182.
8. I. D. E., *Industrial Democracy in Europe* (Oxford: Clarendon, 1981) pp. 339–40.

CHAPTER 9   CHANGE

1. L. L. Lederman, 'Foresight Activities in the U.S.A.: Time for a Reassessment' in *Long Range Planning*, vol. 17, no. 3. (June 1984) p. 41.
2. 'By transforming the national mood from apathy to action, the New Deal was invigorating its enemies as well as its friends', A. M. Schlesinger, jnr, *The Age of Roosevelt: the Politics of Upheaval*, vol. 3. (London: Heinemann, 1961) p. 3.
3. J. D. Thompson, *Organisations in Action* (New York: McGraw-Hill, 1967) p. 35.
4. Ibid., pp. 20–23.
5. B. Levin, 'The Iceberg that Snowballed' *The Times*. 1984.
6. P. R. Drucker, *The Practice of Management* (London: Heinemann, 1955) p. 127.
7. J. Pfeffer, *Power in Organizations* (Boston; Pitman, 1981) p. 326.
8. C. F. Carter & B. R. Williams, *Industry and Technical Progress* (London: Oxford University, 1957) pp. 108–110.
9. M. Kogan, *The Politics of Education* (Harmondsworth: Penguin, 1971) p. 167.
10. L. R. Sayles, *Leadership: What Effective Managers Really Do and How They Do It* (New York: McGraw-Hill, 1979) pp. 180–183.

CHAPTER 10   MANAGEMENT SUCCESSION, PROMOTION AND EDUCATION

1. M. Edwardes, *Back from the Brink* (London: Collins, 1983) p. 56.
2. E. Ginzberg, *What Makes an Executive?* (New York: Columbia University, 1955) p. 148.
3. J. Pfeffer, *Power in Organizations* (Boston: Pitman, 1981) pp. 349–50.
4. C. E. Lindblom and D. K. Cohen, *Usable Knowledge* (New Haven, Conn.: Yale University Press, 1979)
5. C. Argyris and D. A. Schon, *Theory in Practice: Increasing Professional Effectiveness* (San Francisco: Jossey-Bass, 1974) pp. 3–34.

CHAPTER 11   INTERORGANISATIONAL RELATIONSHIPS

1. 'Baby Boomers Push for Power', *Businessweek*, 2 July, 1984.
2. J. D. Thompson, *Organizations in Action* (New York: McGraw-Hill, 1967) pp. 67–73.
3. K. E. Weick, *The Social Psychology of Organizing* (Reading, Mass.: Addison-Wesley, 1969) p. 64.
4. C. Perrow, *Complex Organizations*, 2nd edn. (Glenview: Scott, Foresman, 1979) pp. 233–7.
5. H. E. Aldrich, *Organizations and Environments* (Englewood Cliffs, N. J.: Prentice-Hall, 1979) p. 329.

6. M. W. Dirsmith and M. A. Covaleski, 'Strategy, External Communication and Environmental Context' in *Strategic Management Journal*, vol. 4, no. 2, pp. 137–41.
7. B. Turner, 'The Organizational and Interorganizational Development of Disasters', *Administrative Science Quarterly*, 21 (September), p. 395.

CHAPTER 12   POLICY AND STRATEGY

1. H. Koontz and C. O'Donnell, *Principles of Management*, 4th edn. (New York: McGraw-Hill, 1968) pp. 177–80.
2. W. F. Glueck, *Business Policy and Strategic Management*, 3rd edn (Auckland: McGraw-Hill, 1980) ch.2.
3. K. G. Banting, *Poverty, Politics and Policy* (London: Macmillan, 1979) p. 4.
4. L. R. Sayles and M. K. Chandler, *Managing Large Systems* (New York: Harper and Rowe, 1971) p. 16.
5. P. Hall *et al.*, *Change, Choice and Conflict in Social Policy* (London: Heinemann, 1975)
6. This theme has received repeated airings in various business magazines.
7. H. Mintzberg, 'The Science of Strategy Making' in B. W. Denning (ed.), *Corporate Planning: Selected Concepts* (London: McGraw-Hill, 1971) p. 98.
8. A. D. Chandler, jr, *Strategy and Structure* (New York: Anchor Books, 1966) pp. 1–21.
9. P. Nokes, *The Professional Task in Welfare Practice* (London: Routledge & Kegan Paul, 1967) pp. 1–16.
10. W. I. Jenkins, *Policy Analysis: a Political and Organisational Perspective* (London: Martin Robertson, 1978) p. 17.
11. Ibid., p. 24.
12. A. Wildavsky, 'Information as an Organizational Problem', *Journal of Management Studies*, vol. 20, no. 1.
13. J. Robinson in E. Penrose, *The Theory of the Growth of the Firm* (Oxford: Basil Blackwell, 1959) p. 3.
14. H. E. Klein and R. E. Linnerman, 'The Use of Scenarios in Corporate Planning: Eight Case Studies', *Long Range Planning*, vol. 14, no. 5 (October 1981) p. 69. R.D. Zetner 'Scenarios, Past, Present and Future', *Long Range Planning*, vol. 15, no. 3 (June 1982) p. 12.
15. H. Muller, *Adlai Stevenson* (London: Hamish Hamilton, 1968) pp. 39–40.
16. M. Gilbert, *Finest Hour: Winston S. Churchill 1939–1941* (London: Heinemann, 1983) p. 7.
17. J. L. Bower, 'Planning within the Firm' in B. Taylor and K. MacMillan (eds), *Top Management* (London: Longmans, 1973) p. 211.
18. H. I. Ansoff, 'Toward a Strategic Theory of the Firm' in H.I. Ansoff (ed.), *Business Strategy* (Harmondsworth: Penguin, 1969) pp. 11–40.

An Illustrative Bibliography

This is a sample of books which directly or tangentially exemplify the ideas discussed and the wide range of activities in which they are displayed.

Abell, P. (ed.), *Organizations as Bargaining and Influence Systems* (London: Heinemann, 1975).

Aldrich, H. E., *Organizations and Environments* (Englewood Cliffs, N.J.: Prentice-Hall, 1979).

Alexis, M. and Wilson, C. Z., *Organizational Decision-Making* (Englewood Cliffs, N.J.: Prentice-Hall, 1967).

Ambrose, S. E., *Eisenhower the Soldier 1890–1952* (London: Allen & Unwin, 1984).

Ansoff, H. I., *Corporate Strategy* (New York: McGraw-Hill, 1965).

Ansoff, H. I. (ed.), *Business Strategy* (Harmondsworth: Penguin 1969).

Argyris, C. and Schon, D. A., *Theory in Practice: Increasing Professional Effectiveness* (San Francisco: Jossey-Bass, 1974).

Bacharach, S. B. and Lawler, E. J., *Bargaining* (San Francisco: Jossey-Bass, 1981).

Bacharach, S. B. and Lawler, E. J. *Power and Politics in Organizations* (San Francisco: Jossey-Bass, 1980).

Ball, G. W., *The Past Has Another Pattern: Memoirs* (New York: Norton, 1982).

Banting, K. G., *Poverty, Politics and Policy* (London: Macmillan, 1979).

Barnard, C., *Functions of the Executive* (Cambridge, Mass.: Harvard University Press, 1938).

Barnett, J., *Inside the Treasury* (London: André Deutsch, 1982).

Barrett, S. and Fudge, C. (ed.), *Policy and Action* (London: Methuen, 1981).

Bate, P. and Mangham, I., *Exploring Participation* (Chichester: John Wiley 1981).

Bazerman, M. H. and Lewicki, R. J., *Negotiating in Organizations* (Beverly Hills; Sage, 1983).

Beckhard, R., *Organizational Development: Strategies and Models* (Reading, Mass.: Addison-Wesley, 1969).

Bell, D. V. J. *Power, Influence and Authority* (New York: Oxford University Press, 1975).

Bell, R., Edwards, D. V., Wagner, R. H. (eds), *Political Power* (New York: Free Press, 1969).

Bennett, R., *Ultra in the West* (London: Hutchinson, 1979).

Bennis, G. W., *Organization Development: Its Nature, Origins and Prospects* (Reading, Mass.: Addison-Wesley, 1969).

Benson, J. K. (ed.), *Organizational Analysis: Critique and Innovation* (Beverly Hills: Sage, 1977).

Berlin, I., *Russian Thinkers* (London: Hogarth, 1978).
Berlin, I., *Against the Current* (London: Hogarth, 1979).
Boorstin, D., *The Image* (Harmondsworth: Penguin, 1963).
Boswell, J. S., *Business Policies in the Making* (London: Allen & Unwin, 1983).
Bottomore, T. B. *Élites and Society* (Harmondsworth: Penguin, 1966).
Brannen, P. *et al.*, *The Worker Directors* (London: Hutchinson, 1976).
B.I.M. *Industrial Democracy* (London: B.I.M., 1968).
B.I.M. *The Board of Directors* (London: B.I.M. 1972).
Brookes, C., *Boards of Directors in British Industry* (London: Department of Employment, 1979).
Brooks, J., *Business Adventures* (Harmondsworth: Penguin, 1971).
Brown, W., *Exploration in Management* (London: Heinemann, 1960).
Brown, W., *Piecework Bargaining* (London: Heinemann, 1973).
Brzezinski, Z., *Power and Principle* (London: Weidenfeld & Nicolson, 1983).
Bullock, A. *The Life and Times of Ernest Bevin*, vol. 1. (London: Heinemann, 1960).
——, *The Life and Times of Ernest Bevin* vol. 2. (London: Heinemann, 1967).
——, *The Life and Times of Ernest Bevin*, vol. 3. (London: Heinemann, 1983).
Bulmer, M. (ed.), *Social Research and Royal Commissions* (London: Allen & Unwin, 1980).
Burns, T. and Stalker, G. M., *The Management of Innovation* (London: Tavistock, 1961).
Burrell, G. and Morgan, G. *Sociological Paradigms and Organisational Analysis* (London: Heinemann, 1979).
Buskirk, R. H., *Modern Management and Machiavelli* (London: Business Books, 1975).
Butler, R. A., *The Art of the Possible* (London: Hamish Hamilton, 1971).
Campbell, C., *Governments under Stress* (University of Toronto Press, 1983).
Carlton, D., *Anthony Eden* (London: Allen Lane, 1981).
Carr, E. H., *The Twenty Years' Crisis 1919–1939* (London: Macmillan, 1946).
Carr, E. H., *What Is History?* (Harmondsworth: Penguin, 1964).
Carter, C. F. and Williams, B. R., *Industry and Technical Progress* (London: Oxford University Press, 1957).
Castle, B. *The Castle Diaries 1974–6* (London: Weidenfeld & Nicolson, 1980).
Castle, G. G. *et al.* (ed.), *Decisions, Organizations and Society* (Harmondsworth: Penguin, 1971).
Channon, D. F., *The Service Industries* (London: Macmillan, 1978).
Child, J., *Organization: a Guide to Problems and Practice* (London: Harper & Row, 1977).
Child, J. and Partridge, B., *Lost Managers* (Cambridge University Press, 1982).
Clegg, S. *The Theory of Power and Organization* (London: Routledge & Kegan Paul, 1979).
Connolly, W. E., *Appearance and Reality in Politics* (Cambridge University Press, 1981).
Cornford, F. M., *Microcosmographia Academica* (London: Bowes & Bowes, 1908).
Coser, L., *The Functions of Social Conflict* (London: Routledge & Kegan Paul, 1956).
Cressey, P. *et al.*, *Industrial Democracy and Participation: a Scottish Survey* (London: Department of Employment, 1981).
Crosland, S., *Tony Crosland* (London: Jonathan Cape, 1982).

Crossman, R., *The Diaries of a Cabinet Minister, vols 1, 2 and 3* (London: Hamish Hamilton and Jonathan Cape, 1975, 1976 and 1977).

Crozier, M., *The Bureaucratic Phenomenon* (London: Tavistock Press, 1964).

Cyert, R. M. and March, J. G., *A Behavioural Theory of the Firm* (Englewood Cliffs, N.J.: Prentice-Hall, 1963).

Dahl, R. A., *Polyarchy* (New Haven, Conn: Yale University Press, 1971).

Dahl, R. A., *Dilemmas of Pluralist Democracy* (New Haven, Conn.: Yale University Press, 1982).

Dalton, M., *Men Who Manage* (New York: John Wiley, 1959).

Dahrendorf, R., *Class and Class Conflict in an Industrial Society* (London: Routledge & Kegan Paul, 1959).

Denning, B. W. (ed.), *Corporate Planning: Selected Concepts* (London: McGraw-Hill, 1971).

Dowling, M. J. *et al.*, *Employee Participation: Practice and Attitudes in North West Manufacturing Industry* (London: Department of Employment, 1981).

Drucker, P. F., *The Practice of Management* (London: Heinemann, 1955).

Duncan, G., *Democratic Theory and Practice* (Cambridge University Press, 1983).

Eccles, T., *Under New Management* (London: Pan, 1981).

Edwardes, M., *Back from the Brink* (London: Collins, 1983).

Ellis, J. *Cassino: The Hollow Victory* (London: André Deutsch, 1984).

Erickson, J., *The Road to Stalingrad* (London: Weidenfeld & Nicolson, 1975).

Erickson, J., *The Road to Berlin* (London: Weidenfeld & Nicolson, 1983).

Etzioni, A. (ed.), *Complex Organizations* (New York: Holt, Rinehart & Winston, 1964).

Etzioni, A., *The Active Society* (New York: Free Press, 1968).

Etzioni-Halevy, E., *Political Manipulation and Administrative Power* (London: Routledge & Kegan Paul, 1979).

Evan, W. M. (ed.), *Interorganizational Relations* (Harmondsworth: Penguin, 1976).

Evans, H., *Good Times, Bad Times* (London: Weidenfeld & Nicolson, 1983).

Flanders, A. (ed.), *Collective Bargaining* (Harmondsworth: Penguin, 1969).

Fox, A., *Industrial Sociology and Industrial Relations* (London: HMSO, 1966).

Fox, A., *Beyond Contract: Work, Power and Trust Relations* (London: Faber & Faber, 1974).

Fraser, D., *Alanbrooke* (London: Collins, 1982).

Gaitskell. H., *The Diary of Hugh Gaitskell 1945–56* (London: Jonathan Cape, 1983).

Galbraith, J. R. and Nathanson, D. A., *Strategy Implementation: the Role of Structure and Process* (St. Paul: West Publishing Co., 1978).

Gaventa, J., *Power and Powerlessness* (Oxford: Clarendon Press, 1980).

Gilbert, M., *Finest Hour: Winston S. Churchill 1939–1941* (London: Heinemann, 1983).

Gilbert, M. (ed.), *The Modern Business Enterprise* (Harmondsworth; Penguin, 1972).

Ginzberg, E. *et al.*, *Democratic Values and the Rights of Management* (New York: Columbia University, 1963).

Glastonbury, B. (ed.), *Social Work in Conflict* (London: Croom Helm, 1980).

Goffman, E., *The Presentation of Self in Everyday Life* (Harmondsworth: Penguin, 1959).

Goodwin, J. (ed.), *Peter Hall's Diaries* (London: Hamish Hamilton, 1983).

Gouldner, A. W., *Patterns of Industrial Bureaucracy* (New York: Free Press, 1954).

Glueck, W. F., *Business Policy and Strategic Management* (Auckland: McGraw-Hill, 1980).

Guest, D. and Knight, K. (eds), *Putting Participation into Practice* (Farnborough: Gower, 1979).

Hall, P. *Great Planning Disasters* (London: Weidenfeld & Nicolson, 1980).

Hall, P. *et al.*, *Change, Choice and Conflict in Social Policy* (London: Heinemann, 1975).

Handy, C. B., *Understanding Organizations* (Harmondsworth: Penguin, 1983).

Hanf, K. and Scharpf, F. W. (eds), *Interorganisational Policy Making* (London: Sage, 1978).

Harvey, J., *The Diplomatic Diaries of Oliver Harvey 1937–1940* (London: Collins, 1970).

Harvey, J., *The War Diaries of Oliver Harvey 1941–1945* (London: Collins, 1978).

Hemingway, J., *Conflict and Democracy* (Oxford: Clarendon Press, 1978).

Hill, W. A. and Egan, D. (eds), *Readings in Organization Theory: a Behavioural Approach* (Boston: Allyn & Bacon, 1967).

Hinsley, F. H. *et al.*, *British Intelligence in the Second World War*, vols 1, 2 and 3 (Part 1), (London: HMSO, 1979, 1981, 1984).

International Research Group, *Industrial Democracy in Europe* (Oxford: Clarendon Press, 1981).

Ilich, J. *Power Negotiating* (Reading, Mass.: Addison-Wesley, 1980).

Jacobs, E., *Stop Press* (London: André Deutsch, 1980).

Jay, A., *Management and Machiavelli* (Harmondsworth: Penguin, 1970).

Jenkins, W. I., *Policy Analysis* (London: Martin Robertson, 1978).

Jones, R. V., *Most Secret War* (London: Hamish Hamilton, 1978).

Jones, T., *A Diary with Letters, 1931–1950* (London: Oxford University Press, 1954).

Kennan, G. F., *The Decline of Bismarck's European Order* (Princeton University Press, 1979).

Kennan, G. F., *Memoirs 1925–1950* (Boston: Little, Brown, 1967).

Kennan, G. F., *Memoirs 1950–1963* (New York: Pantheon Books, 1972).

Kahn, R. L. and Boulding, E. *Power and Conflict in Organizations* (London: Tavistock Press, 1964).

Kissinger, H., *The White House Years* (London: Weidenfeld & Nicolson and Michael Joseph, 1979).

Kissinger, H., *Years of Upheaval* (London: Weidenfeld & Nicholson and Michael Joseph, 1982).

Kogan, M., *The Politics of Education* (Harmondsworth: Penguin, 1971).

Koontz, H., *The Board of Directors and Effective Management* New York: McGraw-Hill, 1967).

Koontz, H. and O'Donnell, C., *Principles of Management* (New York: McGraw-Hill, 1968).

Lawrence, J. R. (ed.), *Operational Research and the Social Sciences* (London: Tavistock Press, 1966).

Lawrence, P. R. and Lorsch, J. W., *Organization and Environment* (Boston, Mass: Harvard University Press, 1967).

Learned, E. P. *et al.*, *Business Policy* (Homewood: Richard D. Irwin, 1965).

Levitt, H. J. *et al.*, *The Social Science of Organizations* (Englewood Cliffs, N.J.: Prentice-Hall, 1963).

Leftwich, A., *Redefining Politics* (London: Methuen, 1983).

Lewin, L. and Vedung, E. (eds), *Politics as Rational Action* (Dordrecht: D. Reidel, 1980).

Lewin, R., *Ultra Goes to War* (London: Hutchinson, 1978).

Lewin, R., *The Other Ultra* (London: Hutchinson, 1982).

Lindblom, C. E. and Cohen, D. K., *Usable Knowledge* (New Haven, Conn.: Yale University Press, 1979).

Lipset, S. M., *Political Man* (London: Heinemann, 1960).

Lively, J., *Democracy* (Oxford: Basil Blackwell, 1975).

Lukes, S., *Power* (London: Macmillan, 1974).

Machiavelli, N., *The Prince* (Harmondsworth: Penguin, 1961).

Machiavelli, N., *The Discourses* (Harmondsworth: Penguin, 1970).

March, J. G. and Simon, H. A., *Organizations* (New York: John Wiley, 1959).

Marchington, M., *Responses to Participation at Work* (Farnborough: Gower Press, 1980).

McLachlan, S., *The National Freight Buy-Out* (London: Macmillan, 1983).

Mackenzie, W. J. M., *Power and Responsibility in Health Care* (Oxford University Press, 1979).

Macmillan, H., *War Diaries: The Mediterranean 1943–45* (London: Macmillan, 1984).

MacMillan, I. C., *Strategy Formulation: Political Concepts* (St. Paul: West Publishing Co., 1978).

Mailick, S. and Van Ness, E. (eds), *Admininstrative Behaviour* (Englewood Cliffs, N.J.: Prentice-Hall, 1962).

McGregor, D., *The Professional Manager* (New York: McGraw-Hall, 1967).

Medawar, P., *Pluto's Republic* (Oxford University Press, 1984).

Merton, R. K. *et al.* (eds), *Reader in Bureaucracy* (New York: Free Press, 1952).

Meyer, M. W. *et al.*, *Environments and Organizations* (San Francisco: Jossey-Bass, 1978).

Michels, R., *Political Parties* (Toronto: Free Press, 1966).

Miles, R. E. and Snow, C. C., *Organizational Strategy, Structure, and Process* (New York: McGraw-Hill, 1978).

Mintzberg, H. *The Nature of Managerial Work* (New York: Harper & Row, 1973).

Mintzberg, H., *Structure in Fives* (Englewood Cliffs, N.J.: Prentice-Hall, 1983).

Mintzberg, H., *Power in and around Organizations* (Englewood Cliffs, N.J.: Prentice-Hall, 1983).

Mueller, R. K., *New Directions for Directors* (Lexington Books, 1978).

Muller, H., *Adlai Stevenson* (London: Hamish Hamilton, 1968).

Morgan, J. (ed.), *The Backbench Diaries of Richard Crossman* (London: Hamish Hamilton and Jonathan Cape, 1981).

Morgan, K. O., *Labour in Power 1945–51* (Oxford University Press, 1984).

Partridge, P. H., *Consent and Consensus* (London: Macmillan, 1971).

Pruessen, R. W. *John Foster Dulles: the Road to Power* (New York: Free Press, 1982).

Mumford, E. and Pettigrew, A., *Implementing Strategic Decisions* (London: Longmans, 1975).

Nokes, P., *The Professional Task in Welfare Practice* (London: Routledge & Kegan Paul, 1967).

Parker, H. *et al.*, *Effective Boardroom Management* (London: B.I.M. 1971).

Parkinson, C. N., *The Law of Delay* (Harmondsworth: Penguin Books, 1978).

Pascale R. T. and Athos, A. G., *The Art of Japanese Management* (Harmondsworth: Penguin, 1982).

Penrose, E. T., *The Theory of the Growth of the Firm* (Oxford: Basil Blackwell, 1959).

Perrow, C., *Complex Organizations* (Illinois: Scott, Foreman, 1979).

Pettigrew, A., *The Politics of Organizational Decision-making* (London: Tavistock Press, 1973).

Pfeffer, J., *Organizational Design* (Illinois: AHM Publishing Co., 1978).

Pfeffer, J., *Power in Organizations* (Boston, Pitman, 1981).

Pfeffer, J., *Organizations and Organization Theory* (Boston: Pitman, 1982).

Pfeffer, J. and Salancik, G. R., *The External Control of Organizations* (New York: Harper & Row, 1978).

Pitt, D. C. and Smith, B. C., *Government Departments* (London: Routledge & Kegan Paul, 1981).

Pliatzky, L., *Getting and Spending* (Oxford: Basil Blackwell, 1982).

Porter, R. B., *Presidential Decision-Making* (Cambridge University Press, 1980).

Reilly, P. A., *Participation, Democracy and Control* (London: B.I.M., 1979).

Rhenman, E., *Industrial Democracy and Industrial Management* (London: Tavistock Press, 1968).

Rhenman, E. *et al.*, *Conflict and Cooperation* (London: John Wiley, 1970).

Romasco, A. U., *The Politics of Recovery* (Oxford University Press, 1983).

Salaman, G. and Thomson, K., *People and Organizations* (London: Longmans, 1973).

Salaman, G. and Thompson, K. (eds), *Control and Ideology in Organizations* (Milton Keynes: Open University Press, 1980).

Sayles, L., *Managerial Behaviour* (New York: McGraw-Hill, 1964).

Sayles, L., *Leadership. What Effective Managers Really Do ... and How They Do It* (New York: McGraw-Hill, 1979).

Sayles, L. and Chandler, M. K., *Managing Large Systems* (New York: Harper & Row, 1971).

Schien, E. H., *Process Consultation* (Reading, Mass: Addison-Wesley, 1969).

Schelling, T. C., *The Strategy of Conflict* (London: Oxford University Press, 1960).

Schon, D. A., *Beyond the Stable State* (Harmondsworth: Penguin, 1971).

Scott, D., *A. D. Lindsay: a Biography* (Oxford: Basil Blackwell, 1966).

Selznick, P., *T.V.A. and the Grass Roots* (New York: Harper Torchbooks, 1966).

Sherwood, R. E. (ed.), *The White House Papers of Harry L. Hopkins, vols 1 and 2.* (London: Eyre & Spottiswoode, 1948).

Silverman, D., *The Theory of Organisations* (London: Heinemann, 1970).

Simon, H., *Reason in Human Affairs* (Oxford: Blackwell, 1983).

Skinner, Q., *Machiavelli* (Oxford University Press, 1981).

Sloan, A. P., *My Years with General Motors* (London: Sidgwick & Jackson, 1965).

Smith, B., *Policy Making in British Government* (London: Martin Robertson, 1976).

Sobel, R., *I.B.M. Colossus in Transition* (New York: N.Y. Times Book, 1981).

Srivastva, S. *et al.*, *The Executive Mind* (San Francisco: Jossey-Bass, 1983).

Stewart, R., *Choices for Managers* (Maidenhead: McGraw-Hill, 1982).

Strauss, A., *Negotiations* (San Francisco: Jossey-Bass, 1978).

Strother, G. B., *Social Science Approaches to Business Behaviour* (London: Tavistock Press, 1962).

Tannenbaum, A. *et al.*, *Hierarchy in Organizations* (San Francisco: Jossey-Bass, 1974).

Taylor, B. and MacMillan, K., *Top Management* (London: Longmans, 1973).

Tayler, B. and Sparkes, J. R. (eds), *Corporate Strategy and Planning* (London: Heinemann, 1977).

Thomas, J. M. and Bennis, W. G. (eds), *Management of Change and Conflict* (Harmondsworth: Penguin, 1972).

Thompson, J. D., *Organizations in Action* (New York: McGraw-Hill, 1967).

Thompson, J. D. (ed.), *Approaches to Organizational Design* (University of Pittsburg Press, 1966).

Tivey, L., *The Politics of the Firm* (London: Martin Robertson, 1978).

Tolstoy, L., *War and Peace* (London: Pan Books, 1972).

Tuchman, B. W., *The Zimmermann Telegram* (London: Macmillan, 1981).

Tuchman, B. W., *Practising History* (London: Macmillan, 1982).

Turner, G., *Business in Britain* (Harmondsworth: Penguin, 1971).

Vance, C., *Hard Choices* (New York: Simon & Schuster, 1983).

Vickers, G., *The Art of Judgement* (London: Chapman & Hall, 1965).

Walker, K. F., *Industrial Democracy* (London: Times Newspapers, 1970).

Warner, M., (ed.), *Organizational Choice and Constraint* (Farnborough: Saxon House, 1978).

Wildavsky, A., *The Art and Craft of Policy Analysis* (London: Macmillan, 1979).

Wiener, M. J., *English Culture and the Decline of the Industrial Spirit 1850–1980* (Cambridge University Press, 1981).

Wilensky, H., *Organizational Intelligence* (New York: Basic Books, 1967).

Wilson, G., *Special Interests and Policy Making* (London: John Wiley, 1977).

Woodward, J., *Industrial Organization, 2nd edn* (Oxford University Press, 1980).

Wrong, D., *Power* (Oxford: Basil Blackwell, 1979).

Zey-Ferrell, M. and Aiken, M. (eds), *Complex Organizations: Critical Perspectives* (Illinois: Scott, Foresman, 1981).

Zuckerman, S., *From Apes to War Lords 1904–46* (London: Hamish Hamilton, 1978).

Index

action
  arising from language, 81
  multiplier, 179
  policy and strategy, 222, 238
  political, 83
administration, costs of change, 176
agenda
  defining, in participation, 160
  hidden, 190
  key problems, 140
  manipulation through the, 44, 45, 51
Alexander, General, Harold, relations
    with General Mark Clark, 3
'anticipated reaction', rule by, 83
anti-intellectualism in business, 139
Archilochus, 1
Argyris, Chris, organisation
    development, 6–7
authority, hierarchical, 3, 5
  coalitions in, 51
  failure of, 3, 5
  participation and, 161
  power and, 70–2

bargaining, *see also* negotiating
  breakdown of, 104
  coalition, in, 53–4
  conflict and, 86–7, 104–5
  implicit, 91, 101
  influences on, 86–7, 89
  language and, 81
  nature of, 87–9
  perceptions, 94–6
  planning for, 96–9
  procedure and substance, 89–90
  relationships in, 18–19, 25–7
  representation in, 92–4
  skills in, 160, 200
  stages in, 96–7

tactics of, 99–101, 102, 103
territorial, 134–5
trade-offs, 90
uncertainty in, 95
Barnett, Joel
  decision-making, 132, 145
bear baiting tactic, 49
behaviour
  adaptive, 9
  authentic, 11–12
  choice in, 26–8
  limited rationality of, 131–3
  meaning for individual, 9, 17, 18
  political, and large-scale change,
    191
  political ingredient, 36
  prestige and, 77
  structures and, 112
behavioural scientists
  o.d. and, 6
  participation and, 156
bluff in bargaining, 99
  counters to, 100
board of directors
  formal functions of, 120–1
  reality of operation, 121–2
  senior management and chief
    executive, 119, 128–9
boundary
  activities of units, 209–10
  organisational, 140
  power of personnel, 211
  roles influenced by technology and
    markets, 212
  spanning, 209
Boyle, Lord, decision-making style,
    133
BIM and industrial democracy, 157
budgets, 68
  bargaining and, 104

256